# Q&A

Routledge•Cavendish Questions & Answers Series

# Evidence
## 2007–2008

# Routledge-Cavendish Q&A series

Each Routledge-Cavendish Q&A contains 53 questions on topics commonly found on exam papers, with comprehensive suggested answers. The titles are written by lecturers who are also examiners, so the student gains an important insight into exactly what examiners are looking for in an answer. This makes them excellent revision and practice guides. With over 500,000 copies of the Routledge-Cavendish Q&As sold to date, accept no substitute.

New editions publishing in 2007:

CIVIL LIBERTIES & HUMAN RIGHTS 4/E
COMPANY LAW 5/E
COMMERCIAL LAW 4/E
CONSTITUTIONAL & ADMINISTRATIVE LAW 5/E
CONTRACT LAW 7/E
CRIMINAL LAW 6/E
EMPLOYMENT LAW 5/E
ENGLISH LEGAL SYSTEM 7/E
EQUITY & TRUSTS 5/E
EUROPEAN UNION LAW 6/E
FAMILY LAW 4/E
INTELLECTUAL PROPERTY LAW
JURISPRUDENCE 4/E
LAND LAW 5/E
TORTS 7/E

For a full listing, visit www.routledgecavendish.com/revisionaids.asp

# Q&A

Routledge•Cavendish Questions & Answers Series

# Evidence
## 2007–2008

CHRISTOPHER ALLEN, LLM, MA, PHD
*Barrister, Formerly Senior Lecturer Inns of Court School of Law*

Routledge·Cavendish
Taylor & Francis Group

Seventh edition first published 2007
by Routledge-Cavendish
2 Park Square, Milton Park, Abingdon, Oxon OX14 4RN

Simultaneously published in the USA and Canada
by Routledge-Cavendish
270 Madison Ave, New York, NY 10016

*Routledge-Cavendish is an imprint of the Taylor & Francis Group,
an informa business*

© 1994, 2007 Christopher Allen

Previous editions published by Cavendish Publishing Limited
First edition 1994
Second edition 1996
Third edition 1998
Fourth edition 2000
Fifth edition 2002
Sixth edition 2005

Typeset in Garamond by
Newgen Imaging Systems (P) Ltd, Chennai, India
Printed and bound in Great Britain by
MPG Books Ltd, Bodmin, Cornwall

All rights reserved. No part of this book may be reprinted or
reproduced or utilised in any form or by any electronic,
mechanical, or other means, now known or hereafter
invented, including photocopying and recording, or in any
information storage or retrieval system, without permission in
writing from the publishers.

*British Library Cataloguing in Publication Data*
A catalogue record for this book is available
from the British Library

*Library of Congress Cataloging in Publication Data*
A catalog record for this book has been requested

ISBN 10: 0–415–42721–5
ISBN 13: 978–0–415–42721–0

# PREFACE

A reviewer of the first edition of John Pitt Taylor's *Treatise on the Law of Evidence* (1848) described the writer's subject as one:

> ... that peculiarly requires to be read in the spirit rather of the philosopher than of the mere lawyer. It has the unchanging laws of nature and reason for its foundation; it is less liable to the infringements of legislation; there is less of reference to cases, and more of principle, than in almost any other subject to which the studies of the lawyer extend; and in its practical application he is almost always obliged to adduce the principle in support of his argument, instead of finding refuge for fallacy within the all-compassing defence of cases.

This happy state of affairs did not last long. The law governing evidence in civil trials became increasingly subject to *stare decisis* during the 19th century. The law governing evidence in criminal trials did not develop so rapidly because there was no effective appellate system before the Court of Criminal Appeal was established in 1907. But after that date rules established by appellate decisions developed and multiplied. Statute was a relatively rare source of evidence law until the last decades of the 20th century, when the rules affecting both civil and criminal trials began a period of rapid change. In civil trials the rules have been substantially relaxed. The same is less true of criminal trials, where the position now is that statute governs a substantial part of the subject.

I have emphasised problem questions in this book in order to give students as much practice as possible in reasoning with facts as well as with law. The practising lawyer is concerned most of the time with facts rather than law. Even in law exams, analysis of a factual situation is essential to the application of the law, and it is often at this stage that students go astray.

When considering problems of law it may be useful to remember that these can be of two kinds. First, of course, there are questions of admissibility – a traditional concern of evidence law. But the law can also have something to say about how a trial judge should direct a jury in relation to evidence that has been admitted. This was originally a matter for the judge's discretion, but discretion has been giving way to rules. There are now things that a judge must say, for example, concerning the significance of a defendant's good character, evidence of identification, or a defendant's silence, when questioned by police, about a matter subsequently relied on in his defence. If a problem question ends with words such as, 'Discuss the evidential issues that arise,' remember that this requires you to tell the examiner about judicial directions as well as admissibility. Further, you must know not only the principal occasions that require a judicial direction but also the essential elements of the appropriate direction. Students who tell the examiner, without more, that a *Turnbull* direction will be necessary, gain little credit. You must be able to say what is required by a *Turnbull* direction.

I hope that this book may be of value as a way of achieving an overall view of a subject. The emphasis on criminal evidence is intentional; it is here that the subject is most lively and this is reflected in examination questions. I hope that the book may also be a means of revision, and a guide in the practice of answering examination questions. I considered dedicating it 'to those who have better things to do', but gravitas prevailed. I like to think, though, that it will be helpful not only to those whose devotion to their mistress the law is total, but to those who spread their favours more widely: to student poets and musicians, to actors and oarsmen and to many more. Nor do I forget those mature students, often with widely different concerns in their daily work, whose opportunity for study is inevitably limited. To all my readers I wish enjoyment and success.

Christopher Allen<br>January 2007

# CONTENTS

*Preface* v
*Table of Cases* ix
*Table of Legislation* xix

| | | |
|---|---|---|
| 1 | Basic Concepts | 1 |
| 2 | Burden and Standard of Proof | 15 |
| 3 | Presumptions, Competence and Compellability | 31 |
| 4 | Hearsay I | 41 |
| 5 | Hearsay II | 59 |
| 6 | Hazardous Evidence | 75 |
| 7 | Confessions and Ill–Gotten Evidence | 97 |
| 8 | Character Evidence I | 127 |
| 9 | Character Evidence II | 147 |
| 10 | The Course of Testimony | 167 |
| 11 | Opinion Evidence | 177 |
| 12 | Privilege and Public Policy | 183 |
| 13 | Revision | 195 |

*Index* 207

# Table of Cases

A [2001] 3 All ER 1 .................................................................................7, 168, 175, 205
Abadom [1983] 1 WLR 126; [1983] 1 All ER 364; (1983) 76 Cr App R 48.........178, 181
AG v Hitchcock (1847) 1 Exch 91.................................................................................80
A-G of Hong Kong v Lee Kwong-Kut [1993] 3 WLR 329 .............................................18
Agar [1990] 2 All ER 442; (1990) 90 Cr App R 318;
 (1989) 139 NLJ 1116 .........................................................................................190–191
Ainscough [2006] Crim LR 635 .................................................................................136
Air Canada v Secretary of State for Trade [1983] 2 AC 394;
 [1983] 2 WLR 494; [1983] 1 All ER 161 ..................................................................188
Alfred Crompton Amusement Machines Ltd v Customs & Excise Commissioners
 (No 2) [1974] AC 405; [1973] 3 WLR 268; [1973] 2 All ER 1169........................188
Alladice (1988) 87 Cr App R 380 .......................................................105, 107, 112, 114
Allan [1969] 1 WLR 33; [1969] 1 All ER 91 ................................................................21
Anastasiou [1998] Crim LR 67 ....................................................................................89
Anderson [1993] Crim LR 447 ...................................................................................110
Andreae v Selfridge & Co Ltd [1938] Ch 1 .................................................................10
Andrews [1987] AC 281; [1987] 2 WLR 413; [1987] 1 All ER 513;
 (1987) 84 Cr App R 382 ..............................................................................60, 69, 72
Argent [1997] 2 Cr App R 27 .....................................................................................124
Ashburton (Lord) v Pape [1913] 2 Ch 469; (1913) 82 LJ Ch 527;
 (1913) 109 LT 381; (1913) 29 TLR 623 ...................................................................194
Aziz and others [1995] 3 All ER 149, HL ...........................................................111, 204

B(C) [2004] 2 Cr App R 570...............................................................................150, 159
Bailey and Smith (1993) 97 Cr App R 365................................................................125
Bathurst [1968] 2 QB 99; [1968] 2 WLR 1092; [1968] 1 All ER 1175;
 (1968) 52 Cr App R 251 ............................................................................................101
Batt [1994] Crim LR 592............................................................................................66
Batt [1995] Crim LR 240............................................................................................98, 126
Beck [1982] 1 WLR 461; [1982] 1 All ER 807; (1982) 74 Cr App R 221 ................77, 82
Beckles [200] EWCA Crim 2766................................................................................125, 201
Bentley (DW) (Deceased) [2001] 1 Cr App R 307 .....................................................21
Betts and Hall [2001] 2 Cr App R 257 .......................................................................125, 201

Birks, [2003] 2 Cr App R 122 ................................................................................................72
Blake and Tye (1844) 6 QB 126; 115 ER 49 ..................................................................98
Blastland [1986] AC 41; [1985] 2 All ER 1095; [1985] 3 WLR 345;
    (1985) 81 Cr App R 266..........................................................................................8, 83
Bliss (1837) 7 LJQB 4 ........................................................................................................62
Bowman v DPP [1990] Crim LR 600 ................................................................................9
Boyson [1991] Crim LR 274, CA ...................................................................................137
Bratty v Attorney General for Northern Ireland [1963] AC 386;
    [1961] 3 WLR 965; [1961] 3 All ER 523; (1961) 46 Cr App R 1 ........................22
Brigden [1973] Crim LR 579 ..........................................................................................101
Britzman [1983] 1 All ER 369; [1983] 1 WLR 350; (1983) 76 Cr App R 134 ............165
Brown (1987) 87 Cr App R 52 ...............................................................................190, 192
Buckley (1873) 13 Cox CC 293 ........................................................................................72
Burge and Pegg [1996] 1 Cr App R 163 ........................................13, 52, 77, 80, 84, 198
Byrne [1960] 2 QB 396; [1960] 3 WLR 440; [1960] 3 All ER 1 .................................181

Calcraft v Guest [1898] 1 QB 759; (1898) 67 LJ QB 505; (1898) 78 LT 283..............194
Callender [1998] Crim LR 337 .........................................................................................72
Campbell v Thameside Metropolitan Borough Council (MBC) [1982] QB 1065;
    [1982] 3 WLR 74; [1982] 2 All ER 791 ................................................................189
Carnall [1995] Crim LR 944..............................................................................................70
Carr Briant [1943] KB 607; [1943] 2 All ER 156; (1943) 29 Cr App R 76 ...................22
Chalkley and Jeffries [1998] QB 848; [1998] 3 WLR 146; [1998] 2 All ER 155...104–106
Chard v Chard [1956] P 259; [1955] 3 WLR 954; [1955] 3 All ER 721 ..................33, 39
Chenia [2003] 2 Cr App R 83 .........................................................................................122
Christie [1914] AC 545; (1914) 111 LT 220; (1914) 83 LJ KB 1097;
    (1914) 30 TLR 471; (1914) 24 Cox CC 249 .........................................................169
Christou [1992] QB 979; [1992] 3 WLR 228; [1992] 4 All ER 559 ....................105, 113
Coles [1995] 1 Cr App R 157 .................................................................................177, 202
Comptroller of Customs v Western Lectric Co Ltd [1966] AC 367;
    [1965] 3 WLR 1229; [1965] 3 All ER 599 .........................................................52–53
Condron [1997] 1 Cr App R 185....................................................................................125
Constantine (Joseph) Steamship Line Ltd v Imperial Smelting Corp Ltd [1942]
    AC 154; [1941] 2 All ER 165; 110 LJ KB 433; 165 LT 27; 57 TLR 485 ..............24
Conway v Rimmer [1968] AC 910; [1968] 2 WLR 998; [1968] 1 All ER 874..............185
Cooke [1995] 1 Cr App R 318 ................................................................................122, 124
Cowan [1996] 1 Cr App R 1 .............................................................149, 154, 156, 161
Crawford [1998] 1 Cr App R 153....................................................................................159

Davies [1962] Crim LR 314 .................................................................................................... 178
Davies [2002] EWCA Crim 2949 ...................................................................................... 18–19
Davies v DPP [1954] AC 378; [1954] 2 WLR 343; [1954] 1 All ER 507;
    (1954) 38 Cr App R 11 ...................................................................................................... 82
Dervish [2002] 2 Cr App R 105 ............................................................................................ 115
Desmond (1999) unreported ................................................................................................. 165
Devonport and Pirano [1996] 1 Cr App R 221 ............................................................. 67, 199
Dillon v R [1982] AC 484; [1982] 2 WLR 538; [1982] 1 All ER 1017;
    (1982) 74 Cr App R 274 .................................................................................................... 34
Dix (1982) 74 Cr App R 306 ................................................................................................. 180
Dodson [1984] 79 Cr App R 220 ............................................................................................ 54
Donald [2004] Crim LR 841 ........................................................................................... 89, 137
DPP v A and BC Chewing Gum Ltd [1968] 1 QB 159; [1967] 3 WLR 493;
    [1967] 2 All ER 504 ................................................................................................ 181, 202
DPP v Boardman [1975] AC 421; [1974] 3 WLR 673; [1974] 3 All ER 887;
    (1974) 60 Cr App R 165 .................................................................................................. 138
DPP v Camplin [1978] AC 705; [1978] 2 WLR 679; [1978] 2 All ER 168;
    (1978) 67 Cr App R 14 .................................................................................................... 5–7
DPP v Majewski [1977] AC 443; [1976] 2 WLR 623; [1976] 2 All ER 142;
    (1976) 62 Cr App R 262 .................................................................................................. 5–7
DPP v Marshall [1988] 3 All ER 683 .................................................................................... 105
Duff Development Co Ltd v Government of Kelantan [1924] AC 797 .............................. 10
Duncan [1981] 93 Cr App R 359 ................................................................................... 111, 115

E [2005] Crim LR 227 ........................................................................................................... 205
Edwards [1975] QB 27 ....................................................................................................... 27–28
Edwards [1991] 2 All ER 266; [1992] Crim LR 549 ........................................................... 168
Edwards [2006] Crim LR 531 ................................................................................................ 128
Elson (1994) The Times, 30 June .......................................................................................... 109
Evans [1965] 2 QB 295; [1964] 3 WLR 1173; [1964] 3 All ER 401;
    (1964) 48 Cr App R 314 .................................................................................................... 82
Everett [1988] Crim LR 826 .................................................................................................. 119
Exall [1866] 4 F & F 922; (1866) 176 ER 850 ...................................................................... 146

Fernandez, Ex p (1861) 10 CBNS 3; (1861) 30 LJ CP 321; (1861) 4 LT 324 ............. 36–38
Forbes [2001] 1 AC 473; [2001] 2 WLR 1 (HL); [2001] 1
    All ER 686 ........................................................................................... 88–89, 93–94, 99
Fowler (1988) 86 Cr App R 219 ............................................................................................ 140
Fulcher [1995] 2 Cr App R 251 ............................................................................................. 128

Fulling [1987] QB 426; [1987] 2 WLR 923; [1987] 2 All ER 65;
  (1987) 85 Cr App R 136 .................................................................. 100, 109, 114, 119–120
Funderburk [1990] 1 WLR 587 ............................................................................................ 80

Gayle [1999] 2 Cr App R 130 ......................................................................................... 93–94
George v Davies [1911] 2 KB 445 ....................................................................................... 10
Gilfoyle [1996] 1 Cr App R 302 .......................................................................................... 72
Gill [1963] 1 WLR 841 ...................................................................................................... 121
Gill [2001] 1 Cr App R 160 ........................................................................................ 122, 172
Glendarroch, The [1894] P 226; (1894) 70 LT 344; (1894) 10 TLR 269 ......................... 25
Goddard v Nationwide Building Society [1987] QB 670;
  [1986] 3 WLR 734; [1986] 3 All ER 264 ..................................................................... 194
Goldenberg (1988) 88 Cr App R 285 ........................................................................ 117–119
Goss [2005] Crim LR 61 .................................................................................................. 127
Gowland-Wynn [2002] 1 Cr App R 569 .......................................................................... 122
Grannell (1990) 90 Cr App R 149 .............................................................................. 87, 100
Grant [1996] 1 Cr App R 73 .................................................................... 5–6, 11–12, 66, 198
Gray [2004] 2 Cr App R 498 ....................................................................... 127, 132, 200
Gray and Others [1995] 2 Cr App R 100 ..................................................................... 66, 98
Grayson [1993] Crim LR 864 .......................................................................................... 100
Greer [1998] Crim LR 572 ................................................................................................. 65
Griffiths [1998] Crim LR 567 ......................................................................................... 6, 68
Gummerson and Steadman [1999] Crim LR 680 ....................................................... 93–94
Gunewardene [1951] 2 KB 600; [1951] 2 All ER 290; [1951] 2 TLR 315;
  (1951) 35 Cr App R 80 ........................................................... 99, 100, 112, 115, 121, 198
Guney [1998] 2 Cr App R 242 ................................................................................... 5–6, 66

H and Others, Re [1996] 1 All ER 1 ................................................................................. 25
H, W and M [2001] Crim LR 818 ..................................................................................... 64
Hacker [1994] 1 WLR 1659; [1995] 1 All ER 45 ............................................................ 141
Halpin [1996] Crim LR 112 ..................................................................................... 5–6, 11, 13
Hanson [2005] Crim LR 787 ............................................. 128–130–132, 135, 138, 141, 143,
                                                            145, 150, 152, 155, 158, 162–163, 165, 199
Harvey [1988] Crim LR 241 ..................................................................................... 118–119
Hasson [1997] Crim LR 579 .............................................................................................. 67
Hayes [1977] 1 WLR 234; [1977] 2 All ER 288;
  (1977) 64 Cr App R 194 ............................................................................................ 36–37
Hennessey (1978) 68 Cr App R 419 ........................................................................ 190–191

Hepworth [1955] 2 QB 600; [1955] 3 WLR 331; [1955] 2 All ER 918;
  [1955] 39 Cr App R 152 .................................................................................................22
Hersey [1998] Crim LR 281 ..........................................................................................93–94
Hetherington v Hetherington (1887) 12 PD 112; (1887) 57 LT 533 .................................33
Hickin and Others [1996] Crim LR 584 ....................................................................89, 95
Highton [2006] Crim LR 52 ...........................................................142, 149, 155, 162–163
Hoare [2004] EWCA Crim 784 ................................................................................125, 201
Hornal v Neuberger Products Ltd [1957] 1 QB 247; [1956] 3 WLR 1034;
  [1956] 3 All ER 970 .......................................................................................................25
Hoskyn v Commissioner of Police for the Metropolis, [1979] AC 474 .......................202
Howell [2003] EWCA Crim 1 ..................................................................................125, 201
Hulbert (1979) 69 Cr App R 243 (CA) ...........................................................................53
Hunt [1987] AC 352 ......................................................................................................19, 28
Hurst [1995] 1 Cr App R 82 ............................................................................................178

Islam [1999] 1 Cr App R 22 ......................................................................................80, 204
Ismail (1990) 92 Cr App R 92; [1990] Crim LR 872 ....................................................110

Jelen and Katz (1990) 90 Cr App R 456 ..................................................................97, 100
Johnson (1988) 1 WLR 1377; [1989] 1 All ER 121; (1988) 88 Cr App R 131 ......190, 192
Johnson [1995] 2 Cr App R 41; [1995] Crim LR 242 ..............................................84, 138
Johnstone [2003] 1 WLR 1736 .........................................................................................18
Jones and Others [1997] 2 Cr App R 119 .....................................................................100

Kearley [1992] 2 AC 228; [1992] 2 WLR 656; [1992]
  2 All ER 345 ..........................................................................................42, 45, 47, 69, 71
Keenan [1990] 2 QB 54; [1989] 3 WLR 1193; [1989] 3 All ER 598;
  (1989) 90 Cr App R 1 ..........................................................................................105–106
Kelly [1992] Crim LR 181 .........................................................................................88, 93–95
Khan (1981) 73 Cr App R 190 .........................................................................................37
Khan [1997] AC 558; [1996] 2 Cr App R 440 .............................................105, 107, 126
Knight [2003] EWCA Crim 1977 ............................................................................125, 201
Kritz [1950] 1 KB 82; [1949] 2 All ER 406; (1949) 33 Cr App R 169 .........................21

L v DPP [2002] 2 All ER 854 .....................................................................................22–23
Lamb (1980) 71 Cr App R 198 .........................................................................................91
Lambert [2002] 2 AC 545 ............................................................................................27, 29
Lee [1996] 2 Cr App R 266 .............................................................................................137

Levison v Patent Steam Carpet Cleaning Ltd [1978] QB 69;
    [1977] 3 WLR 90; [1977] 3 All ER 498 .................................................................. 26
Lilley [2003] EWCA 1789 ........................................................................................ 73
Lobban v R [1995] 1 WLR 877; [1995] 2 All ER 602;
    [1995] 2 Cr App R 573 ................................................................................... 99, 121
Lobell [1957] 1 QB 547; [1957] 2 WLR 524; [1957] 1 All ER 734 ........................ 22, 202
Looseley [2001] 4 All ER 897 ............................................................................ 105, 107
Lovelock [1997] Crim LR 821 ................................................................................... 67
Lowery v R [1974] AC 85; [1973] 3 WLR 235; [1973] 3 All ER 622 ......................... 182
Lucas [1981] QB 720; [1981] 3 WLR 120;
    [1981] 2 All ER 1008 .............................................................. 13, 52, 77, 81, 84, 198
Lupien (1970) 9 DLR (3d) 1 ..................................................................................... 182
Lydon [1986] 85 Cr App R 221 ................................................................................. 50

M(T) and Others (2000) unreported ......................................................................... 128
McGovern [1991] Crim LR 124 ........................................................... 108, 110, 117–119
McIntosh [1992] Crim LR 651 .................................................................................. 57
Makanjuola [1995] 1 WLR 1348 ........................................................................... 77–78
Makanjuola v Commissioner of Metropolitan Police [1992] 3 All ER 617 ................ 188
Malashev [1997] Crim LR 587 .............................................................................. 89, 95
Malindi v R [1967] 1 AC 439; [1966] 3 WLR 913; [1966] 3 All ER 285 ............ 154, 163
Maqsud Ali [1966] 1 QB 688; [1965] 3 WLR 229; [1965] 2 All ER 464 ............. 57, 125
Marcus [2005] Crim LR 384 ...................................................................................... 95
Marks v Beyfus [1890] 25 QBD 494; (1890) 59 LJ QB 479;
    (1890) 63 LT 733; (1890) 6 TLR 406; (1890) 17 Cox CC 196 .................... 190–191
Martinez-Tobon (1993) 98 Cr App R 375 ................................................................. 101
Mason [1988] 1 WLR 139; [1987] 3 All ER 481;
    (1988) 86 Cr App R 349 ........................................................... 97, 105, 110, 118
Matto v Wolverhampton Crown Court [1987] RTR 337;
    [1987] Crim LR 641 ............................................................................... 105–106, 124
Mawaz Khan [1967] 1 AC 454; [1966] 3 WLR 1275;
    [1967] 1 All ER 80 ................................................................... 45, 51, 56, 80, 83
Mequaker v Goddard [1940] 1 KB 687 ...................................................................... 10
Mertens [2005] Crim LR 301 ............................................................................ 150, 159
Middleton [2001] Crim LR 251 ................................................................................. 84
Miller v Howe [1969] 1 WLR 1510; [1969] 3 All ER 451 ........................................... 50
Miller v Minister of Pensions [1947] 2 All ER 372; (1947) 177 LT 536;
    (1947) 63 TLR 474 ................................................................................................ 25

Moghal [1977] 65 Cr App R 56 ................................................................................72, 83
Mountford [1999] Crim LR 575 ...................................................................................122
Mullen v Hackney LBC [1997] 1 WLR 1103; [1997] 2 All ER 906 ................................9
Murray v DPP (1993) 97 Cr App R 151 ...............................................................101–102
Murrell [2005] Crim LR 869 ..............................................................................150, 159
Myers v DPP [1965] AC 1001; [1964] 3 WLR 145; [1964] 2 All ER 881 ................46–47

Napper [1996] Crim LR 591 .........................................................................................148
Nash [2005] Crim LR 232..................................................................................... 89, 94
Neil [1994] Crim LR 441..........................................................................108, 110, 118
Neill v North Antrim Magistrates' Court [1992] 1 WLR 1220 ......................................64
Nelson [1998] 2 Cr App R 399 ....................................................................................111
Nickolson [1999] Crim LR 61 ......................................................................................122
Nye v Nilblett [1918] 1 KB 23 .......................................................................................10

O'Connor (1987) 85 Cr App R 298 ..............................................................................105
Oyesiku (1971) 56 Cr App R 240..........................................................................171–172

Paraskeva (1983) 76 Cr App R 162 ..............................................................................170
Paris (1993) Cr App R 104.................................................................................104, 121
Parker [1995] Crim LR 233...........................................................................................100
Patel v Comptroller of Customs [1966] AC 356; [1965] 3 WLR 1222;
    [1965] 3 All ER 593.................................................................................................50
Patrick (1999) unreported..............................................................................................84
Pattinson and Exley [1996] 1 Cr App R 51 .........................................................89, 92–93
Payton [2006] Crim LR 997 .........................................................................................127
Pearce (1979) 69 Cr App R 365 ................................................................... 66, 198, 204
Peart v Bolckow Vaughan & Co Ltd [1925] 1 KB 399 ....................................................9
Perry [1984] Crim LR 680 ...........................................................................................140
Peters [1995] 2 Cr App R 77........................................................................................198
Petkar [2004] 1 Cr App R 270.........................................84, 115, 122, 125, 171–172, 201
Pettman (1985) unreported .........................................................................................134
Phillips (1936) 26 Cr App R 17; (1936) 156 LT 80; (1936) 30 Cox CC 536 ..................170
Pieterson [1995] 1 WLR 293; [1995] 2 Cr App R 11 .....................................................56
Podola [1960] 1 QB 325; [1959] 3 WLR 718; [1959] 3 All ER 418 ..............................22
Popat [1998] 2 Cr App R 208 ..................................................................................94–95
Popat (No 2) [2000] Crim LR 54 ..................................................................................94

Price [2005] Crim LR 304..................................................................................................150, 159
PS v Germany [2002] Crim LR 312. ...............................................................................73

Qadir [1998] Crim LR 828...........................................................................................92, 94

R v Chief Constable of West Midlands Police ex p Wiley (1995) 1 AC 274;
    [1994] 3 All ER 420.................................................................................................188
R v DPP ex p Kebilene [2000] 2 AC 326..............................................................18–19, 27, 29
Rankine [1986] QB 861; [1986] 2 WLR 1075; [1986] 2 All ER 566;
    (1986) 83 Cr App R 18......................................................................................190–191
Redgrave (1982) 74 Cr App R 10...............................................................................151–152
Reference Re R v Truscott [1967] SCR 309; [1967] 2 CCC 285 (Canada).......................146
Renda [2006] Crim LR 534...............................................................................................128
Rennie [1982] 1 WLR 64; [1982] 1 All ER 385; (1982) 74 Cr App R 207...........112, 114
Reynolds [1989] Crim LR 220..........................................................................................182
Reynolds v Llanelly Tinplate Co Ltd [1948] 1 All ER 140 ...................................................9
Rice [1963] 1 QB 857..........................................................................................................51
Roberts [1942] 1 All ER 187; (1942) 28 Cr App R 102.................................169, 171–172
Roberts [1997] 1 Cr App R 217..........................................................................................99
Robertson [1968] 1 WLR 1767; [1968] 3 All ER 557......................................................22
Robinson [2003] EWCA Crim 2219........................................................................125, 201
Robinson (Dennis) [2006] Crim LR 431; EWCA Crim 3233.................................150, 159
Robinson (Wayne) [2006] Crim LR 427; EWCA Crim 1940..........................................52
Rodley [1913] 3 KB 468; (1913) 9 Cr App R 69....................................................143–144
Rogers v Home Secretary [1973] AC 388; [1972] 3 WLR 279;
    [1972] 2 All ER 1057..............................................................................................187
Rowton (1865) Le & Ca 520; (1865) 169 ER 1497.........................................151–152, 169
Rudd (1948) 32 Cr App R 138..................................................................................99–100
Rush and Tomkins Ltd v GLC [1989] AC 1280; [1988] 3 WLR 939;
    [1988] 3 All ER 737.................................................................................................184
Ryder [1993] Crim LR 601 ..............................................................................................138

Salabiaku v France (1988) 13 EHRR 379 ..........................................................................17
Samuel [1988] 2 WLR 920..............................................................................................121
Sang [1980] AC 402 ...........................................................5, 54, 64, 106, 128, 131, 135, 137,
                                                                                    141, 147, 150, 157, 162, 164
Savage v Chief Constable of the Hampshire Constabulary [1997] 2 All ER 631 .............188
Selvey v DPP [1970] AC 304; [1968] 2 WLR 1494; [1968] 2 All ER 497....................158

Senat v Senat [1965] P 172; [1965] 2 WLR 981; [1965] 2 All ER 505 ..........................172
Sharp [1988] 1 WLR 7; [1988] 1 All ER 65;
   (1988) 86 Cr App R 274 ..........................................100, 108, 111–112, 115, 204
Shaw (1888) 16 Cox CC 503 ..........................................................................170
Sheldrake v DPP [2004] 3 WLR 976 ...............................................................18–19
Silverlock [1894] 2 QB 766; (1894) 63 LJ MC 233; (1894) 72 LT 2981;
   (1894) 10 TLR 623; (1894) 18 Cox CC 104 ..............................................182
Singh [2006] Crim LR 647 ..........................................................42, 46, 48, 71–72
Slater [1995] 1 Cr App R 584 ....................................................................92–93
Slowcombe [1991] Crim LR 198 .............................................................190–191
Smith (1976) 64 Cr App R 217 ......................................................................140
Smurthwaite and Gill [1994] 1 All ER 898; (1994) 98 Cr App R 437 ............105–106
Somanathan [2005] EWCA Crim 2866, [10]-[54], sub nom RS .........................138
Sparks v R [1964] AC 964; [1964] 2 WLR 566; [1964]
   1 All ER 727 ....................................................................................46–47, 71
Spencer [1986] AC 128; [1986] 3 WLR 348; [1986] 3 All ER 928 ........................77
Stagg (1994) unreported ...............................................................................111
Stanton [2004] 3 TLR 1 ..................................................................................94
Stewart [1995] Crim LR 500 ..................................................................105, 107
Stone [2005] Crim LR 569 ........................................................................77, 82
Subramaniam v Public Prosecutor [1956] 1 WLR 965 ...................42, 44, 70, 175

T and H [2002] 1 All ER 683 ..........................................................................80
Taylor v Chief Constable of Cheshire (1987) 1 WLR 1479;
   [1987] 1 All ER 225; (1986) 84 Cr App R 191 .....................................53–54, 57
Taylor, Weaver and Donovan (1928) 21 Cr App R 20 ........................................55
Teeluck and John [2005] Crim LR 728 ..........................................................127
Teper v R [1952] AC 480; [1952] 2 All ER 447 ..................................................47
Thompson (1976) 64 Cr App R 96 ................................................................173
Thompson v R [1918] AC 221; (1918) 87 LJ KB 478; (1918) 118 LT 418;
   (1918) 34 TLR 204; (1918) 13 Cr App R 1 .................................................139
Thomson [1912] 3 KB 19 ................................................................................72
Thornton [1995] 1 Cr App R 578 .............................................................92–93
Tomlin v Standard Telephones and Cables Ltd [1969] 3 All ER 201;
   [1969] 1 WLR 1378; [1969] 1 Lloyd's Rep 309 ..........................................184
Toohey v Commissioner for Metropolitan Police [1965] AC 595;
   [1965] 1 All ER 506; [1965] 2 WLR 439 ....................................................182
Tripodi v R (1961) 104 CLR 1 ........................................................................98

Turnbull [1977] QB 224; [1976] 3 WLR 445;
[1976] 3 All ER 549 ...................................................................77–78, 89, 92–95, 137, 196
Turner [1975] QB 834; [1975] 2 WLR 56; [1975] 1 All ER 70 .................8, 130–131, 180

Vye (1993) Cr App R 134 ..........................................................81, 127, 132, 151, 153, 199

W [2005] Crim LR 965.............................................................................................205
Wainwright (1875) 13 Cox CC 171 ...........................................................................72
Walker [1998] Crim LR 211 ....................................................................................119
Walsh (1990) 91 Cr App R 161......................................................................105–106, 114
Walters [1979] RTR 220; (1979) 69 Cr App R 115 ....................................................60
Walters v R [1969] 2 AC 26; [1969] 2 WLR 60 .........................................................21
Ward [2001] Crim LR 316 ........................................................................................71
Warner (1993) 96 Cr App R 324...............................................................................67
Watkins, Re [1953] 1 WLR 1323; [1953] 2 All ER 1113 ...........................................40
Waugh v British Railways Board [1980] AC 521; [1979] 3 WLR 150;
[1979] 2 All ER 1169.........................................................................................193–194
Weir [2006] Crim LR 433; [2005] EWCA Crim 2866............................................128, 131
Wertherall v Harrison [1976] 1 QB 773 ......................................................................9
White v R [1998] 1 Cr App R 153 ...........................................................................174
Wickham (1971) 55 Cr App R 199 ..........................................................................148
Wilkins [1975] 2 All ER 724; (1975) 60 Cr App R 300 ..........................................140
Willis [1916] 1 KB 933; (1916) 12 Cr App R 44; (1916) 25 Cox CC 397;
(1916) 85 LJ KB 1129.................................................................................................82
Woolmington v DPP [1935] AC 462; (1935) 104 LJ KB 433; (1935) 153 LT 232; (1935)
51 TLR 446; (1935) 30 Cox C 234;(1935) 25 Cr App R 72 .................................15, 17
Wright (1934) 25 Cr App R 35 ..................................................................................91
Wright [1994] Crim LR 55 .................................................................................11–12, 66, 198
Wright v Doe d Tatham (1837) 7 Ad & El 313; (1837) 112 ER 488........................69

# TABLE OF LEGISLATION

## STATUTES

Children Act 1989
   s 96(2) .................................................................................................36, 38
Civil Evidence Act 1972
   ss 1(1), 3(2) ..............................................................................................178
Civil Evidence Act 1995 ...............................................................................59
   s 1(1) ..........................................................................................................41
   s 1(2) ...................................................................................................41, 44
Civil Partnership Act 2004
   s 84 (1) ......................................................................................................32
Contempt of Court Act 1981
   s 10 ..........................................................................................................184
Criminal Evidence Act 1898
   s 1(f)(ii) ..............................................................................154–155, 158, 163
   s 1(f)(iii) ...................................................................................................159
Criminal Justice Act 1967
   s 9 ............................................................................................................136
   s 10 ............................................................................................................12
Criminal Justice Act 1988
   s 10 ............................................................................................................12
   s 23 ....................................................................................59, 65, 71, 171
   ss 25–26 .............................................................................................59, 71, 73
   s 30 ..........................................................................................................178
   s 34(2) .......................................................................................................77
   s 139 ..........................................................................................................22
Criminal Justice Act 2003
   Pt 11, Ch 1 .........................................................................127, 129, 134, 147
   Pt 11, Ch 2 ..........................................................................................41, 59,
   s 98 ................................................................................130–131, 134, 137, 139, 145
   s 99(1) .....................................................................................................159
   s 100 .................................................................................................149, 170

xix

| | |
|---|---|
| s 100(1) | 149 |
| s 100(1)(a) | 128, 170 |
| s 100(1)(b) | 128, 170 |
| s 100(1)(c) | |
| s 100(4) | 149, 170 |
| s 101(1) | 139, 142 |
| s 101(1)(a), (b) | 128 |
| s 101(1)(c) | 61, 128, 133–134, 137 |
| s 101(1)(d) | 13, 128, 131, 133–135, 137–138, 141, 143, 145, 150, 152, 154–159, 161–164, 199 |
| s 101(1)(e) | 128, 150, 157–160 |
| s 101(1)(f) | 128, 154–155, 160, 162–163 |
| s 101(1)(g) | 128, 142, 149–150, 154, 156–158, 161–165, 170 |
| s 101(3) | 128, 135, 142, 149–150, 153, 156–157, 159, 162–165, 199 |
| s 101(4) | 128 |
| s 102 | 61, 128, 134, 137 |
| s 103 | 128, 150 |
| s 103(1)(a) | 12, 131, 134, 157–158, 163 |
| s 103(1)(b) | 130, 132, 134, 157–158, 163–164 |
| s 103(2) | 157, 164 |
| s 103(3) | 128, 135, 141, 143, 145, 150, 163, 199 |
| s 103(4) | 128 |
| s 103(4)(b), (5) | 164 |
| ss 104, 105 | 128, 159 |
| s 105(1), (2), (a) | 154 |
| s 105(3) | 154, 162 |
| s 105(4), (5) | 155 |
| s 105(4) | 163 |
| s 106 | 128, 158 |
| s 106(1)(t) | 162 |
| s 106(2) | 164 |
| s 109 | 138 |
| s 112 | 130–131 |
| s 112(1) | 134, 137, 139, 145 |
| s 114 | 42–43, 46, 60 |
| s 114(1) | 41, 43–44 |
| s 114(1)(d) | 48, 51, 70–72 |

| | |
|---|---|
| s 114(2) | 48, 72 |
| s 115(2) | 41, 53–54, 87 |
| s 115(3) | 42, 44, 46, 48, 51, 57, 71 |
| s 115(3)(a) | 69 |
| s 116 | 42–43, 49, 51, 59, 60–64, 69, 71 |
| s 116(1) | 51 |
| s 116(1)(a) | 51, 64 |
| s 116(1)(b) | 51, 62, 64, 71 |
| s 116(2) | 51, 64 |
| s 116(2)(c) | 204 |
| s 116(2)(d) | 204 |
| s 116(2)(e) | 71, 173, 202 |
| s 116(3) | 202 |
| s 116(4) | 72, 173, 202 |
| s 117 | 59–60, 62–65 |
| s 117(1)(a) | 62 |
| s 117(2)(a)–(c) | 62, 65 |
| s 117(2)(c) | 65 |
| s 117(5) | 62 |
| s 117(7) | 72 |
| s 118 | 46, 59–62, 71–72 |
| s 118(1) | 63, 67, 83, 175, 199 |
| s 118(1) 4(a) | 63 |
| s 118(1) 4(b) | 62 |
| s 119 | 64, 167 |
| s 119(1) | 173 |
| s 120 | 64, 167, 174 |
| s 120(1) | 86–87 |
| s 120(2) | 172 |
| s 120(3) | 173 |
| s 120(4) | 79–80, 86–87, 169, 174, 204 |
| s 120(5) | 86–87, 169, 174 |
| s 120(7) | 80, 174 |
| s 120(7)(a)–(f) | 80, 204 |
| s 120 (7) (d) | 70, 72 |
| s 120(8) | 80, 167 |
| ss 121–25 | 60 |

s 121 .................................................................................................................62–65
s 121(1) ....................................................................................................................48
ss 121(1)(c), 124, 126(2) ..........................................................................64, 72, 204
s 139 ........................................................................................................................87
s 139(1) ...........................................................................................................172–173
Sched 37 pt 6 ..........................................................................................................59

Criminal Justice and Public Order Act 1994
s 32 ..........................................................................................................................77
s 34 ..............................................................................78, 84, 100–102, 103–104,
115, 120, 122, 124–125,
171–172, 196, 201
s 34(2A) ..............................................................................................84, 115, 122
s 35 ..................................................................................................100–102, 161
s 35(3) ............................................................................................................148, 161
ss 36, 37 ..............................................................................................100–101, 103–104
s 38 ........................................................................................................................100

Criminal Procedure Act 1865
s 3 ..........................................................................................................................173
s 6 ..........................................................................................................................170

Criminal Procedure (Insanity) Act 1964
s 4(1) .......................................................................................................................23

Evidence Amendment Act 1853
s 1 .......................................................................................................................36–37

Family Law Reform Act 1969
s 26 ....................................................................................................................35, 40

Fatal Accidents Act 1976 ..............................................................................................193

Health and Safety at Work Act 1974
s 40 ..........................................................................................................................18

Homicide Act 1957
s 2 .................................................................................................................179–181

Human Rights Act 1998 ..................................................................................................7
s 3 ..........................................................................................................................175

Investigatory Power Act 2000 ....................................................................................126

xxii

# Table of Legislation

Law of Property Act 1925
- s 184 .................................................................................................39–40
- s 184(1) .............................................................................................33–34

Magistrates' Courts Act 1980
- s 101 ..................................................................................................27–29

Police and Criminal Evidence Act 1984
- s 58 ...................................................................................................110, 121
- s 58(8) ..............................................................................................114, 121
- s 58(8)(c) ................................................................................................121
- s 62(10) ..................................................................................................102
- s 62(11) ....................................................................................................78
- s 66 ..........................................................................................................87
- s 67(11) ...............................................................................................77, 87
- s 73 .........................................................................................................170
- s 73(2) ....................................................................................................141
- s 74 .........................................................................................................137
- s 74(3) ..............................................................................................140–142
- ss 76 and 78 .....................................................................................112–113
- s 76 ..........................................................86, 97, 100, 108–110, 118, 120
- s 76(1) ..............................................................................53, 87, 121, 204
- s 76(2) ..............................................................................................99, 121
- s 76(2)(a) ........................................................................................120–121
- s 76(2)(b) .............................................97, 110, 112, 114–115, 117–121
- s 76(4) .............................................................................................115, 120–121
- s 76(8) .........................................................................................100, 109, 120
- s 76A(1) ..................................................................................................160
- s 78 ......................................................71–72, 77, 87, 97, 99–100, 104, 110, 113,
  120–124, 126, 131, 163
- s 78(1) ...................................46, 51, 53–54, 64, 88, 91, 93–94, 104–107,
  122–125, 128  129, 137, 145, 155, 162
- s 80 ...................................................................................................32, 36–37
- s 80(3)(a) ..............................................................................................36–37
- s 82(1) ............................................................83, 98, 108–109, 113, 115, 117, 120
- s 82(3) ................................................................................................105, 107
- s 116 ....................................................................................................53–54
- s 116(3) ....................................................................................................63

xxiii

Police and Criminal Evidence Act 2004
  s 80(2A) .................................................................................................................. 202
Prevention of Crime Act 1953
  s 1 ...................................................................................................................... 20–22
Public Order Act 1986
  s 3(1) ....................................................................................................................... 84
Readers (Protection) Act
  s 1 ...................................................................................................................... 26–27
  s 2 ...................................................................................................................... 26–29
Rehabilitation of Offenders Act 1974 ............................................................... 157–158
Road Traffic Act 1988
  ss 6(4), 7(6) ................................................................................................................
Theft Act 1968
  s 8 ........................................................................................................................... 38
  s 27(3) ............................................................................................................. 129, 140
  s 27(3)(b) .............................................................................................................. 140

Workmen's Compensation Act 1943 ......................................................................... 9

Youth Justice and Criminal Evidence Act 1999
  ss 41–43 ......................................................................................................... 167–168
  s 41 ........................................................................................ 6–8, 80, 175, 204–205
  s 41(1) ................................................................................................................... 204
  s 41(1)(c) ............................................................................................................... 205
  s 41(2), (2)(b), (3)(b) .................................................................................. 175–176, 205
  s 41(3)(c)(ii), (5) ......................................................................................... 175–176, 204
  s 43(3)(c) ............................................................................................................... 175
  ss 53–56 .................................................................................................................. 32
  s 53(1) ................................................................................................ 36–37, 83, 202
  s 53(3) ....................................................................................................... 37, 83, 202
  s 55(2) ..................................................................................................................... 83
  s 55(2)(a) ........................................................................................................... 36–37

# OTHER LEGISLATION

Civil Procedure Rules 1998
  r 31.20 ............................................................................................................ 184, 194

Criminal Justice Act 2003 (category of offences) order 20004............................................11
   SI 3346, sched, pt 1 ....................................................................................165

European Convention on the Protection of Human Rights and
   Fundamental Freedoms 1951
   Art 6................................................................................................................7, 175
   Art 6(2).........................................................................................16–17, 19, 27, 29
   Art 6(3) (d)............................................................................................................48
   Art 8 .....................................................................................................................107

# Chapter 1

# Basic Concepts

## INTRODUCTION

The biggest obstacle to doing well in an evidence examination is failure to realise that this is very largely a practical subject, and that when you are faced with a problem question you need to think as carefully about the facts as about the law – perhaps even more carefully, because quite often what you think about the facts will affect the legal position. It would therefore be a good idea to make it a rule that you think about a problem question first as a story.

Somebody is trying to prove something. How is he doing this? First, he should have in mind a clear idea of what is to be proved. Suppose we take a famous murder trial which took place in 1910 – that of Dr Crippen. The prosecution was trying to prove that Crippen had murdered his wife. The story, according to them, was that Crippen had fallen in love with his young secretary, Ethel Le Neve, and had decided to kill his wife so as to leave him free to marry Ethel. One night, therefore, he put poison in a glass of stout – his wife's regular nightcap. The poison might have been sufficient to kill her, or it might merely have rendered her unconscious. At any rate, by the time Crippen had finished with the body she must have been dead. According to the prosecution, he cut the flesh from the bones and buried it in pieces in the cellar of the house where they lived. He burned the bones, and the head was never found. To explain his wife's absence, he told friends at first that she was staying with relations. Later, when the police began to make inquiries, he told them that she had left him and that he had been too embarrassed to tell people this. Crippen had not yet been arrested, and shortly after his interview with the police, he hurriedly left the country with Ethel Le Neve. Meanwhile, the police dug up the cellar floor and discovered the human remains that had been buried there. Crippen was followed and brought back to England to stand trial.

You know, of course, what constitutes murder in English law. But from the standpoint of someone studying evidence, you must now decide precisely what it was that the prosecution had to prove in this particular case.

The first thing they had to prove was that Mrs Crippen was dead. Crippen maintained throughout that his wife had left him and that he knew nothing of the remains in the cellar. It was therefore necessary for the prosecution to establish that the remains were those of Mrs Crippen. They had also to show that her husband had killed her intentionally.

It is at this stage that the prosecution had to start thinking carefully in terms of relevance. Ideally, each item of evidence they presented should have had a probative job to do in the overall task of proving that Crippen had murdered his wife. For example, by proving that Mrs Crippen had had the mark of an operation on her body, and by showing that one of the pieces of buried flesh had the same mark, the prosecution was able to establish that the remains in the cellar were those of Mrs Crippen and that therefore she was in fact dead.

The evidence of Crippen's flight was also relevant, but it's worth pausing to consider why this was so. What probative job did this item of evidence do for the prosecution? The prosecution suggested that it showed guilty knowledge. But why should it do that? One answer is that people who suddenly leave the country when the police are making inquiries about them are likely to do so because they fear that their criminal activities are about to be discovered.

Notice two important points at this stage. The first is that if you press sufficiently the question why an item of evidence is relevant, your explanation will often take the form of a generalisation about the way things are in the world *which itself may or may not be true*. I tried to make my explanatory generalisation about people who run away appear true by using the words 'are likely to do so'. It leaves room for alternative explanations – they may be innocent but fear that the police will frame them; they may have a rich aunt dying in Brazil – but I put my explanation forward as one that is likely. If I am right in this, it follows that the evidence of the flight was relevant, admissible and had significant probative weight.

Now, let's look at a question of relevance in another famous murder case. Edith Thompson and her husband were not very happily married. They took in a young lodger, Freddie Bywaters. One night, when Mr and Mrs Thompson were walking home, Freddie sprang out from a place where he had been waiting and stabbed Mr Thompson to death. But the prosecution story was that Freddie was not the only culprit. He and Edith, it was alleged, were having an affair, and she had plotted the murder with him and had encouraged him to carry it out.

Among the many items of evidence relied on at trial by the prosecution was the disparity in age between Freddie and Edith. She was 28 years old at the time of the murder; he was only 20. What was the relevance of this? What probative job did this information do? At the time, nobody seems to have had any clear thoughts on the matter. But we need to ask this question: what generalisation about the way things are in the world has to be true for this item of evidence to be relevant? Here is a suggestion: 'In a sexual relationship, an older woman is likely to dominate a younger man.' That, if true, would help the prosecution because it would add to the probability that Edith persuaded Freddie to murder Mr Thompson. But *is* it true? If it is not true, and no satisfactory substitute can be found, then surely the evidence is irrelevant, and so inadmissible. (See Twining, W, *Theories of Evidence: Bentham and Wigmore*, 1985, pp 143–144; and Twining, W, *Rethinking Evidence: Exploratory Essays*, 1994, pp 290–293.)

I said earlier that there were two important points to be made about the sort of answer which I suggested to the question of why evidence of Crippen's flight was relevant at his trial. One was the point which I have just been making about the *form* the answer takes – that of a generalisation. The second important point is this. The weaker a generalisation is, the more likely it is to be true. But the weaker the generalisation, the less probative weight will attach to the item of evidence in question. This may be very important where admissibility depends on assessing the probative weight of a piece of evidence and the improperly prejudicial effect that it might have on a jury if they heard it. For example, some cats are Siamese. I have three cats. But, this is not much evidence that I have a Siamese cat. One or more of them *may* be a Siamese, but the likelihood is not great because there are many other breeds, as well as non-pedigree cats.

Later, you will see the importance in other areas of evidence law of the question: what is the probative job that this item of evidence is put forward to do? (Hearsay is a particularly good example. See Chapters 4 and 5.) But being able to answer this question, and being able to say why an item of evidence is relevant by pointing to an appropriate generalisation, can be done only if you have first thought carefully about the *story* the examiner is telling you in the particular problem question.

If you get a question directly on relevance in the examination, it will almost certainly be an essay question involving theory, and I have tried in the answer to Question 1 to give some idea of how such an essay might be tackled. But you don't *have* to be able to write an answer to a theoretical question about relevance to do well in an examination. What you *do* have to be able to do is understand how the idea *works*.

As well as relevance, there are a few other basic concepts that you ought to know about; I have referred to these in the Checklist and you should find them adequately dealt with in your textbook. You will find that this is a subject that has attracted quite a complicated terminology, about the use of which there is not complete agreement on the part of either judges or writers. A lot of this terminology can in practice be avoided, but you should take care to understand how the writer of the textbook you are using employs his terminology, and you should be particularly careful when reading cases to make sure that you understand what a particular judge is getting at by the language he uses.

## Checklist

Students should be familiar with the following areas:
- relevance;
- admissibility;
- what facts are in issue in criminal cases;
- how to discover what facts are in issue in a civil case;
- formal admissions in civil and criminal cases;
- judicial notice.

# Question 1

Is a concept of legal relevance useful in the law of evidence?

## Answer plan

Begin by setting out the two different ways in which a legal concept can be 'useful': one is connected with what the law is, the other with what it ought to be. The question raises a classic problem on which the two great American writers on evidence, Thayer and Wigmore, had different views; these are outlined. Note that there are some cases where judges do appear to have laid down rules about what is or is not relevant and at least one occasion where Parliament has tried to do so. Note also the practice of the courts of rejecting evidence of only minimal weight on the ground that it is 'irrelevant'. But, the point is then made that none of this justifies acknowledging a concept of 'legal relevance' in existing law because:
- such a concept would be impossible to define; and
- it would be difficult to develop a body of case law on the subject.

In addition, such a concept would be undesirable because:
- if a body of case law could after all be developed, it would be cumbersome and restrictive;
- it would make it even more difficult than it is at present for the law to respond to changing conditions.

In summary, therefore, the essay is constructed as follows:
- two ways in which a legal concept can be 'useful';
- outline of the argument to be put forward;
- Thayer's rejection of 'legal relevance';
- Wigmore's contrary view;
- judicial decisions about relevance, for example, *DPP v Camplin (1978)*; *DPP v Majewski (1977)*;
- the connection made by courts between relevance and weight;
- apparent 'rules' about relevance: *Grant (1996)*; *Halpin (1996)*; *Guney (1998)*;
- difficulties presented by 'legal relevance'.

# Answer

A legal concept may be useful either because it helps us to understand the law as it is, or because if it were to be introduced, it would improve the state of the law. I shall argue that a concept of legal relevance is scarcely to be found in the existing state of the law and that it would not be useful to introduce it.

Thayer defined the law of evidence as 'a set of rules and principles affecting judicial investigations into questions of fact', but he pointed out that these rules and principles do not regulate the process of reasoning, save to the extent of helping to select the factual material upon which the processes of reasoning are to operate. Chiefly, in addition to prescribing the manner of presenting evidence and fixing the qualifications and privileges of witnesses, these rules and principles determine what classes of things shall not be received in evidence. There is one principle of exclusion, however, which Thayer described as not so much a rule of evidence as a presupposition involved in the very conception of a rational system of evidence: this was the principle which forbids receiving anything irrelevant.[1] But the law, according to Thayer, furnishes no test of relevance. For this, it tacitly refers to logic and general experience, the principles of which are presumed to be known.

Wigmore, on the other hand, questioned the idea that the law furnished no test of relevance. He argued that although relevance is originally a matter of logic and common sense, there are still many instances in which the evidence of particular facts as bearing on particular issues has been so often the subject of discussion in courts of law, and so often ruled upon, that the united logic of a great many judges and lawyers may be said to furnish evidence of the sense common to a great many individuals, and so to acquire the authority of law. It is thus proper, he argued, to talk of legal relevance.

It is certainly the case that in some instances, judges have laid down rules about what is relevant or irrelevant. For example, they have decided that age and sex are always relevant when considering the defence of provocation (*DPP v Camplin (1978)*). And intoxication is, as a matter of law, irrelevant in considering whether the *mens rea* for a crime of basic intent was present (*DPP v Majewski (1977)*). And in s 41 of the Youth Justice and Criminal Evidence Act 1999 Parliament attempted to lay down what the government minister in the House of Lords referred to as 'a statutory framework for determining relevance' in trials where a sexual offence is alleged.

But, apart from specific rules such as these, it is necessary to take into account the practice of the courts of rejecting evidence that has minimal weight on the ground that it is 'irrelevant'. Is this because the evidence falls short of the minimum requirement of something which can be called 'legal relevance'? There are good reasons why data of very slight weight should be excluded. Doing justice according to law is not the same as doing a piece of historical research. Concessions have to be made to what Justice Holmes referred to as 'the shortness of life', as well as to the financial resources of the litigants or the legal aid fund. Moreover, if the field of judicial inquiry were too wide, it might make decisions more unreliable because a mass of evidence would more readily lead to confusion.[2]

It is also possible for the courts to develop something that can appear at first glance to be a rule about relevance in a particular type of situation, but which is really something else. Over the last few years, there has been a cluster of cases concerned with the precise significance to be attached to the discovery of large sums of cash in the possession of persons charged with possession of drugs with intent to supply. In one of these cases, *Grant (1996)*, it was said in the Court of Appeal that if there was any possible reason other than drug dealing for the defendant's possession of cash, the finding of the cash was to be treated as irrelevant, and juries should be so directed. And, in *Halpin (1996)*, the Court of Appeal said that evidence of a defendant's possession of large amounts of money, or of his extravagant lifestyle, could not be relevant where the issue in the case was possession, rather than intent to supply. However, this was later rejected in *Guney (1998)*, where the Court of Appeal said that although evidence of cash or lifestyle might only rarely be relevant where there was a charge of simple possession of drugs, such evidence could not be excluded as irrelevant as a matter of law. The relevance of any item of evidence is to be decided 'not on abstract legal theory but on the circumstances of each individual case' (see also *Griffiths (1998)*). It appears that the courts, at any rate, are reluctant to acknowledge a concept of 'legal relevance', higher and stricter than logical relevance. In fact, two main difficulties lie in the way of such development.

The first is that a concept of this kind would defy definition. The second is that since each case would be decided on its own facts, there would be considerable difficulty in developing a body of case law about what was legally relevant. The examples cited earlier of *DPP v Camplin* and *DPP v Majewski* are better seen as defining the substantive law in relation to particular offences than in saying something about a concept called 'legal relevance'.[3]

Not only does there seem to be little support for the proposition that a concept of legal relevance – despite the language of some judges – can be found in the law; there appear to be good reasons why such a concept should not be recognised.

In the first place, there is an inherent conflict between a theory that all logically relevant evidence should be admitted unless excluded by a clear ground of policy, and a theory of legal relevance, which would require a minimum quantity of probative value for each item of evidence in any particular case. There is a danger that a concept of legal relevance, if consistently applied, would exclude logically relevant evidence unless legal precedent authorised its admission. If, despite difficulties, a body of case law were to develop, it would give rise to a large number of cumbersome rules and exceptions.

The second reason why a concept of legal relevance ought not to be recognised is that to fix relevance in a straitjacket of case law would make it even more difficult than it already is to adapt the law to changing circumstances.

Necessarily, judges' decisions about relevance reflect the prevailing value judgments of the society in which they live. Relevance can become a useful instrument for discarding arguments and evidence that challenge important, though perhaps unexpressed, values. Thus, in the 19th century, the courts upheld a notion of freedom of contract which allowed them to argue that an aggrieved worker could have protected his position by insisting on an appropriate contractual stipulation. Evidence of inequality of bargaining power would have been ruled 'irrelevant'. That what is relevant depends on the basic assumptions of a particular society becomes even clearer when one considers the evidential significance of marks on the bodies of those formerly suspected of witchcraft, or of the appearance in their vicinity of such creatures as a cat, a toad or a wasp.[4]

No one, of course, could argue a case from a standpoint wholly outside the beliefs of his own society. And it may well be that arguments about relevance will be constrained by the way in which the substantive law is defined. What one can reasonably hope is that the ability to argue from a critical standpoint in particular cases should not be easily frustrated. A further obstacle in the way of such arguments would be likely to emerge if a concept of legal relevance were to become fully developed in the law of evidence.[5]

A concept of legal relevance could also lead to unfairness to defendants, who might be prevented from adducing relevant and weighty evidence in support of their defence. This was recognised, in effect, by the House of Lords in *A (2001)*, when the law lords interpreted s 41 of the Youth Justice and Criminal Evidence Act 1999 in the light of the Human Rights Act 1998 and the defendant's right to a fair trial under Article 6 of the European Convention on Human Rights.

### References

1. Cf *Turner (1975)*, *per* Lawton LJ: 'Relevance, however, does not result in evidence being admissible: it is a condition precedent to admissibility.'
2. Cf the observations of Lord Bridge in *Blastland (1986)*.
3. But see s 41 of the Youth Justice and Criminal Evidence Act 1999. It looks very much as if the government accepted that some facts can be *logically* relevant, but, to preserve a 'balance' between the interests of the complainant and the defendant, they are not allowed to be *legally* relevant.
4. Thomas, K, *Religion and the Decline of Magic*, 1971, p 530.
5. See Thayer, JB, *A Preliminary Treatise on Evidence at the Common Law*, 1898, Chapter 6; James, GF, 'Relevancy, probability and the law' (1941) 29 *California Law Review* 689, pp 689–705; Trautman, HL, 'Logical or legal relevancy – a conflict in theory' (1952) 5 *Vanderbilt Law Review* 385, pp 385–413; Weyrauch, WO, 'Law as mask – legal ritual and relevance' (1978) 66 *California Law Review* 699, pp 699–726.

# Question 2

How satisfactory is the law on judicial notice?

### Answer plan

The law on this subject is in a mess – albeit an interesting one. The following points should be made:

- the distinction (if any) between taking judicial notice and using local or special knowledge;
- the different rationales that have been suggested for judicial notice;
- the effect of those rationales on the way the law is viewed;
- the failure of English law to commit itself unequivocally to a single rationale;
- the ambiguity of the relationship between judicial notice and evidence.

# Answer

The problem with the law of judicial notice is that it is underdeveloped. As a result of this, there is confusion about the principles on which it rests and about its scope.

There is confusion about its scope because it is unclear whether a distinction should be made between taking judicial notice and using special or local knowledge. In *Wetherall v Harrison (1976)*, the Divisional Court held that magistrates were entitled to use their own special or local knowledge when trying cases, but Lord Widgery CJ saw this as a necessary concession to the layman's inability to exclude such factors from his deliberations. He thought that, in this respect, magistrates were unlike trained judges and were more like members of a jury. In line with this approach, the Divisional Court in *Bowman v DPP (1990)* said that a bench of magistrates using its local knowledge of a particular piece of land was not taking 'judicial notice'. But in *Mullen v Hackney LBC (1997)*, the Court of Appeal held that a county court judge had been entitled to take judicial notice of his own special or local knowledge about the defendant council's failure to honour undertakings given to the court in other cases. This decision was almost certainly wrong. There is a line of cases to the effect that county court judges can rely on their own local knowledge 'properly and within reasonable limits': see, for example, *Reynolds v Llanelly Tinplate Co Ltd (1948)*. But all these cases were decided under the *Workmen's Compensation Acts*, under which the county court judge sat as an arbitrator. There is no doubt that an arbitrator can, in certain circumstances, make use of his own knowledge and experience to determine issues in dispute between the parties to the arbitration, without hearing expert evidence. This was held to be within the judge's powers under those Acts: see, for example, *Peart v Bolckow Vaughan & Co Ltd (1925)*. But the cases do not establish that county court judges sitting in any other capacity have the same freedom that they had as arbitrators in workmen's compensation cases. Nor do those cases suggest that judges were taking 'judicial notice' of anything.

There are two main theories about the rationale of judicial notice. On one view, it is a device for filtering out evidence about matters that are really unarguable. If you regard judicial notice in this light, you will tend to want its scope to be restricted to notorious, or readily ascertainable facts; its application to be mandatory rather than discretionary; and the effect of its application conclusive.[1]

Another view is that judicial notice is simply a labour saving device in litigation. If seen in this way, its scope can be wider, and its application discretionary. Its effect can even be defeasible in the light of further evidence.[2] A controversial variant of this view is that any process of judicial reasoning about facts assumes the truth of a mass of material that has not been formally proved. For example, a judge assumes that trains run on rails, that France is outside the United Kingdom, and that there is a law of gravity. If this analysis is right, 'the tacit applications of the doctrine of judicial notice are more numerous and more important than the express ones'.[3] But this is a controversial view. Others have acknowledged that both judges and juries must make use of general knowledge to interpret evidence. But, they argue, this is not a question of judicial notice; it is the tribunal relying on its own experience of the ordinary course of human affairs.[4]

A limited view of judicial notice should require mandatory application. This line has been taken in cases relating to political and constitutional matters. For example, in *Duff Development Co Ltd v Government of Kelantan (1924)*, the House of Lords said that where the question of the sovereignty of a foreign State is in issue, it is the practice of the courts to treat as conclusive the information that they obtain on the matter from a Secretary of State. But in other cases the courts have taken the view that they have a discretion whether or not to take judicial notice of a particular fact. In *George v Davies (1911)*, for example, it was tacitly accepted by the Divisional Court that a judge had a discretion to decide whether to take judicial notice of an employment custom that had been established by evidence in earlier cases.

A further problem with judicial notice is its relationship to evidence. Where judicial notice is taken without inquiry, for example, that cats are kept for domestic purposes (*Nye v Niblett (1918)*) or that people who go to hotels do not like having their nights disturbed (*Andreae v Selfridge & Co Ltd (1938)*), it is clear that no process of proof is involved, because no material containing information is produced by either party. But is judicial notice after inquiry based on a process of proof? The opinions of judges have been divided. In *McQuaker v Goddard (1940)*, at least one member of the Court of Appeal (Clauson LJ) took the view that a judge was entitled to disregard the rules of evidence and look at materials that would otherwise have been inadmissible, on the basis that he was merely 'refreshing his memory' about the ordinary course of nature – a subject of which, by a legal fiction, judges had complete knowledge.

It is clearly unsatisfactory to have a situation where it is unclear whether rules about admissibility are going to be applied or not. The truth of the matter is that, in principle, scope and effect, the law about judicial notice is underdeveloped and ripe for clarification.

### References

1. Morgan, EM, *Some Problems of Proof under the Anglo-American System of Litigation*, 1956, p 42.
2. Thayer, JB, *A Preliminary Treatise on Evidence at the Common Law*, 1898, p 278.
3. Tapper, C, *Cross & Tapper on Evidence*, 10th edn, 2004, p 94.
4. See, for example, Eggleston, R (Sir), *Evidence, Proof and Probability*, 2nd edn, 1983, pp 143–144.

## Question 3

The police suspect that Alex and Ben are dealing separately in drugs. They lawfully search Alex's house. There they find a large quantity of cannabis resin hidden

# BASIC CONCEPTS

behind a wardrobe. They also find £3,420 in cash in Alex's coat pockets, and a pair of diamond earrings worth £35,000 in a jewel box belonging to Alex's wife. Alex tells the police that he frequently smokes cannabis and that the supply was solely for his own use. He adds that he had the cash in his coat because he runs a firm of builders and had to pay his staff their wages that afternoon. He is nevertheless charged with possession of cannabis with intent to supply.

The police lawfully search Ben's house. They find a small amount of cocaine in an old tobacco tin on a shelf in his garage, and £345 in cash in a desk in Ben's study. Ben says, 'I'd no idea there was cocaine in that old tin. It must have been left there by Cedric. He used to be a lodger, and I let him keep his motor cycle in the garage.' The police trace and interview Cedric, who tells them that he has never owned a motor cycle and that he never went into the garage when he was Ben's lodger. Ben is charged with possession of cocaine.

Discuss the evidential issues arising.

## Answer plan

The defendants are not suspected of operating together, so deal with each separately.

### Alex

- You are told that the search was lawful, so there is no point to be taken about improperly obtained evidence. Obviously, evidence of finding the cannabis can be given, and it can be produced as an item of real evidence if necessary. Is there anything the prosecution could do to avoid having to produce the cannabis in court? Is there any reason for the defence to insist that it should be produced?

- The discovery of the cash in Alex's coat. You must first decide if this is relevant to the prosecution case. If it is relevant, and admissible, what directions should the judge give to the jury about the use they can make of this evidence? The cases of *Wright (1994)* and *Grant (1996)* are helpful here. A first-class answer might refer to the strength of those decisions after the passing of the **Criminal Justice Act 2003**, which has made it much easier to adduce evidence of criminal disposition on the part of the accused.

- The wife's diamond earrings. Are they relevant? Is there any other evidence of 'lavish lifestyle'? Even if there were, would it be likely to be regarded as relevant? See *Halpin (1996)*.

*Ben*
- Obviously, evidence can be given of discovering the tin containing cocaine, and it can be produced at trial if necessary.
- Is the cash in Ben's desk relevant to the charge against him? Remember that though initially he was suspected of supplying, he has been charged with possession only.
- What is the significance of the evidence that Cedric can give? What direction should the judge give to the jury about it?

# Answer

The prosecution will have no difficulty in adducing evidence of the search at Alex's house or of the discovery of the cannabis, which should be produced as an item of real evidence, unless the defence is prepared to make a formal admission in respect of its discovery under s 10 of the Criminal Justice Act 1967.

The discovery of the cash in Alex's coat is more problematic. In *Wright (1994)* the discovery of £16,000 in cash and a gold necklace worth about £9,000 was held to be relevant and admissible where the defendant was charged with possession of cocaine with intent to supply. In *Grant (1996)* the defendant, charged with possession of crack cocaine with intent to supply, was found with just over £900 in cash in his possession. The Court of Appeal held that the finding of money in conjunction with a substantial quantity of drugs was capable of being relevant to intent to supply, and could properly be admitted. But a proper direction must be given to the jury about the use to be made of such evidence. Any innocent explanation for possession of the cash must be rejected before its possession can be relevant to the offence of possession with intent to supply. But if innocent explanations are rejected, and the presence of the cash indicates not merely past dealing, but ongoing dealing in drugs, it can be taken into account in deciding whether the prosecution has proved intent to supply. It seems clear that the discovery of the cash will be relevant and admissible, but the jury will have to be satisfied that Alex did not have it for his stated purpose before they can take it into account in deciding whether the prosecution has proved intent to supply. It is unclear whether the judge should now also direct them to be satisfied that the money does not indicate merely past dealing, but is evidence of ongoing dealing. At the time when *Wright* was decided there were severe restrictions on the use of evidence of past matters to show the accused's disposition to commit the offence charged. Since the Criminal Justice Act 2003 those restrictions have been substantially reduced,[1] and it may now be sufficiently relevant if the cash is evidence only of past dealing.

The wife's diamond earrings would probably be regarded as either irrelevant, or inadmissible as possessing insufficient probative value. She is not charged, and there is no evidence even that they were a present from her husband. In *Halpin (1996)* the Court of Appeal said that a 'lavish lifestyle' would only rarely be relevant to intent to supply drugs found in the possession of the accused, and there is nothing on the facts to show that there was anything other than the earrings to indicate such a lifestyle.

In Ben's case, evidence will be given of the discovery of the cocaine, which can be produced as an item of real evidence in the same way as the earlier discovery at Alex's house. It appears that Ben has given no explanation for the presence of cash in his desk. But it is a relatively small sum; he is not charged with possession with intent to supply; and it is difficult to see how possession of this money could be relevant to the question whether he was also in possession of the cocaine. Cedric's denials of possession of a motor cycle or of using the garage suggest that Ben might have been lying to the police. Cedric would have to give evidence at Ben's trial and the judge would have to warn the jury, in accordance with *Lucas (1981)* and *Burge and Pegg (1996)*, that before they can use Cedric's evidence against Ben, they must be satisfied that Ben had indeed lied, and was not simply mistaken, and that even if he had lied, he might have done so for an innocent reason.[2]

## References

1 See ss 101(1)(d) and 103(1)(a).
2 See Chapter 6.

# Chapter 2

# Burden and Standard of Proof

## INTRODUCTION

The burden and the standard of proof are matters that must be kept distinct, and judges have a duty to direct the jury in respect of each of them. Problems are therefore most likely to arise in criminal jury trials because a wrong direction, or no direction at all, could provide a successful ground of appeal.

You must be able to distinguish between a legal and an evidential burden. The latter is not strictly a burden *of proof* at all. It is best seen as a rule of common sense which says that there must be *some* evidence for a particular issue to become a live one, so that it is fit for consideration by a jury or other tribunal of fact. Because of this, whether an evidential burden has been satisfied or not in a jury trial is a matter for the judge alone, and consequently there should never be a need to refer to it in a summing up.

In civil cases, it will generally be clear from the statements of case where the burden of proof lies. Although you will find fascinating cases where it wasn't clear at all discussed in the textbooks, don't get bogged down with them when you first approach this topic.

It is important to understand why in criminal cases it is impossible to say for certain when the well known *Woolmington* principle will *not* apply. As you will see from the answer to Question 4, there can be no simple list of exceptions.

The *standard* of proof is less likely to occur as an essay topic because it raises too many theoretical issues. For example, should we reduce the standard of proof in (some) criminal cases if there were to be a significant increase in a particularly unpleasant type of crime? Does it make sense to talk of 'standards' of proof at all? Aren't things either proved or not, more or less easily, depending on their inherent probability? All good fun, but not to be attempted in the examination if you haven't studied these problems as part of your course.

What you may get is a 'dud direction' question, covering both burden and standard of proof, where you are asked to examine an excerpt from a summing up and say whether there are grounds for appeal. It is important to remember that there is no magic form of words about either the burden or standard of proof that *must* be used, though judges are wise to follow one of the two accepted forms and it is clear that some directions will not suffice. It's a good idea to look at the cases which have approved various forms of words so as to get their general sense and compare those with cases where there was held to have been a misdirection.

It is particularly important to remember that the legal burden of proof remains with the prosecution where defences such as provocation, self-defence, duress, non-insane automatism and alibi are in issue. In cases where the defendant *does* have the legal burden of proving something, that burden will be discharged if the civil standard of proof is satisfied. Remember also that where there is a burden on the defence on a particular issue, there cannot also be a burden on the prosecution on that same issue. Sometimes, candidates try to have the best of both worlds and say, for example, that the defence in an offensive weapon case has to prove on the balance of probabilities that there was a reasonable excuse, and the prosecution has to prove beyond reasonable doubt that there was not. This is gibberish.

## Checklist

Students should be familiar with the following areas:
- the distinction between the burden and standard of proof;
- the meaning of 'evidential burden';
- factors affecting the burden of proof in civil cases;
- the burden of proof in criminal cases;
- the standard of proof in civil and criminal cases.

# Question 4

When will the imposition of a legal burden on an accused person be compatible with Art 6(2) of the European Convention on Human Rights?

## Answer plan

Note, first, that the question is about the developments after the Human Rights Act. It should be obvious, therefore, that a discussion of the law before that Act will be irrelevant. And don't try to make it appear relevant by saying that in order to understand recent developments it's necessary to look at the development of the law since *Woolmington*! In this case it's not. The following points could be made:

- The basic principle established in *Salabiaku v France (1988)*;
- The six factors that may be taken into account, supported by reference to decided cases, when deciding whether a reverse burden is compatible with the **European Convention on Human Rights**:

    the distinction between *mala in se* and *mala prohibita* in relation to offences;

    deference to Parliament's decision;

    a distinction between elements of the offence and defences;

    maximum penalties;

    ease of proof and defendant's peculiar knowledge;

    the presumption of innocence itself.

# Answer

Article 6(2) provides that everyone charged with a criminal offence shall be presumed innocent until proved guilty according to law. English law has not consistently followed the 'golden thread' principle referred to in *Woolmington v DPP (1935)*. There are statutes expressly providing that an accused shall bear the burden of proof in relation to some matter; other statutes have in the past been interpreted as doing so by implication. Since the passing of the **Human Rights Act 1998**, it has become clear that not every reversal of the burden of proof will infringe Art 6(2) of the European Convention on Human Rights, but that each statutory provision must be considered on its merits. The European jurisprudence accepts that reverse burdens do not infringe Art 6(2) so long as they are confined within reasonable limits, which take into account the importance of what is at stake and maintain the rights of the defence (*Salabiaku v France, 1988*). Prediction has become an uncertain task, but Dennis has identified six elements that may be taken into account in reaching a decision where the court is faced with legislation that apparently reverses the burden of proof in any respect.[1]

The first element is based on a classification of offences that distinguishes, in the traditional terminology, between *mala in se* and *mala prohibita*. For example, in *Lambert (2002)* Lord Clyde said that a strict responsibility might be acceptable in the case of statutory offences that were concerned to regulate the conduct of a particular activity in the public interest. A licence could be required to carry out certain activities, or controls might be imposed to promote health and safety and avoid pollution. Such cases, he said, could properly be seen as not truly criminal. Many might be relatively trivial and carry no real social disgrace. This approach was adopted by the Court of Appeal in *Davies (2002)*, where the Court upheld s 40 of the Health and Safety at Work Act 1974. This provision imposed a legal burden on a defendant to prove that it had not been reasonably practicable to do more than he had done to ensure that employees were not exposed to risks to their health and safety. The difficulty with classification of offences as a criterion for reverse burdens of proof is, as Dennis pointed out, that the moral quality of regulatory offences is variable. For example, where a regulatory offence leads to someone's death, as was the case in *Davies*, it might not be easy to maintain that the breach involved no real social disgrace. The same could also be true of a regulatory offence that led to widespread pollution of the environment.

A second consideration is the deference that should be shown to Parliament's decision. In *Lambert (2002)* Lord Steyn said that the burden is on the state to show that the legislative means adopted were not greater than necessary. He added that there must be a 'pressing necessity' to impose a legal burden on the accused. But other judges have been more inclined to give weight to the decision of the elected body that passed the legislation. For example, in *R v DPP, ex p Kebilene (2000)* Lord Hope said that such deference would be particularly appropriate where the issues involved questions of social or economic policy. In *Johnstone (2003)* Lord Nicholls pointed out that Parliament had the primary responsibility for deciding, as a matter of policy, what should be the constituent elements of a criminal offence, and courts should reach a different conclusion from the legislature only where it was apparent that the latter had attached insufficient importance to the individual's fundamental right to be presumed innocent until proved guilty.

However, in *Sheldrake v DPP (2004)* Lord Bingham doubted whether there should be an assumption that Parliament would not have made an exception to the basic rule without good reason. Such an approach might lead the court to give too much weight to the enactment under review, and too little to the presumption of innocence. Dennis has suggested that the court's approach should depend on drawing a clear distinction between the two criteria referred to in *Salabiaku*. Deference to the democratic body should be due when considering whether it was in fact pursuing a legitimate aim; less deference should be due when considering whether a reverse onus was a proportionate method of achieving that aim.

A third consideration is based on drawing a distinction between elements of the offence and available defences. For example, in *A-G of Hong Kong v Lee Kwong-Kut (1993)*, a decision of the Privy Council, Lord Woolf said that if the prosecution retains responsibility for proving the essential ingredients of the offence, a reverse burden is more likely to be acceptable. But, recognising the difficulty of isolating the essential ingredients, he added that the substance and reality of the language creating the offence should be regarded, rather than its form.

However, the distinction between elements of an offence and defences has often been criticised. Lord Steyn in *Lambert* said that the distinction would sometimes be 'unprincipled and arbitrary'. He observed that sometimes the distinction was based simply on the drafting technique. A constituent element of an offence can be removed from the definition and cast as a defensive issue. Further, any definition of an offence can be reformulated so as to include all possible defences within it. A good example of the difficulty in applying this criterion is *Hunt (1987)*, where an element of the offence was found in what appeared at first sight to be a list of exceptions contained in a statutory instrument that had been made pursuant to powers contained in the primary legislation.

Maximum penalties are another consideration. In *Davies (2002)* Tuckey LJ said that the absence of any risk of imprisonment was 'undoubtedly an important factor' in determining whether there was a legitimate reverse burden of proof. Conversely, in *Lambert* Lord Steyn was clearly influenced by the fact that the maximum sentence was life imprisonment. In *Johnstone* Lord Nicholls said that the more serious the punishment, the more compelling must be the reasons for imposing a reverse burden. But in *Sheldrake* the House of Lords upheld a reverse onus where the maximum penalty for the offence was only six months' imprisonment. Dennis has noted that maximum penalties are a very uncertain guide, and that the nature of the penalty, whether custodial or pecuniary, is not conclusive either way.

The ease of proof and the defendant's peculiar knowledge can also be taken into account. For example, in *ex p Kebilene* Lord Hope said that one of the considerations was the nature of the burden on the accused. Did it relate to something that it was likely to be difficult for him to prove, or to something likely to be within his knowledge or to which he had access? The same point was made by Lord Nicholls in *Johnstone*. On the other hand, as Dennis has pointed out, there are very many cases where the accused's state of mind is of crucial importance, but where the burden of proving it is on the prosecution.

A final consideration is the presumption of innocence itself. As Lord Bingham said in *Sheldrake*, the underlying rationale of the presumption is that it is repugnant to ordinary notions of fairness for a prosecutor to accuse a defendant of crime and for the defendant to be then required to disprove the accusation, on pain of conviction and punishment if he fails to do so. The closer a legislative provision is to that situation, the more objectionable it is likely to be. Approaching the problem from a slightly different angle, Lord Nicholls in *Johnstone* said that a sound starting point for considering a reverse burden in the light of Art 6(2) is to remember that if a defendant is required to prove a fact on the balance of probability in order to avoid conviction, a conviction can follow in spite of the fact-finding tribunal having a reasonable doubt as to his guilt.

It will be seen that there can be no straightforward answer to the question initially posed. It is possible to identify a number of considerations, but the weight the court will give to them in any particular case is unlikely to be readily predictable. The problem is substantial. In 1996, 40 per cent of offences triable in the Crown Court appeared to violate the presumption of innocence.[2]

# References

1. Ian Dennis, 'Reverse Onuses and the Presumption of Innocence: In Search of Principle,' [2005] *Criminal Law Review* 901–936.
2. Andrew Ashworth and Meredith Blake, 'The Presumption of Innocence in English Criminal Law,' [1996] *Criminal Law Review* 306, 314.

# Question 5

Answer all FOUR parts of this question:

(a) Alice was convicted of theft. In her summing up, the judge said to the jury: 'The prosecution brings this case and it is for the prosecution to prove it. Unless, having heard all the evidence, you are sure that the defendant is guilty, she must be acquitted.' Advise Alice whether she has grounds for appeal.

(b) Bertha was convicted of having an offensive weapon with her in a public place, contrary to s 1 of the Prevention of Crime Act 1953. In her summing up, the judge said to the jury: 'Members of the jury, it is not contested that this defendant had with her an offensive weapon in a public place. But she says she had it with her for her own protection. She has to satisfy you that that was a reasonable excuse for having the weapon with her, and unless you are satisfied of that, you must convict.' Advise Bertha whether she has grounds for appeal.

(c) Charlene is charged with murder. There is medical evidence suggesting that she is under a mental disability which renders her unfit to plead and stand trial. What is the law relating to the burden and standard of proof in this situation?

(d) Dora was convicted of wounding with intent to do grievous bodily harm. In her summing up, the judge said to the jury: 'The defence in this case is self-defence. That means that the defendant has an evidential burden, but no more, to satisfy you that what she says about acting in self-defence is more probable than not.' Advise Dora whether she has grounds for appeal.

## Answer plan

Part (a) obviously deals with the burden and standard of proof. The question is whether the judge has directed the jury adequately. The answer is that she has, but note how you can show your knowledge effectively to the examiner when saying so. Without being at all irrelevant, the following points can be made:

- the need to provide a correct direction on both the burden and the standard of proof;

- the proper direction on the burden of proof;
- the application of that test to what was said in this case;
- the proper direction on the standard of proof;
- it is not a particular formula but the effect of the summing up as a whole that matters;
- *Kritz (1950)* and *Walters v R (1969)*.

Don't forget to advise Alice – this is done in the final sentence.

Part (b) is a bit more complicated. You need to know about s 1 of the Prevention of Crime Act 1953, but this is a fairly well cited example of a statutory provision that expressly puts a burden of proof on the defendant. It is important to remember that a direction on the *burden* of proof and a direction on the *standard* of proof are two different things. The following points should be made:

- whether there has been a correct direction on the burden of proof;
- standard of proof where a burden is placed on a defendant in a criminal trial;
- ambiguity of the language used in Bertha's case.

Part (c) provides an example of the operation of different standards of proof, depending on which side raises the issue.

Part (d) requires you to make the following points:

- basic rule about burden of proof;
- self-defence available as a defence;
- no *legal* burden on the accused;
- the evidential burden.

# Answer

(a) Every summing up should contain a correct direction on both the burden and the standard of proof (*Bentley (Deceased) (2001)*). Here, there is a direction on each. The judge has rightly told the jury, in effect, that the burden is on the prosecution. No particular form of words is necessary, and this is the clear sense of the words actually used. There has also been a correct direction on the standard of proof. Again, it is not the particular formula that matters, but the effect of the summing up (*Allan (1969)*). One of the well established forms of direction, however, is to tell the jury that in order to find the accused guilty they must be 'sure', or 'satisfied so that they feel sure' (*Kritz (1950)*; *Walters v R*

(1969))). Here, the former expression has been used. It is entirely adequate and Alice has no grounds for appeal on this part of the summing up.

(b) Section 1 of the Prevention of Crime Act 1953 provides a defence of reasonable excuse to a charge of having an offensive weapon in a public place, but the section places the burden of proving this defence on the accused. It would be possible to argue, following *Lambert (2002)*, that the effect of s 1 is to impose only an evidential burden on defendants. But this interpretation is unlikely to be applied. In *L v DPP (2002)*, the Divisional Court upheld the traditional interpretation of s 139 of the **Criminal Justice Act 1988**, saying that there was a strong public interest in bladed articles not being carried in public without good reason, and that it was not obviously offensive to the rights of the individual to require him to prove a good reason for carrying one. The same approach is very likely to be adopted towards having an offensive weapon in a public place. The judge has almost certainly got her direction on burden right. However, in all cases where the law puts a burden of proving something on a defendant, it can be discharged merely by proof on the balance of probabilities – the civil, rather than the criminal standard (*Carr-Briant (1943)*). What has happened here is that the judge has told the jury that Bertha has to 'satisfy' them that she had a reasonable excuse. But this is ambiguous, for it could refer either to the civil or to the higher criminal standard (*Hepworth (1955)*). Thus, the jury might have applied the wrong standard in deciding whether Bertha had made out her defence. Accordingly, she has a good ground of appeal.

(c) The answer depends on who raises the issue.[1] If the prosecution says that Charlene is under this disability and the defence disputes this, the burden of proof will be on the prosecution to satisfy the jury beyond reasonable doubt that its contention is correct (*Robertson (1968)*). If, on the other hand, it is the defence which puts forward this contention and the prosecution disagrees, the defence will have the burden of proof, but only to the civil standard – on a balance of probabilities (*Podola (1960)*).

(d) Where the defendant is charged with wounding with intent to cause grievous bodily harm, the burden of proof, as is usual in criminal cases, rests throughout on the prosecution. In certain circumstances, self-defence may be a defence to this charge, but the accused bears no legal burden on the issue. Thus, in *Lobell (1957)*, where the appellant had been convicted on such a charge after the trial judge had directed the jury that it was for the defence to establish its plea of self-defence, the conviction was quashed on the ground that there had been a misdirection. What the defendant does have is an evidential burden, but this means no more than that he must be able to point to some evidence in the trial which makes self-defence a live issue for the jury's consideration. As Lord Morris put it in *Bratty v Attorney-General for Northern Ireland (1963)*, where the accused bears the evidential burden alone, he must adduce such evidence as would, if believed and left uncontradicted, induce a reasonable doubt in the mind of the jury as to whether his version might not be true.[2]

Whether a party has discharged an evidential, as opposed to a legal, burden is a matter for the judge and not the jury. It was therefore wrong of the judge to refer to the evidential burden in her summing up. If possible, it was even more wrong to refer in that connection to the standard of proof which is applicable where a defendant has a *legal* burden. The jury have been misled and Dora has a good ground of appeal.

## References

1 Either the prosecution or the defence may do so: see s 4(1) of the Criminal Procedure (Insanity) Act 1964.
2 Although Lord Morris used the word 'adduce', this does not mean that the defendant must call such evidence himself. It could be obtained from prosecution witnesses under cross-examination, or it might even emerge during their examination-in-chief. See *L v DPP (2002)*.

# Question 6

Annie hired a removal firm, XY & Co, to move the contents of her house in Plymouth to a house which she had bought in Worcester. The removal van and all its contents were destroyed by fire in a layby just outside Exeter. Some time after the loss, Annie was told by an employee of XY & Co that the van had been deliberately set on fire so that XY & Co could claim from their insurers for its loss.

Annie is suing XY & Co for the value of her destroyed property, which she estimates to be £250,000. She claims first in respect of their deliberate destruction by the defendants; alternatively, she alleges that they were destroyed by reason of the defendants' negligence. By their defence, XY & Co deny deliberately setting fire to the van and plead that their contract with Annie had an exclusion clause, which said that they would not be liable for loss by fire provided that their servants were not negligent. They also plead that it was a term of the contract that they would not be liable for any loss in excess of £5,000. Annie says that she never agreed to this term and that XY & Co are liable for the full loss.

Discuss the burden and standard of proof in relation to the issues that arise.

> ### Answer plan
>
> The first step is to sort out what the issues are likely to be. A rough and ready way of doing this is to think of what matters each side would have to prove in order to win, assuming there is no response from their opponents.
>
> Annie must prove the existence of the agreement with the defendants for the carriage of her goods, the consignment of her goods to the defendants in accordance with the agreement, the fact that non-delivery was due to deliberate destruction of the goods by the defendants, and the amount of the loss. In view of the exclusion clause, the burden of proof in relation to negligence is uncertain.
>
> The defendants must prove the existence of the exclusion clause and, if need be, that the loss falls within it. They may also have to prove that they exercised all proper care of the goods while they were in their possession. In addition, they will have to show that the provision limiting their liability to £5,000 was part of the contract.
>
> Broadly speaking, it will be seen that this ties in with the maxim that he who asserts must prove, but there are problems with the interpretation of the exclusion clause which require discussion of bailment.
>
> The allegation of arson raises the question of the standard to be applied where a crime is alleged in a civil action.

# Answer

Although the burden of proof in any particular case depends on the circumstances under which the claim arises, in a civil action, the burden normally lies on the party who affirms something to be the case, and not upon the party who makes a denial. As Viscount Maugham said in *Constantine (Joseph) Steamship Line Ltd v Imperial Smelting Corp Ltd (1942)*, it is 'an ancient rule founded on considerations of good sense and it should not be departed from without strong reasons'.

Annie will therefore bear the legal burden of establishing the essential elements of her claim. With one exception, these are readily defined.

She will first have to prove the existence of a contract made between herself and the defendants for the carriage by the defendants of her goods from Plymouth to Worcester. She will then have to prove that, pursuant to this contract, she consigned her goods to the defendants. Her principal claim is that the defendants deliberately destroyed her goods by fire whilst they had possession of them. Clearly, the burden of proving this rests on Annie. She will also have to prove the value of the goods which have been lost.

Since this is a civil action, all these matters will have to be proved according to 'the preponderance of probability' (*Miller v Minister of Pensions (1947)*). Even where Annie is alleging matters that would amount to the criminal offence of arson, she does not have to prove them beyond reasonable doubt. In *Hornal v Neuberger Products Ltd (1957)*, the plaintiff was sold a lathe by the defendants. One of their directors was alleged to have stated falsely that the machine had been reconditioned by a named firm. Had this representation been made by the director with knowledge of its falsehood, he would have been guilty of fraudulent misrepresentation. In a civil action for damages for breach of warranty, alternatively for fraud, the trial judge found that the claim in respect of fraud had been proved on the balance of probabilities, but added that he would not have been satisfied had the criminal standard been applicable. The Court of Appeal held that he had correctly applied the civil standard.

In *Hornal*, Denning LJ said that the more serious the allegation, the higher the degree of probability required, and in some later cases, the judge appears to have applied a slightly loaded civil standard.[1] However, Morris LJ said in *Hornal* that the gravity of the allegation was simply part of the whole range of circumstances that had to be weighed when deciding on the balance of probabilities. He did not favour variations of standard in civil cases, and current opinion prefers his view. In *Re H and Others (1996)*, the majority of the House of Lords supported the view that the more serious the allegation, the less likely it was to be true, and the weightier the evidence needed for a court to find it proved. But it was emphasised that where a serious allegation was in issue, the standard of proof was not higher than the ordinary civil standard. If a third standard were to be substituted in some civil cases, it would be necessary to identify what that standard was, and when it applied. Confusion and uncertainty would result. Any earlier observations to the contrary were not accurate statements of the law.

As an alternative to deliberate destruction, Annie pleads negligence on the part of the defendants. Does she have the legal burden of proving this? Two arguments might be used to show that she does. It could be said that this is just another instance of the application of the basic maxim that it is for the person who affirms something to be the case to bear the burden in respect of that issue. The defendants might also argue by analogy from the way in which an exclusion clause was interpreted in *The Glendarroch (1894)*. In that case, the plaintiffs claimed damages from shipowners for the latter's failure to carry goods safely. The shipowners relied on an exemption clause which excluded their liability for loss or damage occasioned by perils of the sea. It was held that the defendants had the burden of proving this provision and that the loss fell within it, but that the plaintiffs, who wished to rely on a proviso to the exemption clause which excluded its operation in the event of the shipowners' negligence, had the burden of establishing that the facts were such as to bring the proviso into effect.

There is, however, an argument that, instead of Annie's having to prove negligence, the defendants have a burden to show that they used all proper care in the carriage of the goods. This is the basic common law rule in cases of bailment for reward, of which this contract is an instance. It could be argued that any ambiguity as to the burden of proof should be resolved in Annie's favour because this basic principle has not been clearly excluded, and its rationale is clearly present here: after the goods were consigned to the defendants, they, and not Annie, were in a better position to explain what happened to them. This was a consideration which proved persuasive in *Levison v Patent Steam Carpet Cleaning Ltd (1978)*. In this case, the defendant carpet cleaners lost the plaintiff's Chinese carpet in unexplained circumstances. A clause in the contract would have exempted them from liability for negligence, but not for any fundamental breach of contract. The burden of proof on the latter issue was held by the Court of Appeal to lie on the defendants. They had to show that they had not been guilty of fundamental breach because they could more easily discharge this burden than could a plaintiff who had a burden to prove that there had been such a breach.

It will of course be for XY & Co to establish the existence of the exclusion clause and, if need be, that the goods were destroyed by fire. Similarly, if they wish to rely on the limitation of damages clause, they will have to prove it formed part of the contract.

### Reference

1  See, for example, *The Michael (1979)*.

# Question 7

After a vigorous press campaign prompted by a sudden increase in accidents to customers in book shops, Parliament passes a new piece of legislation: the **Readers (Protection) Act**. Section 1 provides: 'A book shop owner shall be guilty of an offence if any person suffers injury while on the book shop owner's premises.' Section 2 provides: 'No offence is committed under s 1 if the book shop owner took reasonable precautions to prevent the injury from occurring.' The Act provides that a book shop owner shall be liable on conviction on indictment to an unlimited fine, the closure of his premises for such period as the court shall think fit, and to a sentence of imprisonment for a maximum of two years. Fergus, the owner of a book shop, has been charged under s 1 of the Act after Gerald, a customer, fell downstairs and broke three ribs while moving from one floor of Gerald's shop to another. Fergus says that he took reasonable precautions to prevent injury to customers by ensuring that the stairs were well lit. He says that when he went to Gerald's assistance he could smell alcohol on Gerald's breath. He suspects that the reason for Gerald's fall was that he was unsteady on his feet after drinking too much at lunch on the day in question.

Advise Fergus on the burden of proof.

> ## Answer plan
>
> The problem raises two substantial questions of interpretation; you are going to have to be selective in the amount of law to which you refer. At the same time, you must be careful to apply the law to the facts that you have been given.
>
> The first question to deal with is whether the statute imposes an implied reversal of the burden of proof. At this stage you do not have to consider Art 6(2) of the *European Convention on Human Rights*. If you can persuade the judge that the effect of s 2 is to provide an essential element of the offence, the prosecution will have to prove that Fergus failed to take reasonable precautions; there will be no burden on the defendant at all.
>
> Start with s 101 of the *Magistrates' Courts Act 1980*, and show by reference to *Edwards* that its principles apply in this case. *Hunt* is an obvious case on which to rely so as to show that there is some flexibility in applying the s 101 principles. Refer to Lord Griffiths's guidelines and try to apply them in this situation.
>
> Then turn to the problem that will arise if the judge holds that the effect of s 2 *is* to impose a reverse burden on the defendant. Will that be compatible with Art 6(2)? Again, there are guidelines to which you can refer, and which can be found in cases such as *ex p Kebilene*, *Lambert*, *Davies*, and *Johnstone*. Remember to try to apply these guidelines to the facts that you have been given. You should come to some conclusion, but there can be no question of its being right or wrong. The decision could go either way.

# Answer

The first question that arises is whether s 1 of the Act creates an offence to which s 2 can be relied on as a defence, or whether the sections must be read together, so that the book shop owner's failure to take reasonable precautions is one of the elements of the offence. If the latter is the correct interpretation, the prosecution will have the burden of proving beyond reasonable doubt that there had been a failure to take reasonable precautions. If the first suggestion is correct, the court will have to consider whether any, and if so what, burden has been imposed by Parliament on the defendant.

Section 101 of the Magistrates' Courts Act 1980 can be taken as a convenient starting point. Although the offence with which Fergus is charged is triable only on indictment, it was held in *Edwards (1975)* that s 101 was a statutory statement of the common law applicable in all criminal courts. Section 101 provides that where the defendant relies for his defence on any 'exception, exemption, proviso, excuse or qualification', whether or not it is part of the description of the offence, the burden of proving such a defence shall be on him.

However, as Lawton LJ observed in *Edwards*, when applying this principle it is necessary to 'construe the enactment under which the charge is laid'. This was subsequently emphasised by the House of Lords in *Hunt (1987)*. In that case the prosecution proved that the defendant had been in possession of powder containing morphine, but their evidence did not prove whether the quantity of morphine was more than 0.2 per cent. The relevant legislation exempted from its provisions preparations containing not more than that quantity. The House of Lords held that, on a correct interpretation of the statute, the rule contained in s 101 of the Magistrates' Courts Act 1980 did not apply because the 0.2 per cent provision was part of the definition of the offence. The burden therefore lay on the prosecution to prove that the powder contained more than that quantity of morphine. It was not for the defence to show that it contained only 0.2 per cent or less. In reaching this conclusion, the House of Lords said that the classification of defences was not constrained by the form of words used or their location in the statute creating the offence.

Lord Griffiths suggested certain guidelines for interpretation. First, he said that courts should be very slow to classify a defence as falling within s 101, because Parliament can never lightly be taken to have intended to impose an onerous duty on a defendant to prove his innocence. Probably the Readers (Protection) Act does not impose an onerous duty on owners of book shops. They are the persons most familiar with their premises and are in the best position to do what needs to be done to ensure the safety of their customers. Making sure that your premises are safe can hardly be regarded as an onerous duty.

Secondly, Lord Griffiths said that the ease and difficulty to be encountered by the parties in discharging the legal burden are of great importance. Probably it is no more difficult for a book shop owner to show what precautions he took than for the prosecution to establish that he did not take all reasonable precautions. It may indeed be easier for the book shop owner to establish that he took all reasonable precautions because he is likely to be aware of current practices in his trade. Although following common practice will not conclusively establish that all reasonable precautions were taken, it may go some way towards doing so.

Thirdly, the gravity of the offence should be considered. The more serious the offence, the more likely it will be that any ambiguity will be resolved in favour of the defendant. In this case we note that the offence is triable only on indictment; that an unlimited fine can be imposed; that the premises can be forced to close indefinitely; and that a sentence of imprisonment of two years can also be imposed. The financial penalties are potentially very severe; in contrast the maximum term of imprisonment is light. Taking these matters into consideration, the offence seems not to be among the gravest, though it is by no means trivial.

Although a court might well interpret s 2 as an essential element of the offence, to be proved by the prosecution, there is some danger that it will be regarded as falling within the s 101 rule. The question that would then arise is whether it imposes a legal burden on the defendant, or only an evidential burden. If the imposition of a legal burden would infringe Art 6(2) of the European Convention on Human Rights, it is likely to be interpreted as imposing an evidential burden only.

It was suggested in *Lambert (2002)* and in *Davies (2002)* that a strict responsibility might be placed on a defendant where the legislation was concerned to regulate the conduct of a particular activity in the public interest, for example, to promote health and safety. This might suggest that a legal burden on Fergus would not infringe Art 6(2). On the other hand, it was said in *Davies* that the absence of a risk of imprisonment was an important factor in deciding whether a reverse burden was legitimate. In this case there is a danger of imprisonment.

Deference should be shown to Parliament's decision. In *Johnstone (2003)* Lord Nicholls pointed out that Parliament had the primary responsibility for deciding what should be the constituent elements of an offence, and the courts should depart from this only if satisfied that the legislature had attached insufficient importance to the presumption of innocence. Ease of proof and a defendant's special knowledge can also be taken into account, as Lord Hope observed in *ex p Kebilene (2000)*.

It seems on balance likely that if a court decides that the statute does impose a reverse burden on the defendant, it will decide that this is a legal, not just an evidential, burden.

# Chapter 3

# Presumptions, Competence and Compellability

## INTRODUCTION

Presumptions fit awkwardly into an evidence course. When lawyers first started to write books on evidence, they used to include large amounts of substantive law on such subjects as trespass, nuisance, bailment, actions on the case, and so forth. The object of these writers was to include not only what we should recognise as rules of evidence, relating to such matters as the competence of witnesses and hearsay, but rules about what had to be proved in order to establish particular claims or defences. There was no unifying principle other than the convenience of the arrangement for practitioners. (See, for example, Gilbert's *The Law of Evidence*, 2nd edn, 1760. This was the leading work on the subject in the second half of the 18th century; the last edition was published in 1801. See generally William Twining, 'The Rationalist Tradition of Evidence Scholarship', in *Rethinking Evidence: Exploratory Essays*, 2nd edn (2006) pp 35–98.)

Modern evidence textbooks deal with some, but by no means all, presumptions. (See the Checklist for details.) However, this is really no more than a hangover from the older way of writing. No successful attempts have been made to find an all-embracing theme that would make 'presumptions' a true part of evidence law. What you will be looking at will be several quite distinct bits of substantive law that have little or no connection with each other.

Because this is an area where attempts to find unifying features have been made so unsuccessfully, you may find classification confusing. When a writer refers to a presumption, you need to be sure about how he is using the word. The sort of presumption that you will be trying to learn about (of death, legitimacy, etc) is what is often called a 'rebuttable presumption of law'. In my view, it confuses things to talk about anything else as a 'presumption'. If someone refers to a 'presumption of fact' he should mean an *inference* about facts which is part of an ordinary reasoning process, having nothing specially to do with law at all. And, if he refers to an 'irrebuttable presumption of law', that is just the same as referring to some rule of substantive law.

Thus, to refer to 'the presumption of innocence' is the same thing as referring to the rule which places the burden of proof on the prosecution.

Questions of competence and compellability are mainly governed by statute. You should note that the Youth Justice and Criminal Evidence Act 1999 contains new provisions relating to the competence of witnesses and their capacity to be sworn in criminal trials (ss 53–56). It also amends s 80 of the Police and Criminal Evidence Act 1984. Spouses and children are the obvious subjects for examination questions; for details, see the Checklist.

But note that the protection given to spouses has been extended to civil partners by the Civil Partnership Act 2004, s 84(1).

## Checklist

Students should generally be familiar with the following areas but check your syllabus, because it may provide a narrower or wider range:

- classifications of presumptions;
- presumption of marriage;
- presumption of legitimacy;
- presumption of death;
- presumption of regularity;
- *res ipsa loquitur*;
- conflicting presumptions;
- general rule of universal competence and compellability;
- how a co-accused can become competent for the prosecution;
- comment on an accused's failure to testify;
- competence and compellability of an accused's spouse: for the prosecution, the accused or a co-accused;
- competence of children in civil and criminal cases.

# Question 8

'The theoretical basis for recognising presumptions is that the presumed fact would, in the usual course of events, flow naturally from the existence of the primary fact, so that there is a rational connection between the two so strong that it is unnecessary to require evidence of the presumed fact in the absence of unusual circumstances.'

Discuss.

# Presumptions, Competence and Compellability

## Answer plan

This is an essay question which requires you to consider a subject that has already been referred to in the Introduction. Is it possible to say something that is true about the way in which all rebuttable presumptions of law behave? If it is, is this the common factor which is to be found? It is important to emphasise that this question, like many other essay questions, cannot be answered on knowledge of statutes and cases alone. You need to have read something of the theory of the subject, and in order to answer this question, you should at least have read what is said in Tapper, C, *Cross & Tapper on Evidence*, 10th edn, 2004, pp 148–151, and Roberts, P and Zuckerman, A, *Criminal Evidence*, 2004, pp 329–344.

You need to cover the following topics:

- the superficial attractiveness of the proposition;
- presumptions that appear to increase artificially the probative worth of the basic facts, for example, presumption of death;
- presumptions designed simply to resolve difficulties of proof, for example, s 184(1) of the Law of Property Act (LPA) 1925;
- the argument that all presumptions may operate simply as techniques for allocating the burden of proof;
- the diversity of ways in which the 'same' presumption can operate.

The conclusion is that, at best, the quotation tells only part of the story and it may be positively misleading.

## Answer

The theoretical basis suggested in the quotation is superficially attractive. For example, according to the presumption of legitimacy, it is presumed that a child born during lawful wedlock is legitimate in the absence of evidence to the contrary (*Hetherington v Hetherington (1887)*). Given the fact of a birth in those circumstances, it would seem most unreasonable not to presume the legitimacy of the child.

But not all presumptions provide such a ready illustration of this sort of rational process. According to the presumption of death, a person will be presumed to have died if it is proved that: (a) there is no acceptable evidence that he has been alive at some time during a continuous period of at least seven years; (b) there are persons likely to have heard of him, had he been alive, who have not heard of him during that period; and (c) all due inquiries have been made with a view to finding the person in question, but without success (*Chard v Chard (1956)*).

The presumption in this case appears to operate so as to increase artificially the probative value of the basic facts in the absence of any contrary evidence. So far as probative worth goes, there is nothing special about seven years' absence as opposed, say, to one of six years. Yet, the former period gives rise to a rebuttable presumption of law, while the latter gives rise to no more than an inference of fact that may be made or not.[1]

In other cases, it seems clear that a presumption has been designed simply in order to resolve a difficulty of proof. An example is s 184(1) of the LPA 1925. This provides that where two or more persons have died in circumstances rendering it uncertain which of them survived the other or others, such death shall (subject to any order of the court), for all purposes affecting the title to property, be presumed to have occurred in order of seniority and, accordingly, the younger shall be deemed to have survived the elder. Here the probative worth of the basic fact is non-existent; the whole effect of the presumption is to allocate the burden of proof.[2]

It has been suggested in fact that a presumption is in all cases simply a technique whereby the substantive law distributes the risk of losing on a given issue, and that it is misleading to try to develop a rationale based on the probative force of the basic facts of the presumption. This misleading approach, it is argued, leads to the conclusion that presumptions such as that of death are simply presumptions of fact to which the law gives artificial weight. If, however, the rationale of presumptions is to be found in the allocation of the burden of proof, the charge of artificiality is misconceived. The rights of someone who has disappeared cannot remain suspended indefinitely; what the law does is to provide, by a rule affecting the burden of proof, a limitation period. The basic fact may, of course, have some probative weight, but it has this by virtue of common sense and experience rather than by virtue of the presumption.[3]

This view of presumptions as devices for allocating the burden of proof receives considerable support from the fact that a particular presumption does not always affect the burden of proof in exactly the same way; the way in which a presumption operates depends on the context in which it may be relevant. This would not be the case if, from a primary fact, there flowed naturally in the usual course of events a particular presumed fact. One would expect a rational process such as that to operate regardless of context.

That this is not the case is shown by the operation of presumptions in a criminal context. According to the presumption of regularity, upon proof of the fact that some official or public act has been performed, or that a person acted in an official capacity, it is presumed that the act which was done complied with any necessary formalities, or that the person so acting had been properly appointed. In *Dillon (1982)*, a police officer had been charged in Jamaica with the offence of negligently permitting two prisoners, lawfully in his custody, to escape. The prosecution failed to call any evidence to show that the officer had authority to hold the prisoners in custody, a matter which they had the burden of proving. On a defence submission of no case to answer, the magistrate held that the prosecution was entitled to rely on the presumption of regularity to establish that such authority existed. This decision was upheld by the Court of Appeal of Jamaica but rejected by the Privy Council, which held that the prosecution was not entitled to rely on a presumption to establish a central element of the offence.

There seems little doubt that the presumption of legitimacy would also affect the burden of proof in different ways, depending on the nature of the proceedings. In a civil case, once birth in lawful wedlock is established, the court must find the child legitimate unless the party opposing legitimacy proves on the balance of probabilities that the child is illegitimate.[4] But suppose a defendant is charged with committing incest with his daughter and his defence is that, though conceived and born in wedlock, she is actually the child of another man. It is most unlikely to be held that the defendant has a legal burden of proof on that issue. It would surely be enough to raise in the minds of the jury a reasonable doubt about whether the woman in question might have been the daughter of another man.[5]

It might be objected that in these criminal examples, there is a conflict of presumptions which produces a different outcome, the presumption with which the others conflict being the presumption of innocence. But this would be to mislead by language. The so called presumption of innocence is not a rebuttable presumption of law like the others, but is simply a way of stating the rule that in criminal cases the burden of proof is on the prosecution.

At best, therefore, it appears that the theoretical basis for recognising presumptions which is suggested in the quotation does not tell the whole story. At worst, it may be positively misleading.

## References

1. Tapper, C, *Cross & Tapper on Evidence*, 10th edn, 2004, p 149.
2. *Ibid*, p 150.
3. Paul Roberts & Adrian Zuckerman, *Criminal Evidence* (Oxford: Oxford University Press, 2004) p 343.
4. Section 26 of the Family Law Reform Act 1969.
5. *Andrews and Hirst on Criminal Evidence*, 4th edn, 2001, para 4.17.

# Question 9

Charlie, while driving his motor car, was involved in a collision with Doris, a cyclist aged 14, who suffered a broken leg as a result.

(a) Charlie is charged with dangerous driving. The CPS wish to call the following, both of whom have made statements to the police, as witnesses for the prosecution:

  (i) Ethel, Charlie's wife. She was travelling in the car with Charlie. Shortly after the accident, she made a statement saying that her husband was distracted by a violent argument with her just before he hit Doris's bicycle. Recently, she has been in touch with the officer in the case and has told him that she does not want to give evidence because she loves her husband despite everything.

  (ii) Freddie, aged nine, who saw the accident while he was waiting for a bus to take him to church, where he sings in the choir.

  Advise the CPS on the competence and compellability of Ethel and Freddie.

(b) Charlie has been prosecuted and acquitted. Civil proceedings have now been begun against him on behalf of Doris for negligence. The claimant's solicitors wish to call Ethel and Freddie as witnesses. Advise the solicitors on the competence and compellability of these potential witnesses.

## Answer plan

This is one of the topics where evidence law depends on whether the proceedings are criminal or civil. Deal with the criminal trial first, and then the civil trial.

### The criminal trial

(i) *Ethel.* For competence, see s 53(1) of the Youth Justice and Criminal Evidence Act (YJCEA) 1999. For compellability, see s 80 of the Police and Criminal Evidence Act 1984, as amended by the YJCEA 1999. Is this a 'specified offence'? Note Doris's age at the time of the accident. How should 'involves' in s 80(3)(a) be interpreted?

(ii) *Freddie.* For competence, see s 53(1) of the YJCEA 1999. Note s 55(2)(a).

### The civil trial

(i) *Ethel.* For competence, see *Ex p Fernandez (1861)*. For compellability, see s 1 of the Evidence Amendment Act 1853.

(ii) *Freddie.* Note the possibility of giving sworn evidence. Your starting point will be the *Hayes* test, with s 96(2) of the Children Act 1989 as a fall-back position.

# Answer

## The criminal trial

Ethel is competent by virtue of s 53(1) of the YJCEA 1999, which provides that, at every stage in criminal proceedings, all persons are (whatever their age) competent to give evidence.

Her compellability will be governed by s 80 of the Police and Criminal Evidence Act 1984, as amended. She will be compellable only if the offence with which her husband is charged is a 'specified' offence. At the time of the accident, Doris was under the age of 16. It might be arguable that the offence fell within s 80(3)(a), and so was a specified offence, because it involved injury to a person who was at the material time under the age of 16. The interpretation of 'involves' in this provision is uncertain. It might mean 'involves as a matter of legal definition', as robbery, for example, involves the use of force or a putting in fear of force.[1] If this approach is adopted, dangerous driving is clearly not a specified offence. On the other hand, 'involves' could mean 'involves as a matter of fact in the circumstances of the particular case'. If that were the interpretation adopted, the offence with which Charlie is charged would be a specified offence, and Ethel would be compellable.[2]

Freddie is in principle competent by virtue of s 53(1) of the Youth Justice and Criminal Evidence Act 1999. There is nothing to suggest that he falls into the category of persons who are not competent that is set out in s 53(3). However, because he is under 14, his evidence will be given unsworn: see s 55(2)(a).

## The civil trial

The basic rule, set out in *Ex p Fernandez (1861)*, is that all persons are competent to give evidence and may be compelled to testify. By s 1 of the Evidence Amendment Act 1853, it is specifically provided that the husbands and wives of the parties to civil proceedings are competent *and compellable* to give evidence on behalf of *any* of the parties to the proceedings. Ethel will therefore be a compellable witness for the claimant.

Because this is a civil action, Freddie may give either sworn or unsworn evidence. The question whether he understands the nature of an oath so as to be able to give sworn evidence will presumably be decided by applying the tests formerly used when children gave evidence in criminal proceedings. The judge will question Freddie in open court before he gives evidence. In *Khan (1981)*, the Court of Appeal said that although much depended on the type of child before the court, generally, inquiry should be made in the case of a child under 14. The conditions to be satisfied were stated in *Hayes (1977)* to be that the child had a sufficient appreciation of the solemnity of the occasion, and understood that an oath involved an added responsibility to tell the truth over and above the social duty to do so. Understanding of a divine sanction is not required.

If these conditions are not satisfied, Freddie may give unsworn evidence. Section 96(2) of the Children Act 1989 provides that a child's evidence may be heard, even if he does not understand the nature of an oath, if he understands that it is his duty to speak the truth, and he has a sufficient understanding to justify his evidence being heard. Freddie is likely to be competent, and so also compellable (*Ex p Fernandez (1861)*).

### References

1 See s 8 of the Theft Act 1968.
2 For further discussion, see Tapper, C, *Cross & Tapper on Evidence*, 10th edn, 2004, p 265.

# Question 10

Eight years ago, Mr and Mrs Austin set off from England to spend an indefinite period of time travelling in South America. They left behind them three adult children: Basil, Cynthia and Darren. At first Mr and Mrs Austin wrote regularly to all the children, but after a time they did so erratically and infrequently. After two years, nothing further was heard from them by any of the children. The letters that had been received showed that Mr and Mrs Austin were travelling through parts of South America where from time to time there was civil unrest and also danger from natural disasters such as flooding and earthquakes.

Some years before leaving England, both Mr and Mrs Austin had made wills. Mr Austin left everything to his wife, but he also provided that, if she should predecease him, his estate should be divided equally between 'the legitimate children of my family'. Mrs Austin left everything to her husband; in the event of his predeceasing her, the estate was to be divided between various charities.

Basil and Cynthia say that their parents must by now have died and wish to know what rights of inheritance they have. They say also that Darren, though born to Mrs Austin during her marriage, was not the child of Mr Austin but of a man with whom Mrs Austin was having an affair while their father was in prison.

Discuss the evidential issues that arise.

PRESUMPTIONS, COMPETENCE AND COMPELLABILITY

> ### Answer plan
>
> Three problems of law need to be considered here:
> - the presumption of death;
> - the presumption created by s 184 of the Law of Property Act 1925;
> - the presumption of legitimacy.
>
> In dealing with these points, you should bear in mind the inferences that might be drawn from the evidence without the aid of presumptions, and also any gaps there may be which necessitate requests for further information.

# Answer

A person will be presumed to have died if it is proved that:

(a) there is no acceptable evidence that he has been alive at some time during a continuous period of at least seven years;

(b) there are persons likely to have heard of him, had he been alive, who have not heard of him during that period; and

(c) all due inquiries have been made with a view to finding the person in question, but without success (*Chard v Chard (1956)*).

In the case of Mr and Mrs Austin, nothing has been heard for the last six years only, so the presumption cannot be applied. In any case, it does not appear whether there are any other persons who might have heard from Mr and Mrs Austin, or what inquiries, if any, have been made. Thus, even if Basil and Cynthia were to wait for a period of seven years to have elapsed, a court might not be satisfied that all conditions for the operation of the presumption had been complied with.

Quite apart from the presumption, it would be open to a court to infer from appropriate circumstantial evidence that Mr and Mrs Austin had died, but Basil and Cynthia would have the burden of proving their parents' death on the balance of probabilities. Thus, if the evidence were sufficient, there would be no need to wait for the expiry of seven years.[1] Whether the evidence is sufficient is likely to depend largely on what inferences can be drawn as to the presence of Mr and Mrs Austin in areas of natural disaster or insurrection and their likelihood of survival in such circumstances.

Section 184 of the Law of Property Act 1925 provides that, in all cases where two or more persons have died in circumstances rendering it uncertain which of them survived the other or others, such death shall (subject to any order of the court), for all purposes affecting the title to property, be presumed to have occurred in order of seniority, and accordingly the younger shall be deemed to have survived the elder. For the children to inherit, it would be necessary for Mr Austin to have survived his wife. By s 184, he will be presumed to have done so if he was the younger of the two; it will therefore be necessary to discover their respective ages. There appears to be no reason why s 184 should not apply where the court makes a finding of death by virtue of the presumption of death.

On the assumption that Mr Austin was younger than his wife and that he therefore survived her, the question of Darren's legitimacy arises. There is a presumption of legitimacy in respect of any child who is proved to have been born or conceived in lawful wedlock. However, s 26 of the Family Law Reform Act 1969 provides that this presumption may be rebutted by evidence which shows that it is more probable than not that the person in question is illegitimate or legitimate as the case may be. Darren will have the advantage of the presumption because he was born while his parents were lawfully married. It will therefore be for Basil and Cynthia to prove on the balance of probabilities that he is illegitimate in order to exclude him from sharing in the distribution of Mr Austin's estate.

One item of evidence in their favour may be the provision itself in Mr Austin's will; it suggests that he believed that there was at least one child of the family who was not legitimate. Clearly, the evidence of his imprisonment will be of the utmost importance. If, for example, Darren was conceived at a time when Mr Austin could have had no access to his wife, this would seem to rebut the presumption conclusively.

## Reference

1 See, for example, *Re Watkins (1953)* for a case where the presumption of death could not be applied, but where the fact of death was nevertheless inferred.

# CHAPTER 4

# HEARSAY I

## INTRODUCTION

Section 1(2) of the Civil Evidence Act 1995 defines hearsay, for the purposes of that Act, as 'a statement made otherwise than by a person while giving oral evidence in the proceedings which is tendered as evidence of the matters stated'. That definition is, in effect, adopted in s 114(1) of the Criminal Justice Act (CJA) 2003, which states, 'In criminal proceedings a statement not made in oral evidence in the proceedings is admissible as evidence of any matter stated if, but only if . . . ', and then goes on to set out the circumstances in which such evidence will be admissible.

Different approaches to the rule against hearsay have been taken in civil and criminal proceedings. The Civil Evidence Act 1995 boldly enacts in s 1(1) that 'in civil proceedings evidence shall not be excluded on the ground that it is hearsay'. In criminal proceedings the law is governed by Part 11, Chapter 2 of the CJA 2003. This does not abolish the rule against hearsay. Instead, it defines the rule and codifies the exceptions; but it achieves the latter task in a half-hearted way by preserving a number of existing common law exceptions. At least for criminal trials it is necessary to understand the scope of the rule, because it would be absurd to develop an argument that evidence should be included as a hearsay exception if the rule does not apply in the first place. It is necessary to concentrate on two features in order to understand the scope of the rule: the definitions of 'statement' and 'a matter stated', and the purpose for which evidence of an out-of-court statement is being adduced.

Section 115(2) of the CJA 2003 defines a statement as 'any representation of fact or opinion made by a person by whatever means; and it includes a representation made in a sketch, photofit or other pictorial form'. The representation can therefore be made by any method. Under the common law, sketches and photofit images were held to be unaffected by the rule. This was illogical, and the Act now brings them, and representations by any other pictorial form, within the rule.

Section 115(3) provides as follows:

A matter stated is one to which this Chapter applies if (and only if) the purpose, or one of the purposes, of the person making the statement appears to the court to have been –

(a) to cause another person to believe the matter, or
(b) to cause another person to act or a machine to operate on the basis that the matter is as stated.

The common law rule against hearsay was held in *Kearley (1992)* to cover non-assertive utterances, such as questions, commands and greetings, where the maker did not intend to communicate any information at all, but where inferences as to the existence of some fact could be drawn from what was said. The decision was widely criticised and the Law Commission recommended that this development should be reversed. Section 115(3) corresponds to clause 2(3) in the bill drafted by the Law Commission to achieve this result. Its effect is to remove 'implied assertions' from the scope of the hearsay rule by making it essential, for the operation of the rule, that the person whose words or actions are reported should have had as at least one purpose that of causing another person to believe the matter that he stated. This effect was confirmed by the Court of Appeal in *Singh (2006)*.

The rule against hearsay excludes an item of evidence *only if the purpose of adducing that evidence is to establish the truth of the facts stated*. It follows that in relation to any item of evidence that you suspect may be caught by the rule, you need first to ask: 'What is the *job of proof* that this item of evidence is being put forward to do?' Only when you know what this is can you see whether the evidence is caught by the hearsay rule, which is brought into operation not by any particular form of words, but by the use that is going to be made of them. Putting it another way, you need to know the *relevance* of the evidence being considered.

Don't try to avoid the problem by saying that an item of evidence might be excluded for offending the rule against hearsay, but might be admitted to prove that the assertion was made. This will discredit you in the eyes of the examiner. If you think that somebody might want to show simply that an assertion was made, you must explain to the examiner why that is the case. For example, in a case like *Subramaniam v Public Prosecutor (1956)*, you would say that the evidence ought to be admitted because any threats are likely to have affected the mind of the defendant, thus making the evidence relevant to his defence of duress.

This chapter concentrates mainly on the scope of the rule against hearsay, but some reference is also made to the unavailability exception in s 116 of the CJA 2003 and to the 'safety-valve' exception in s 114.

HEARSAY I

> ## Checklist
>
> Students should be familiar with the following areas:
> - the definition of hearsay reflected in s 114(1) of the CJA 2003;
> - the definitions of 'statement' and 'matter stated';
> - statements produced by machines;
> - 'negative hearsay';
> - the importance of relevance in the rule against hearsay;
> - justifications for excluding hearsay evidence;
> - the unavailability exception in s 116 of the CJA 2003;
> - the 'safety-valve' exception in s 114 of the CJA 2003.

# Question 11

Albert Crippen and Charlie Haigh are charged with dishonestly receiving stolen goods, namely 20 bottles of gin belonging to Umbrages plc, knowing or believing the same to be stolen goods. The case for the prosecution is that they bought the gin from a neighbour, Bridget, who was employed by Umbrages, from whom she had stolen the gin. Albert's defence is that he had no idea that the goods were stolen. When questioned by the police, he said that Bridget had told him that the bottles of gin were 'perks' which her employers allowed her and which she did not want to keep because she was teetotal. If Albert testifies in his own defence, will he be allowed to repeat what Bridget told him?

Charlie told the police that he had never taken part in the deal and that he did not even know Bridget. While DS Shovel was lawfully searching Bridget's house, the telephone rang. He picked up the receiver and heard a female voice say: 'Bridget, are you and Charlie Haigh coming to David's party on Saturday?' DS Shovel said nothing and the caller rang off after a few seconds. May evidence of the telephone call be given by DS Shovel to establish a connection between Charlie and Bridget and to show that Charlie lied to the police?

> ## Answer plan
>
> The first part of this question requires you to decide Albert's purpose in wanting to give evidence of what Bridget had told him. It would, of course,

be a defence to the charge if what Bridget said was true because the gin would not then have been stolen. But Albert doesn't need to go that far. He need only raise a doubt about whether he knew or believed the goods to have been stolen. So he wants to give evidence of his innocent state of mind at the time of the sale and show that his account of the matter is likely to be true because of what Bridget said to him. You need therefore to describe how the rule against hearsay operates and to show that this is a situation, like the one in *Subramaniam (1956)*, where the basic condition for applying the rule is absent.

The second half of the question requires you to think about the admissibility of Charlie's statement to the police that he did not know Bridget, and the relevance of what was heard on the telephone. In connection with the latter, you need first to sort out what might be inferred from the caller's question and then to apply s 115(3) of the Criminal Justice Act (CJA) 2003.

# Answer

The effect of s 114(1) of the CJA 2003 is that in criminal proceedings a statement not made in oral evidence in the proceedings is inadmissible as evidence of any matter stated unless certain conditions apply. The sub-section follows s 1(2) of the Civil Evidence Act 1995, which defines hearsay as 'a statement made otherwise than by a person while giving oral evidence in the proceedings which is tendered as evidence of the matters stated'. What Bridget is alleged to have said to Albert amounts to a 'statement' within s 115(3) of the CJA 2003 because it was, on Albert's account, clearly made with the purpose of causing him to believe that she had obtained the gin honestly.

However, evidence of a statement made outside court will be admissible if the purpose of calling the evidence is not to prove the truth of the matters asserted, but some other matter that is relevant in the proceedings. In this case, the purpose of adducing the evidence would not be to prove the truth of what Bridget said, but simply the fact that she made the statement to Albert. This would be relevant because the prosecution must show that Albert knew or believed the gin to have been stolen. If Bridget told him that she had acquired the gin with her employers' consent, the prosecution case in this respect is less likely to be true. For this purpose, it does not matter whether Bridget was telling the truth or not. What matters is the effect her words may have had on Albert's mind.

This distinction was brought out by the Privy Council in *Subramaniam v Public Prosecutor (1956)*. The defendant had been charged with unlawful possession of ammunition; his defence was duress. In support of this defence, he wished to give evidence of what had been said to him by terrorists, but was prevented from doing so by the trial judge on the basis that such evidence would offend the rule against hearsay. The Privy Council said that the evidence should have been admitted, emphasising that the fact that a statement had been made was frequently relevant, quite apart from its truth, in considering the mental state and subsequent conduct of someone in whose presence the statement had been made.

Albert can therefore give evidence of what Bridget told him.

The first question in relation to the telephone call taken by DS Shovel concerns what it is able to prove. The words constituted not a statement but a question. The words uttered by the caller cannot therefore be said to have been either true or false. What could be inferred from what the caller said? Amongst the possibilities are:

(1)  the caller knew Bridget;
(2)  the caller believed that Bridget and Charlie Haigh knew each other;
(2a) Bridget and Charlie Haigh did know each other;
(3)  the caller believed that Bridget was in the habit of going out with Charlie Haigh;
(3a) Bridget was in the habit of going out with Charlie Haigh.

If (2a) or (3a) were true, it could be shown that Charlie had lied to the police when he said that he did not know Bridget. His lie would be relevant because it would be something from which a jury might infer Charlie's guilt.

The fact that Charlie had denied knowing Bridget would be admissible because the rule against hearsay applies only where evidence of an out of court statement is adduced to prove the truth of what was said. It does not apply where the purpose of adducing the evidence is to show that the speaker said something that was false. For example, in *Mawaz Khan v R (1967)*, the two defendants were charged with murder. The Crown relied strongly on the fact that each defendant had made a statement in which he had tried to set up a joint alibi with his co-defendant. Those alibis could be shown to be false. The Privy Council held that the statements were relevant because they tended to show that the makers were acting in concert and that this showed a common guilt. Evidence of these statements was not affected by the rule against hearsay because the prosecution had proposed to establish not their truth, but the fact that they had been made.

Under the earlier law, in the light of the decision of the House of Lords in *Kearley (1992)*, evidence of the telephone call would be inadmissible to enable the jury to infer either (2a) or (3a). In *Kearley*, a majority of the House of Lords held that the beliefs of a number of telephone callers to the defendant's premises that drugs were available from the defendant were irrelevant to the question of whether the defendant could or would supply them. This is a much weaker case than that because the prosecution have to rely on the belief of one caller only that Charlie knew Bridget. Even if relevant, the decision in *Kearley* would make the evidence an implied assertion, and so inadmissible hearsay. The Court of Appeal held in *Singh (2006)* that ss 114 and 118 CJA 2003, when read together, was to abolish the common law hearsay rules, save for those expressly preserved, and to create a new rule against hearsay which did not extend to implied assertions.

The definition of a 'matter stated' in s 114(1) is given in s 115(3). This requires that the purpose, or one of the purposes, of the person making the statement should appear to the court to have been to cause another person to believe the matter, or to cause another person to act, or a machine to operate, on the basis that the matter is as stated.

The purpose of the caller was simply to ask a question, not to cause anyone to believe anything. Subject to the trial judge's general discretion to exclude prosecution evidence, either at common law or under s 78(1) of the *Police and Criminal Evidence Act 1984*, DS Shovel will be able to give evidence of what was said over the telephone in order to rebut Charlie's claim that he did not know Bridget.

# Question 12

Has the hearsay rule been brought closer to its rationale by the reforms in the *Criminal Justice Act 2003*?

## Answer plan

You need to begin by stating the traditional rationale – in fact, a collection of reasons – for having a rule against hearsay. Lord Normand in *Teper v R (1952)* is a useful source. Then go on to show ways in which the rule was formerly applied, despite the fact that the rationale did not operate. It would be helpful to make some reference to challenges to the rationale, and to the effect of *Kearley* in divorcing rule from rationale. Finally, consider the effect of the new provisions in the Criminal Justice Act (CJA) 2003.

In summary, the essay is constructed as follows:

- traditional reasons for the rule against hearsay;
- application of the rule when some reasons were absent: *Sparks v R (1964)*, *Myers v DPP (1965)*;
- questionable validity of some reasons against hearsay;
- effect of extending the rule to implied assertions;
- the suggested rights of confrontation and challenge;
- effect of reforms in the CJA 2003.

# Answer

In *Teper v R* (1952), Lord Normand explained the rationale of the rule against hearsay in this way. Hearsay is not the best evidence, and it is not delivered on oath. The truthfulness and accuracy of the person whose words are recounted by another witness cannot be tested by cross-examination, and the light that the original speaker's demeanour would have thrown on his testimony is lost.

But it is clear that the rule against hearsay has been applied when some of these criticisms have been inapplicable. In *Sparks v R* (1964), for example, the trial judge refused to allow the mother of a girl aged three to give evidence that her daughter had told her that she had been assaulted by 'a coloured boy'. This decision was upheld by the Privy Council. But there was no significant hearsay danger. The child's statement was unambiguous, she was unlikely to have been mistaken, and the danger that she might have lied was surely non-existent.

Another example is *Myers v DPP* (1965). In order to show that cars sold by the defendant had been stolen, the prosecution wished to call an employee who was in charge of records kept by the car manufacturers. These records were microfilms of cards that had been filled in by production line workers. They showed details of numbers stamped on the cylinder blocks of the cars on the production line. The House of Lords held that this evidence was hearsay, and so inadmissible. But the manufacturers' records must have been far more reliable than the memories of the workers, even if they could have been identified and called.

It is arguable that the hearsay rule became divorced from some elements of its rationale because those elements had become obsolete, or at least questionable. The argument that hearsay is not the best evidence has always been unsatisfactory. Where hearsay is the only evidence of some matter, it will be the best evidence of that matter. The Law Commission concluded that there is no clear evidence that an oath or affirmation in itself promotes truthful testimony.[1] Wigmore thought that the oath added little to cross-examination, which he thought was the real test.[2] In any case, the argument that hearsay is not on oath addresses only the danger that the person reported might have made a false statement deliberately. It can be no safeguard against an original observation that was mistaken. Opinions have differed about the value of a witness's demeanour in testing reliability.[3] The difficulty in recapturing the emphasis and tone of voice of the original utterance may be a more significant objection to admissibility. The main element in Lord Normand's explanation that survives today is the absence of an opportunity to cross-examine the original speaker.

The extension of the hearsay rule to implied assertions in *Kearley (1992)* divorced the rule even from the rationale based on absence of cross-examination. Lord Normand's objection was that the truthfulness and accuracy of someone whose words are reported by another witness cannot be tested. But where the words relied on are non-assertive, they cannot have a truth value, and this objection cannot apply. The real objection here is that the original speaker may be mistaken (though hardly dishonest) in the underlying belief that prompted the non-assertive utterance. If A is overheard asking B, 'Have you any bananas for sale today?', that utterance cannot be true or false. What is true or false is A's underlying belief that B is in the business of selling bananas.

Lord Normand's explanation of the rule against hearsay relies solely on the limited probative weight to be given to hearsay evidence. A different kind of argument is based not on rectitude of decision, but on concern for procedural rights.[4] There are two rights that may be relied on in support of the hearsay rule. One is the right of confrontation, by which evidence cannot be given against a defendant behind his back. The other is the right of challenge to witnesses. Although these rights make for rectitude of decision, they also maximise the defendant's participation in his own trial and so promote the legitimacy of the verdict in his eyes and in the eyes of the public generally.

Hearsay evidence appears to infringe both the right of confrontation and the right of challenge. But it is difficult to argue that these rights are part of the rationale of the rule. There is no absolute right of physical confrontation in English law. Evidence may be given by video link, for example. And European decisions show that hearsay evidence can be used against defendants in certain circumstances, despite Art 6(3)(d) of the European Convention on Human Rights, which provides that everyone charged with a criminal offence has the right to examine or have examined witnesses against him.

One of the major reforms effected by the CJA 2003 was, as the Court of Appeal acknowledged in *Singh (2006)*, to remove the concept of 'implied assertions' from the scope of the rule against hearsay. This was done by the definition of 'a matter stated' in s 115(3). In this way the new legislation closed a gap between rule and rationale that the decision in *Kearley* had opened. Further, the decision in *Sparks v R* would almost certainly not be the same today. The reason for this is the existence of the 'safety-valve' contained in s 114(1)(d) of the Act, whereby a hearsay statement is admissible either for the prosecution or the defence if the court is satisfied that it is in the interests of justice for it to be admissible. The court must have regard to the factors set out in s 114(2), but this list is intended to focus attention on whether the circumstances surrounding the making of the hearsay statement show that it can be treated as sufficiently reliable to be admitted, despite the fact that its maker cannot be cross-examined. That Parliament – or at least the Law Commission – was conscious of the real dangers of unreliability is shown by the special provisions relating to multiple hearsay contained in s 121(1). The hearsay rule was made to accord more with its rationale by the provisions permitting documentary hearsay in the Criminal Justice Act 1988. But the position of oral hearsay remained unchanged until s 116 of the CJA 2003 allowed oral as well as written statements to be admissible where a witness was unavailable.

In these respects at least, CJA 2003 has brought the law relating to hearsay closer to the traditional rationale for exclusion.

### References

1 Law Com No 245, Cm 3670, para 3.13.
2 *Wigmore on Evidence*, 3rd edn, 1940, vol 5, para 1,362.
3 Law Com No 245, Cm 3670, paras 3.9–3.12.
4 See Dennis, IH, *The Law of Evidence*, 2nd edn, 2002, pp 555–558.

# Question 13

Oliver Mellors is charged with the murder in London of Connie Chatterley. The case for the prosecution is that they met at Connie's house, and that during a quarrel Oliver struck Connie repeatedly with a cricket bat, thereby causing her death. There is medical evidence that Connie died between 1 pm and 2 pm. The police found a gold cigarette case engraved with the initials 'OM' beside the body. They subsequently interviewed Mellors, who claimed to have been in France on the day that Connie was killed. Later, a neighbour told the police that she had seen Mellors in London on the day in question, but no written statement was taken and the witness cannot now be traced. Connie's gardener has told the police that at about 10.30 am on that day he overheard a conversation between Connie and a man. He did not see either of them, but he recognised Connie's voice and he thought he recognised that of Mellors. He says that Connie said: 'Don't forget to buy some fish, Oliver.' The man replied, 'I'll get some on the way home'.

Discuss the evidential issues that arise.

### Answer plan

You must first decide what items of evidence have to be discussed. They are as follows:

- The discovery of the cigarette case. What is its relevance? Is there a hearsay problem? If there is, can it be avoided?
- The relevance of a false alibi. Is hearsay involved in relating what Mellors said about being in France?

- Can evidence be adduced of what the neighbour said to establish that the alibi was false?
- The gardener's evidence. Note that there are two ways in which what he says may be relevant. There are hearsay problems with only one of them.

# Answer

The first issue concerns the discovery of the engraved cigarette case. This may assist the prosecution by showing that the defendant was present at the scene of the crime at about the time when the murder took place. For this purpose, it would have to be established that the cigarette case belonged to the defendant, and the engraved initials suggest that this was so. But is there a hearsay problem? It is arguable that the context in which the initials appear shows that their function is to assert ownership; this appears to make the prosecution rely on a statement for the truth of its contents, contrary to the rule against hearsay. A similar situation arose in *Patel v Comptroller of Customs (1966)*, where labels on goods which stated the country of origin were held by the Privy Council to be inadmissible as proof of where the goods came from.[1]

The country of origin of the goods was one of the matters in issue in the case of *Patel*, and this serves to distinguish it from *Lydon (1986)*. In the latter case, the prosecution wished to adduce evidence that a piece of paper bearing the words 'Sean rules' had been found near the scene of the crime. This was alleged to be relevant because it tended to connect the defendant, whose first name was Sean, with the commission of the offence. The Court of Appeal held that this evidence was admissible because although the words on the paper constituted an assertion, it was not in itself an assertion of anything that was relevant to the facts in issue. The fact that something relevant to a fact in issue might be inferred from this item of evidence did not affect admissibility.

Here, however, the inscription arguably does amount to an assertion of a matter which the prosecution wishes to establish as part of its case – the ownership of the cigarette case. In principle, therefore, admissibility seems to be in doubt because of the rule against hearsay. However, it may be possible for the prosecution to rely on evidence from acquaintances of Mellors who can recognise the cigarette case as one that Mellors used to carry. *Miller v Howe (1969)* suggests that something that is written will not be caught by the rule against hearsay when it is an identifying part of an object, the identity of which is in issue, and not merely an assertion of a characteristic of the object. This was a case where the question arose whether a particular breath testing device had been the one approved by the Home Secretary, an 'Alcotest 80'. The Court of Appeal indicated that a label to that effect on the device would have been sufficient evidence of its identity, and that even the presence of such a label on the box containing the device would have been enough.

The prosecution could also try to rely on the decision in *Rice (1963)* in order to argue that the cigarette case was admissible as an item of original, as opposed to hearsay, evidence, because a cigarette case with those initials engraved on it is likely to belong to someone with those initials. A last resort would be the 'safety-valve' exception to the rule against hearsay provided by s 114(1)(d) of the **Criminal Justice Act (CJA) 2003**.

The giving of a false alibi may be an indication of guilt. The prosecution will have no difficulty in adducing evidence that Mellors told the police that he was in France on the day of the murder. No breach of the rule against hearsay is involved because the prosecution wishes to rely, as in *Mawaz Khan (1967)*, not on the truth of what was said, but on its falsity.[2]

The policeman to whom the neighbour spoke might be able to give evidence of what he was told by virtue of the unavailability exception in s 116(1) of the CJA 2003. The neighbour, had she been available, could have given evidence of having seen Mellors in London on the relevant day, thus satisfying s 116(1)(a). It is assumed that the neighbour can be identified so as to satisfy s 116(1)(b). In the absence of identification the evidence could not be given. The remaining question would then be whether any of the five conditions mentioned in s 116(2) is satisfied. The obvious condition on which to rely is condition (d). It would be necessary to show that 'such steps as it is reasonably practicable to take' have been taken to find the neighbour. But even if what the neighbour told the police was admissible in principle under s 116, it would be open to the defence to ask the judge to exclude it in the exercise of his discretion, either under the principle confirmed in *Sang (1980)*, or under s 78(1) of the **Police and Criminal Evidence Act 1984**. Since evidence of identification is regarded as peculiarly hazardous, such an application might well succeed on the basis that the absence of opportunity to cross-examine the identifying witness about the circumstances of the identification would make the proceedings unfair.

The probative force of the gardener's testimony is that Mellors was not in France, but with Connie in London on the day in question. Two factors suggest this. First, the fact that Connie addressed 'Oliver' suggests that it was Mellors to whom she was talking. The fact that the words 'Don't forget to buy some fish, Oliver' were not intended as a statement but as an exhortation, or perhaps a command, means that the words would not offend the rule against hearsay, because the purpose of uttering them was not to cause the person to whom they were addressed to believe any matter. The words did not, therefore, constitute 'a matter stated' within s 115(3) of the CJA 2003.

Secondly, however, the fact that the gardener heard a voice which he thought he recognised as that of Mellors also suggests that the latter was in London and not in France. What is relied on here to prove that Mellors was present is not the truth of what the man who made a reply to Connie said, but the fact that whatever words were uttered were in tones which the gardener identified as those of Mellors. No hearsay problem arises, and the gardener should be able to testify that he heard, at the time and place referred to, the voice of Connie and a voice which he thought he recognised as that of Mellors.[3]

### References

1. See also *Comptroller of Customs v Western Lectric Co Ltd (1966)*.
2. For the directions that a judge must give in relation to lies told by a defendant, see *Lucas (1981)*, *Burge and Pegg (1996)* and Chapter 6.
3. For the difficulties with voice identification, see the commentary on *Robinson (Wayne)* [2006] Crim LR 427.

# Question 14

Answer all THREE parts of this question:

(i) Ellen is charged with handling 10 pairs of stolen jeans, knowing or believing them to have been stolen. The prosecution has a confession from Ellen in which she states: 'They were nicked all right. I bought them from a stranger in a pub. He offered them at a very cheap price and I asked if there was anything wrong with them. He said, "No. They're new. The truth is they've been taken off a lorry, but no one will miss them".' The police have been unable to find the owner of the jeans to prove that they were stolen. Can the prosecution rely on Ellen's confession for this purpose?

(ii) Freda is charged with theft. The prosecution alleges that she walked into a chemist's shop, grabbed several bottles of talcum powder and scent from a display, and walked out without paying. She was not stopped at the time, but her actions were filmed by a security camera, and when the manager saw the video tape he recognised Freda and informed the police. Unfortunately, the video tape has since been lost. Can the manager give evidence of what he saw when he watched the tape?

(iii) Gerald is charged with robbery. The prosecution alleges that he walked up to Henry in the street, struck him on the head, and stole his watch. Henry has only a hazy recollection of the incident. However, several hours afterwards a bystander, Ian, told PC Prout that he had seen everything. He said that the attacker was six feet tall, with light brown hair, and had a tattoo of a butterfly on his left cheek. He later gave a more detailed description of the attacker to a police artist, who made a sketch based on what Ian told him. Both the oral description and the sketch match Gerald's appearance quite well. Ian has since disappeared, and no written statement from him can be found by the police. Can PC Prout give evidence of Gerald's oral description of the attacker? Can the prosecution call the police artist to produce the sketch?

## Answer plan

(i) The admissibility of confessions should be dealt with briefly. (On the subject of confessions, see Chapter 7.) The main part of the problem is covered by the principle in *Comptroller of Customs v Western Lectric Co Ltd (1966)*. See also *Hulbert (1979)*.

(ii) Could the video tape have been produced as evidence if it had been available? Remember the definition of statement in s 115(2) of the **Criminal Justice Act (CJA) 2003**, and note *Taylor v Chief Constable of Cheshire (1987)*.

(iii) Are the description and the sketch caught by the rule against hearsay? See s 115(2) again. Can the evidence be admitted under any relevant exception to the rule? Note s 116 and the possibility of defence submissions under *Sang* and s 78(1) of the **Police and Criminal Evidence Act 1984 (PACE)**.

# Answer

(i) Evidence of Ellen's confession can be given in principle under s 76(1) of the PACE, but not for the purpose required here by the prosecution. If Ellen had had first-hand knowledge of the theft, for example, if she had seen the theft take place, her admission could be used to prove that the jeans were stolen. But her admission is based on what the stranger told her and an admission based on hearsay does not prove the truth of what is admitted. For example, in *Comptroller of Customs v Western Lectric Co Ltd (1966)* it was held that an admission by the defendants that they had falsely described the country of origin of certain goods was inadmissible. The information on which the defendants had relied in making this admission was hearsay, because it consisted of markings on the goods indicating a different country of origin from that stated by the defendants. Lord Hodson said that if a man admits something of which he knows nothing, it is of no real evidential value. A similar problem arose in *Hulbert (1979)*. The defendant was charged with handling stolen goods. It was held that her admission that she had been told that the goods were stolen was inadmissible as evidence that the goods were in fact stolen.

(ii) The old rule against hearsay did not exclude tapes, films or still photographs that had directly recorded an incident as it was taking place. So, for example, in *Dodson (1984)* film from a security camera that had been operating during a robbery was admitted in evidence. The reasoning was that the hearsay rule did not apply to evidence produced by a machine that had automatically recorded some process or event. This distinction is preserved by the new law. A 'statement' is confined by s 115(2) to a representation made by a *person*. It follows that information generated by a *machine*, unless based on information provided by a person, is not a statement, and so not caught by the hearsay rule. It follows that that the film could have been adduced in evidence, if it had been available, without infringing the hearsay rule. Accordingly, there seems to be no reason why the manager should not give evidence of what he saw on it, just as he could have given evidence of what he saw if he had been in the store when the thefts took place. Support for this can be found in *Taylor v Chief Constable of Cheshire (1987)*, where witnesses were allowed to give evidence of what they saw on a video recording of an incident, even though the recording had been accidentally erased before the trial. The court's view was that their evidence was direct evidence of the commission of the offence, in the same way as if their observation of the incident had been through binoculars.

(iii) Under the pre-2003 law, it was held that sketches or photofit likenesses made under the direction of an identifying witness were in a class of their own, and were not caught by the rule against hearsay. This was rightly criticised as illogical, and s 115(2) now defines a statement for hearsay purposes so as to include a representation made in a sketch, photofit or other pictorial form. In principle, therefore, not only Ian's oral description but also the police artist's sketch are affected by the rule. But since Ian has disappeared, the prosecution can rely on the unavailability exception in s 116. It will be necessary to prove that such steps as were reasonably practicable to take were taken to find Ian, but without success. The defence could submit that the evidence should nevertheless be excluded, either under the common law discretion confirmed in *Sang (1980)*, or under s 78(1) of PACE.

# Question 15

Percy is being prosecuted for the murder of Edith. He is an Australian visitor to England who was staying in a flat on the third floor of a block known as Shearman Court in West London. Edith lived alone in another flat on the ground floor. The prosecution says that Percy and Edith were having an affair, but that on the evening of 14 July, there was a quarrel between them at Edith's flat, during which Percy strangled her.

Percy was first implicated in the crime when a police tracker dog led detectives to his flat on the third floor. In a properly conducted police interview, he told the police that he had not killed Edith, had never had an affair with her and had never been inside her flat.

Curtis, who lived in another flat on the ground floor of Shearman Court, told police that on the evening of the murder, he had heard a loud argument going on in Edith's flat between Edith and a man with an Australian accent.

When the police lawfully searched Percy's flat, they found an opened letter in a desk drawer. It was addressed to Percy and read as follows: 'Don't be fooled by that tart Edith. She's been screwing Frederick for the last month. Give her up – she's not worth it. With love from Rose.' The prosecution does not wish to call Rose, but it wants to put the letter in evidence as part of their case against Percy.

Lilian, a friend of Edith, was interviewed by Percy's solicitor. She told him that after the murder, she took away from Edith's flat a parrot called Max, which Edith had kept as a pet, in order to look after it. She said that during the day Max was silent, but that when evening came, the bird repeatedly called out, 'Frederick, no, no, no!'.

Discuss the evidential issues that arise.

## Answer plan

The first thing to emphasise is that all the evidence you have been asked to consider is circumstantial and highly inconclusive, *but it is not, merely for this reason, inadmissible.* If you think about it, there is no evidence that proves something conclusively, for there will always exist possible alternative explanations for the item of evidence in question. Far too many students think that a defendant cannot be convicted on purely circumstantial evidence, or at least that such evidence is bound by its very nature to be less substantial than direct evidence, such as the evidence given by a witness of what he saw or heard. This too is completely wrong. In *Taylor, Weaver and Donovan (1928)*, Lord Hewart CJ said: 'It is no derogation of evidence to say that it is circumstantial.' His words should be remembered.

With this in mind, you need to consider five points:

- *Tracker dog evidence.* There is an English authority on this. Note what has to be proved to establish the reliability of such evidence. Of course, there is no hearsay problem here.
- *What Percy said to the police.* What is the purpose of adducing this in evidence? The answer to that question will solve any hearsay difficulties.
- *Curtis's evidence.* Again, what will the prosecution be adducing this to prove? Your answer should be: (a) There was a quarrel that night. (b) It took place at Edith's flat. (c) It was between Edith and a man. (d) The man

was Australian. None of this, of course, points inevitably to Percy, but see the opening paragraph above, and remember that this is only a part of the prosecution case.
- *The letter.* This is an example of what is sometimes called the distinction between hearsay and real evidence. If you treat these expressions as labels which can be instinctively slapped on various items of evidence, you are heading for disaster. The starting point, as always, is not the *label* but the *job of proof* that the evidence can do. Putting it another way, the problem of admissibility can be solved only if you consider carefully what inferences can be drawn from the evidence in question. As part of its case, the prosecution wants to prove a number of propositions. Which of those propositions, if any, does the letter support? The answer to this will tell you if it is relevant. What arguments are needed to move from the letter to the propositions that the prosecution wants to prove? The answer to this will tell you about admissibility.
- *Lilian's evidence.* Is it relevant? Is there a hearsay problem? If it is relevant and there is no hearsay problem, what is to stop it from being admitted?

# Answer

The tracker dog presumably led the police to Percy's flat because the animal picked up Percy's scent in Edith's flat. There might have been a perfectly innocent explanation for this but, in view of Percy's denial that he had ever been inside the flat, the evidence is capable of supporting the prosecution case. *Pieterson (1995)* established that evidence of the activities of tracker dogs will be admissible, provided a proper foundation can be laid to establish reliability. The dog's handler should give evidence about its training, and should also establish that over a period of time, it behaved reliably as a tracker during controlled tests.

Evidence can be given of what Percy said to the police. The prosecution will wish to show that Percy lied about his association with Edith and will invite the jury to infer guilt from this. The purpose in adducing evidence of what Percy said will be to show its falsity, not its truth. In these circumstances, the rule against hearsay does not apply (*Mawaz Khan v R (1967)*).

Curtis can give evidence of the sounds that he heard coming from Edith's flat on the evening of 14 July. A jury would be entitled to infer from this that an argument was going on at the time. Curtis could also say that he heard the accents of an Australian male to show that such a person was present on that occasion. Neither of these items of evidence infringes the rule against hearsay because the purpose of adducing the evidence is not to establish the truth of what was said, but the fact that there was an argument and that one of the participants was an Australian man.

The evidential value of the letter found in Percy's desk is not that it establishes the truth about Edith's love life, but that it enables us to infer that Percy had been having some sort of relationship with a woman called Edith and that he probably had a vengeful state of mind towards her. The argument can be put thus: why should Percy have such an interest in the letter that he kept it in his desk if he did *not* have any such relationship? In other words, it is Percy's reaction to what was written that is relied on, not the truth of what was said in the letter. Evidence was admitted for a similar purpose in *McIntosh (1992)* where the defendant was charged with importing drugs. In a house where he had been living before his arrest, the police found a piece of paper which contained calculations, not in the defendant's hand writing, of the purchase and sale prices of 12 oz of an unnamed commodity. The Court of Appeal held that this evidence had been properly admitted as circumstantial real evidence tending to connect the accused with the crime charged. Though not spelled out by the court, the reason appears to have been that the person in possession of the document kept it because he was interested in the information which it contained.

Given that there was a relationship between Percy and Edith, then, *regardless of the truth of what was said about Edith in the letter*, the fact that the allegation was read and the letter kept suggests that Percy took it seriously, and from that it can be inferred that he may have had vengeful feelings towards Edith.

One possible inference from the parrot's behaviour is that the bird was repeating what it heard Edith shout on the evening when she was murdered. From this it could be inferred that, because Frederick is named rather than Percy, it was not Percy who murdered her. The first point to be made is that what the parrot 'said' was not a statement. If Edith uttered those words, she did not do so for the purpose of causing another person to believe anything, as required by s 115(3) of the **Criminal Justice Act 2003**. As a non-statement, therefore, what Edith said is not caught by the rule against hearsay. Because some parrots tend to repeat human language that they hear, Max might be seen as a recording device. Had a tape recorder been operating at the time, the tape could well have been admissible as direct evidence of what was going on. In *Maqsud Ali (1966)*, the Court of Appeal held that a tape recording is admissible in evidence provided, *inter alia*, the accuracy of the recording can be proved and the voices properly identified.

The real difficulty here is not one of hearsay and, by analogy with *Taylor v Chief Constable of Cheshire (1987)*, Lilian should be allowed to give evidence of what she heard if Max is properly seen as a recording device. The prosecution could legitimately object, however, that as a recording device Max is most unreliable. How could the court be satisfied, even on a *prima facie* basis, that Max did not pick up this expression on some quite different occasion or from someone other than Edith? The truth of the matter is that Max is quite different from the sort of mechanical recording devices whose products have been admitted hitherto by the courts as real evidence. Lilian's evidence is therefore most unlikely to be admissible for the defence.

# Chapter 5

# Hearsay II

## INTRODUCTION

The scope of the rule against hearsay has been much reduced. The Civil Evidence Act 1995 has abolished the rule completely for civil proceedings. In 1995 the Law Commission published a Consultation Paper on the subject of hearsay in criminal cases, and in 1997 published a Report. The recommendations of the Commission have been very largely incorporated in Part 11, Chapter 2 of the Criminal Justice Act (CJA) 2003, which has created four principal categories of admissibility, all of which are available to both the defendant and the prosecution:

- hearsay admissible by statute;
- hearsay admissible under any preserved common law rule;
- hearsay admissible by agreement;
- hearsay admissible in the interests of justice (the 'safety-valve').

Reference has already been made in Chapter 4 to the unavailability exception in s 116 of the CJA 2003 and to the 'safety-valve' exception in s 114. It is important to note that hearsay statements under either section can be oral or written.

Under ss 23 and 24 of the Criminal Justice Act 1988, documentary hearsay statements were admissible under certain conditions. However, the interpretation of ss 23 and 24 gave rise to difficulty, and the powers to admit hearsay statements under them were the subject of a wide judicial discretion, contained in ss 25 and 26, that gave rise to accusations of inconsistency and uncertainty. These provisions were repealed by Sched 37, Part 6 of the CJA 2003 and replaced by an exception in favour of 'business and other documents' in s 117.

With the exception of the rules preserved by s 118, the common law rules governing the admissibility of hearsay evidence in criminal proceedings are abolished. As well as some minor exceptions, two major common law exceptions are preserved: *res gestae* statements and statements in furtherance of a common enterprise.

***Res gestae statements*** are generally taken to include four different categories:

(i) Statements that accompany and explain an action of the person making the statement.
(ii) Spontaneous exclamations made in response to an event so dramatic as to rule out any opportunity for concoction. The leading case is *Andrews (1987)*, and you should know the tests for admissibility that it establishes.
(iii) Declarations about the maker's contemporaneous state of mind or emotion. The law has developed in a haphazard and unsatisfactory way, and is consequently in a state of some uncertainty (and so is a favourite topic for examination questions). It is odd that the CJA 2003 did not attempt to clarify it. You should pay particular attention to the cases on statements of intention.
(iv) Declarations about the maker's contemporaneous physical sensations. Note that the declarations cannot be used to prove what caused the sensations.

***Statements in furtherance of a common enterprise*** made by one party to the enterprise are admissible against others, even where they have had nothing to do with making the statement and may not know that a statement has been made. This rule is not confined to conspiracy cases; it applies wherever the prosecution alleges a joint enterprise. But the statement must have been made in furtherance of the enterprise, so it will not apply to the confession of one party after his arrest: *Walters (1979)*.

The law relating to confessions is also preserved, but this topic is separately considered in Chapter 7.

Do not neglect the supplementary provisions in ss 121–125 of the CJA 2003. The rules about multiple hearsay are particularly important. You should always be aware that admissible hearsay can still be excluded, either at common law or by statute.

## Checklist

Students should be familiar with the following areas:
- the unavailability exception (s 116);
- the business and other documents exception (s 117);
- the preserved common law exceptions (s 118);
- the 'safety-valve' exception (s 114);
- the supplementary provisions (ss 121–125);
- common law and statutory powers of exclusion.

# Question 16

Harold is charged with the murder of his wife, Irene. The case for the prosecution is that he stabbed her repeatedly with a screwdriver because he believed that she was having an affair with Jack, a neighbour. Irene died in hospital from the wounds that she received. A month before the alleged stabbing, Irene called in a distressed state on another neighbour, Kate. Irene brought with her a meat cleaver and an axe and asked Kate to look after them for her. When Kate asked Irene why she wanted her to do this, Irene replied, 'Harold keeps threatening me with these, and I'd feel safer if they were out of the way'. She added, 'I've been feeling sick after meals; I think he's already trying to poison me'. A week before she was stabbed, Irene wrote a letter to Leo, a solicitor, asking for an appointment to see him about getting a divorce. In the letter she stated, 'I hope there won't be any difficulty. Recently he's been threatening to kill me'.

Discuss the evidential issues arising.

## Answer plan

Your first task is to isolate each item of evidence requiring consideration. You should have a list that looks like this:

- Irene visited Kate in a distressed state a month before she was injured.
- She had with her a meat cleaver and an axe and asked Kate to look after them.
- The reason she gave for her request.
- What Irene said about feeling sick after meals.
- The letter to Leo.

In considering these items of evidence, you should bear in mind the provisions of ss 116 and 117 of the **Criminal Justice Act (CJA) 2003**, as well as the law relating to *res gestae* preserved by s 118. You must also consider relevance, the rules relating to evidence of bad character, and the judge's common law and statutory discretion to exclude otherwise admissible evidence. The problem presented by opinion evidence also arises.

# Answer

The purpose of adducing Kate's evidence of Irene's visit would be to establish Harold's murderous intentions towards his wife. It could be argued for the prosecution that this is in principle relevant and admissible as important explanatory evidence under s 101(1)(c) of the CJA 2003.[1] For the defence it could be argued that it is insufficient to satisfy the test in s 102, and is too remote in time from the alleged attack to be relevant. If the judge rules in favour of the defence, the evidence will, of course, be excluded; but if he rules in favour of the prosecution, the question of hearsay will have to be considered. Can evidence be adduced of what Irene said to Kate about her reason for bringing the meat cleaver and the axe, and about feeling sick after meals?

Her reason for bringing the cleaver and the axe is in principle caught by the rule against hearsay. The statement was made out of court and is being adduced for the truth of its contents. The most obvious exception on which to rely is the unavailability exception in s 116. Kate has identified Irene as the maker of the statement; s 116(1)(b) is therefore satisfied. Had she survived, she could have given evidence herself of Harold's threats on the basis that they were expressions of his contemporaneous state of mind, and so admissible under the *res gestae* exception preserved by s 118. The difficulty with this analysis is that the account of Harold's threats is multiple hearsay where Kate is the testifying witness. It would be better to argue that Harold's threats are examples of performative language because they constitute criminal offences in themselves. As such, Kate's repetition of Irene's account will be first-hand hearsay and will not be subject to the restrictions in s 121 of the CJA 2003. There can, of course, be no question of admitting Irene's words on the basis that they accompany and explain a relevant act under s 118(1) 4(b). It was held in *Bliss (1837)* that the act has to be relevant to the facts in issue quite apart from the statement accompanying it, and on these facts that condition is not satisfied.

Irene's statement about feeling sick after meals, and the alleged reason for this, are inadmissible. Harold has not been charged with any offence in connection with poisoning, and the fact that Irene had been feeling sick after meals is irrelevant to the charge that he does face. Her speculation about the reason for feeling sick would, in any case, be inadmissible opinion evidence.[2]

The letter to Leo is further evidence of recent threats by Harold to kill Irene. The statement on this matter should be admissible either under s 116 or s 117 of the CJA 2003. If the threats are treated as examples of performative language, no multiple hearsay problems arise. Section 117(1)(a) is clearly satisfied. The document was received by Leo in the course of his profession as a solicitor, and Irene may reasonably be supposed to have had personal knowledge of the matters dealt with. Section 117(2)(a) and (b) are therefore satisfied. Sub-section (2)(c) does not apply because the information in the letter passed directly from Irene to Leo. The letter was prepared for the purpose of civil proceedings; accordingly, the additional requirements in s 117(5) do not have to be considered.

## References

1 See Chapters 8 and 9.
2 See Chapter 11.

# Question 17

Charles Peace is charged with the burglary on 15 May of a house in Penny Avenue. On the afternoon of 15 May, Alice was walking near Penny Avenue when a man whom she recognised as Eddie, a neighbour's son, ran up to her and shouted, 'It's disgraceful! I've just seen Charles Peace breaking into a house in Penny Avenue! And he was one of my teachers at school!' Alice noticed that Eddie's speech was slurred and that his breath smelled of beer, so she did not stop to hear any more. When she reached home she told her husband, Ben, about the incident. Since then, Eddie has died from an overdose of drugs and Alice has had such a severe stroke that she is likely to be unfit to give evidence at Charles Peace's trial. But Ben remembers clearly what she told him and is willing to give evidence for the prosecution. Shortly after Charles was arrested, his brother David committed suicide. David's girlfriend, Nora, says that the night before he killed himself, David told her that he had committed the burglary in Penny Avenue and that Charles had had nothing to do with it. She gave a statement to this effect to Charles's solicitor, but now she refuses to give evidence because she believes that David's ghost will haunt her if she does so.

Discuss the evidential issues arising.

## Answer plan

The first question is whether Alice could give evidence of Eddie's statement if she is fit enough to testify. You need to consider s 116 of the Criminal Justice Act (CJA) 2003 and the *res gestae* exceptions preserved by s 118(1). Assuming that her evidence will be admissible, can Ben give evidence of what she told him if she is unable to testify? The problem here is one of multiple hearsay, which you will need to consider in the light of s 121.

If Nora can be persuaded to testify for the defence, would her evidence be admissible? You need to consider s 116 again. But if she refuses to testify, can the defence use her written statement instead? See ss 116 and 117.

## Answer

If Alice recovers sufficiently well to give evidence the prosecution could rely either on s 116 of the CJA 2003 or on the *res gestae* 'excited utterance' exception preserved by s 118(1) 4(a).

Section 116 is available because if Eddie had survived, he could have given oral evidence of what he perceived. Section 118(1) 4(a) preserves the law established in *Andrews (1987)*. The judge would have to be satisfied that the event perceived by

Eddie was so unusual or dramatic as to dominate his thoughts to the extent that his utterance was an instinctive reaction to the event, giving no time for concoction or distortion. The judge would have to take into account the fact that Eddie was, apparently, a drug user, and that on the occasion in question his speech was slurred and his breath smelled of beer. Either or both of these matters might constitute special features giving rise to the possibility of error. In *Andrews* it was recognised that such a feature might exist where the original speaker had drunk to excess. If the judge decides that a special feature exists, he must consider whether he can still exclude the possibility of error before admitting the evidence.

Even if a judge decided that Alice's evidence was in principle admissible, the defence could submit that it ought to be excluded, either under the common law discretion, confirmed by *Sang (1980)*, or under s 78(1) of the Police and Criminal Evidence Act 1984. Both discretions are preserved by s 126(2) of the CJA 2003. The evidence is of identification, and so particularly liable to error. In the absence of opportunity for cross-examination about the circumstances in which the identification was made, a defence submission to exclude the evidence could well succeed. If Alice's evidence is admitted, it would be open to the defence to adduce evidence affecting Eddie's credibility, such as his addiction to drugs, under s 124 of the CJA 2003.

If Alice is not sufficiently recovered to give evidence, and the judge decides that in principle her evidence is admissible and should not be excluded in the exercise of his discretion, the additional question arises whether Ben can give evidence of what she told him. Ben's evidence would be second-hand hearsay, and s 121 will apply. If Alice's evidence of Eddie's statement is admissible at all, it will not be by virtue of either s 117, 119 or 120. In the absence of agreement by the defence, which obviously would not be forthcoming, the only route for the admissibility of multiple hearsay would be that contained in s 121(1)(c), under which the court would have to be satisfied that the value of the evidence, taking into account its reliability, was so high that the interests of justice required Ben's evidence to be admissible. For the reasons given in support of discretionary exclusion, it is unlikely that this condition will be satisfied.

If Nora can be persuaded to testify for the defence, would her evidence of what David said be admissible under s 116? David himself could have testified to that effect if he had not died. The conditions in s 116(1)(a) and (b) are satisfied, and the fact that David is dead satisfies a relevant condition under s 116(2). Nora's evidence would therefore be admissible. If Nora cannot be persuaded to testify, can the defence use her written statement as evidence? To do so, reliance could again be placed on s 116, this time on the basis that Nora does not give evidence through fear. Her fear may be irrational, but s 116(3) provides that 'fear' is to be widely construed. The fact that Nora is in fear at the time of the trial (which *H, W and M (2001)* showed to be the relevant time) would have to be proved by admissible evidence. As to this, the pre-2003 law was in some uncertainty, and this has not been clarified by the new legislation. In *Neill v North Antrim Magistrates' Court (1992)*, the House of Lords held, in relation to a similar exception in s 23 of the Criminal Justice Act 1988, that evidence of fear which itself offended the rule against hearsay was inadmissible. However, in *Greer (1998)* the Court of Appeal said that there was no reason why a judge should not hear 'unsworn evidence' from the witness who was in fear.

It should be noted that Nora's statement would constitute second-hand hearsay and would therefore be subject to the restrictions of s 121.

Because of s 121, it would be better if her statement could be admitted under s 117 as a business document. However, this will not be possible because Nora did not herself receive the information from David in the course of a trade, business, profession, etc. The condition in s 117(2)(c) is therefore not satisfied.

# Question 18

Adrian, Billy and Charlie are charged with possession of drugs with intent to supply. In the house where all three lived, police found a large quantity of cocaine and £28,000 in used banknotes. When interviewed, all three defendants said that the money had been the proceeds of successful gambling. They said that they had just moved into the house and had no knowledge of the presence of the cocaine, which had been discovered in the loft. The police also found a diary in Adrian's handwriting, in which there appeared inside the back cover a list containing references to first names, to various quantities of something that was unspecified, and to sums of money. Below the list was written: 'Adrian to get half; Billy and Charlie a quarter each.' There were also various entries for the week before the date when all three were arrested. One of these read: 'Billy and Charlie are getting cold feet. I wish they hadn't persuaded me to let them in on the deals.' For two weeks before the arrests were made, DC Kray kept watch outside the house, which was visited by 26 people. He was able to identify 18 of these as persons with previous convictions for the possession of drugs.

Discuss the evidential matters arising.

## Answer plan

There are three items of evidence that need your consideration:
- Is evidence of finding the money admissible? If so, does the judge need to say anything about it in summing up?
- Are the contents of Adrian's diary admissible? Against whom? Don't forget that the entries should be dealt with separately. Will the judge need to give any special direction?
- Is the evidence of DC Kray admissible for the prosecution?

# Answer

In relation to the cash, two questions arise. Is it relevant to the prosecution case? If it is, what directions should the judge give to the jury about it? In *Wright (1994)*, the Court of Appeal held that the discovery of £16,000 in cash in the defendant's flat was admissible to support a charge of possessing cocaine with intent to supply, on the basis that drug dealers are known to deal in large sums of cash. However, in *Batt (1994)*, the Court of Appeal held that the finding of cash (albeit in that case a much smaller sum) was inadmissible, because it was suggestive only of past dealings. As such, it was unfairly prejudicial because it showed only a disposition to commit such offences. *Batt* seems difficult to reconcile with *Wright*, but later cases have tended to prefer the reasoning in *Wright*. Therefore, the position is that the finding of the cash is likely to be admissible to support the charge, but there are two elements in the charge, both of which the defendants deny. Not only do they deny intent to supply; they also deny *possession* (their case is that they knew nothing of the presence of the cocaine). In *Guney (1998)*, the Court of Appeal said that whether evidence is relevant depends on the circumstances of each case. Where possession with intent to supply is charged, there are many circumstances in which evidence of cash and lifestyle might be relevant and admissible in relation to the issue of possession itself, especially to the issue of knowledge as an ingredient of possession. Thus, the discovery of the cash may be relevant to possession as well as intent to supply.[1]

However, a careful direction will have to be given to the jury about the use they can make of this information. In *Grant (1996)*, the Court of Appeal said that before relying on such evidence, the jury must be satisfied that the money was not in the defendant's possession for any innocent reason that may have been advanced (in this case, as a result of successful gambling) and that, even if they find that it does relate to drug dealing, they must be satisfied that it relates to an ongoing course of dealing, and is not merely the proceeds of past deals. However, at the time when *Grant* was decided there were severe restrictions on adducing evidence that was relevant only to a defendant's disposition. These were substantially reduced in the **Criminal Justice Act 2003**, and it might now be enough for the cash to be taken only as evidence of past dealing.[2]

In *Pearce (1979)*, the Court of Appeal held that wholly exculpatory statements made by suspects when confronted with incriminating evidence are admissible to show their reactions to the accusations being made, but are not evidence of the truth of their contents. Accordingly, the defendants' statements about ignorance of the presence of cocaine, and their explanations for the presence of the money, will be admissible for this limited purpose.

The entries in Adrian's diary should be separately considered. It was held in *Gray and Others (1995)* that a statement made in furtherance of a common purpose by one defendant is admissible as evidence against the others, though made in their absence. The reason for this is that a combination of persons for the purpose of committing a crime is regarded as implying an authority to each to act or speak in furtherance of the common purpose on behalf of the others. For example, in *Devonport and Pirano (1996)*, where the defendants were charged with conspiracy to defraud a bank, a document drawn up by the girlfriend of one of the defendants, at the latter's dictation, showed an intended division of the proceeds of the offence between all the defendants, who were named. It was held that this was evidence against all the defendants, there being evidence in addition to the document to show that they were all parties to the conspiracy. Since the document was a record of *intended* distribution of the proceeds when the conspiracy had been fulfilled, it had been prepared in furtherance of the conspiracy, and was thus admissible. It would have been different if the document had been merely a record, made when everything was finished, of what had happened. This common law exception was preserved by para 7 of s 118(1) of the Criminal Justice Act 2003.

The entries at the back of Adrian's diary show an *intended* distribution between the three defendants, and there is other evidence (the discovery of the drugs and the cash in the house where all three lived) to link Billy and Charlie to a common enterprise, even though not charged as a conspiracy. On this basis, the entry is admissible against all the defendants. But the judge will have to warn the jury that they must be satisfied that the entry was not only evidence of past dealing, but capable of going to intention to supply in the future. In other words, the diary entry must be treated with the same caution as the discovery of the cash: see *Lovelock (1997)*. But the reservation noted in relation to *Grant* in respect of such a direction after the passing of the Criminal Justice Act 2003 might be relevant here also.

The second entry about Billy and Charlie getting cold feet is clearly not made in furtherance of the common enterprise. It is admissible as a confession by Adrian.[3]

The evidence of DC Kray may be relevant because it shows the sort of people frequenting the house, and tends to show that the house was being used for drug dealing. Similar evidence was admitted in *Warner (1993)*, where the prosecution's case was that the pattern of visits was consistent with the method of drug dealing testified to by prosecution witnesses. The defence case was that the visitors had been making only social calls but in *Hasson (1997)*, evidence that the defendants, who were charged with being concerned in the supply of cannabis resin, had associated with persons with drug related convictions was held inadmissible. In contrast to *Warner*, it was not part of the prosecution case that the defendants were supplying drugs to those whose convictions were adduced in evidence. The question on these facts therefore appears to be whether there is a nexus between the defendants' association with these visitors and any specific allegation of dealing made by the prosecution. In the absence of such a nexus, the evidence is likely to be inadmissible.

### References

1 See also *Griffiths (1998)*.
2 See also Question 3.
3 For confessions, see Chapter 7.

# Question 19

Michael, who runs a car hire firm, is charged with manslaughter. The case for the prosecution is that he rented a car to Nick for one week on 1 April. On 2 April, the car was found at the bottom of a cliff with Nick's body inside. The prosecution alleges that when Michael rented the car to Nick, the steering mechanism was, to Michael's knowledge, so faulty that a driver would be likely to lose control of the car. Michael intends to plead not guilty. He denies that the steering mechanism was faulty. He says that if it was faulty, he had no knowledge of this. He says that fog on the night of the accident made visibility very poor, and that this caused Nick to drive off the road and over the cliff. Another explanation, he says, is that Nick drove over the cliff deliberately because he believed that his wife had left him. Michael wishes to testify that one week before the accident, he rented the same car to Olive, a qualified car mechanic. Michael says that he saw Olive examine the car carefully before getting in and taking it on a test drive by herself. Only when she returned did she allow her children to get in as passengers. Michael also wishes to call Patrick, Nick's best friend, who says that he received a call from Nick's mobile telephone on the night of 1 April. According to Patrick, Nick said: 'I'm driving along a cliff road. The fog is frightening, but I can't find anywhere to stop the car.' The prosecution has disclosed that a note was found on Nick's kitchen table. It was from his wife and was dated 31 March. It said: 'I can't stand living with you any more. I have gone to live with Quentin in Ireland. Don't try to contact me.'

Discuss the evidential issues arising.

### Answer plan

There are three items of evidence, to be considered separately:

- the incident involving Olive;
- Patrick's account of the mobile phone call from Nick;
- the note from Nick's wife.

# Hearsay II

# Answer

The significance of the incident involving Olive is that it shows that the car was in good condition only a week before Nick hired it. Olive was a qualified car mechanic, she examined the car carefully before taking it for a test drive, and only on her return did she take her children as passengers. The inference is that she found the car to be in a safe condition. Of course, the fact that the car was safe then does not mean inevitably that there was nothing wrong with it when Nick hired it, but it makes it unlikely.

Under the pre-2003 law, it is possible that evidence about the incident with Olive would have been inadmissible. In *Wright v Doe d Tatham (1837)*, Parke B said *obiter* that the rule against hearsay applied to non-verbal conduct. As an example, he envisaged a trial where the seaworthiness of a ship was in issue. Suppose the deceased captain had first examined every part of the ship, and only when his inspection was complete had he embarked on it with his family. Parke B said that this evidence would be affected by the rule against hearsay just as much as a statement by the captain to a bystander to the effect that he had examined the ship and had found it seaworthy. *Wright v Doe d Tatham* was relied on by the House of Lords when it held in *Kearley (1992)* that the rule against hearsay affected non-assertive utterances. Whether it also caught hearsay by conduct was never finally decided. However, s 115(3)(a) of the **Criminal Justice Act (CJA) 2003** defines 'a matter stated' as one where the purpose, or one of the purposes, of the person making the statement appears to the court to have been to cause another person to believe the matter stated. The effect of this is to abolish the rule that non-assertive utterances are caught by the rule against hearsay, and its effect must also be to abolish Parke B's notion of hearsay by conduct that was not intended to convey any message to observers. The evidence of Olive's behaviour will therefore be admissible.

Patrick can give evidence of what Nick said during the telephone call by virtue of the unavailability exception in s 116, and possibly also by virtue of the preserved *res gestae* exceptions.

If Nick had survived, he could have given evidence of conditions on the cliff road. There are no identification problems, and Nick is unavailable because he is dead. It would be possible to argue, further, that what Nick said amounted to an 'excited utterance'. The leading authority is *Andrews (1987)*. This requires that the circumstances provoking the utterance should have been so unusual, startling or dramatic as to dominate the thoughts of the speaker to the extent that the utterance was an instinctive reaction to those circumstances, with no opportunity for reflection or concoction. The difficulty on these facts is that what Nick appears to have been experiencing, though unpleasant, was not a sudden event; it was, apparently, a continuing state of affairs. As such, it could be argued that it lacked the dramatic quality of something like the sudden and violent attack in *Carnall*

*(1995)*. Thus, it is difficult to predict with certainty whether or not Patrick's evidence would be admitted under this exception.

The note found on the kitchen table will be admissible. One of the defence theories is that Nick committed suicide when he discovered that his wife had left him. The evidence of the note will be admissible quite simply for the effect it might have had on Nick's mind. In *Subramaniam v Public Prosecutor (1956)*, the Privy Council emphasised that a statement will not be caught by the rule against hearsay where it is adduced merely to establish the fact that it was made. This fact, quite apart from the truth of the statement, is frequently relevant in considering the mental state and conduct of someone to whom the statement was made. That is exactly the relevance of the note on these facts. It might have been quite untrue that the wife had gone to Ireland or had decided to leave her husband for another man. The point is that Nick might have believed what he read, and this might have given him a motive for suicide.

# Question 20

How successful was the Criminal Justice Act 2003 in reforming the law relating to hearsay?

## Answer plan

There is a wide range of approaches to this question. But you could make these points, among others:

- abolition of 'implied assertions';
- the 'safety-valve' in s 114(1)(d);
- oral as well as documentary hearsay now available where a witness is unavailable;
- extending the scope of 'recent complaints': s 120(7)(d);
- retention of *res gestae*: a point for criticism;
- the extent of judicial discretion: another possible point for criticism.

# Answer

Hearsay used to be an essentially common law doctrine with some statutory additions. One critic described it as a 'legalistic backwater' which was 'the home of sophistry and the graveyard of common sense.'[1] Since the 2003 Act it has become primarily a statutory doctrine with some common law rules preserved.

A major reform has been the abolition, acknowledged by the Court of Appeal in *Singh (2006)*, of the concept of 'implied assertions', to which the House of Lords had given its authority in *Kearley (1992)*. This decision was much criticised for extending the scope of hearsay to such an extent that, in principle, almost any utterance, or even action, could fall within the exclusionary rule on the basis that it reflected a belief of the speaker or agent in a state of affairs that justified the utterance or action in question. The decision was also criticised for its confusion of implications with inferences. Section 115(3) of the 2003 Act now defines 'a matter stated' as one where the person making the statement appears to the court to have had as one of his purposes either causing another person to believe the matter or causing another person to act (or a machine to operate) on the basis that the matter is as stated. It follows that if A asks B, 'Have you any bananas for sale?' A will not be taken to have had the purpose of asserting that B is a dealer in bananas, and his question, if overheard, can be adduced as evidence of the fact that B is a dealer.

Birch has argued that s 115(3) might have been too radical. She has suggested that as the law now stands, the defence will be able to make free play with non-assertive words and conduct, whereas the prosecution, because of s 78 of **Police and Criminal Evidence Act 1984 (PACE)**, will not.

Another major reform is the availability of the 'safety-valve' in s 114(1)(d), which provides for the admissibility of a hearsay statement where the court is satisfied that it is in the interests of justice for the statement to be admitted. This will not only enable a court to do justice in a case such as *Sparks (1964)*; it will make unnecessary the use of 'hearsay fiddles', such as that adopted in *Ward (2001)*, where it was held that evidence tending to confirm the defendant's presence near the scene of the crime, but which was *prima facie* hearsay, could nevertheless be admitted because of its weight.[2]

By s 116, oral as well as documentary hearsay evidence can now be given where a witness is unavailable; s 23 of the Criminal Justice Act 1988 allowed only documentary hearsay to be given in such circumstances. But by s 116(1)(b) the person who made the statement must be identified to the court's satisfaction; if this condition is not fulfilled, reliance will have to be placed on the safety-valve or on the *res gestae* exception, preserved by s 118. The discretion and leave provisions of ss 25 and 26 of the CJA 1988 do not appear in the 2003 Act. But necessity by itself will not eliminate the weaknesses of hearsay evidence.[3] A defence application under s 78 of PACE can be made, and possible breach of Art 6 of the European Convention on Human Rights must also be considered. The European Court has consistently taken the view that a conviction will not be fair if it is founded 'mainly' on evidence from someone whom the accused has had no opportunity to have examined.[4] Further, leave is required by s 116(2)(e) where a witness does not give evidence through fear.

A small but significant change in the law appears in s 120(7)(d). Recent complaints are now to be made 'as soon as could reasonably be expected after the alleged conduct'. Formerly, the complaint had also to be 'recent' in relation to the offence (*Birks, 2003*). The probable effect of s 120(7)(d) is that this restriction has gone, so that complaints of offences committed against someone who was a child at the time will be more readily admitted. The section extends the scope of recent complaints to offences of any kind. It also provides that previous statements shall now be evidence of the truth of the matters stated, thereby removing a distinction between evidence of truth and evidence of credibility that jurors must have found it hard to appreciate.

A major criticism of the reforms is that they do not go far enough. The retention in s 118 of the old law relating to *res gestae* is unsatisfactory, in particular because the admissibility of statements about contemporaneous mental states remains underdeveloped and obscure. Cases about statements of intention illustrate this well. In *Buckley (1873)*, a decision at first instance, such evidence was admitted, but without reasons. In *Wainwright (1875)*, another decision at first instance, such evidence was excluded, but the basis for the decision is unclear. It may well be that admissibility was sought under a different head of *res gestae*. In *Thomson (1912)* the Court of Criminal Appeal held such evidence inadmissible, but the appellant's argument had been based on the much broader proposition that an accused person is entitled to adduce any relevant evidence in his defence, regardless of the rules of evidence. A more favourable view of admissibility was taken, *obiter*, by the Court of Appeal in *Moghal (1977)*. A still more favourable view was taken by the Court of Appeal in *Gilfoyle (1996)*, which had the apparent effect of removing the requirement of contemporaneity between the utterance and the state of mind under investigation. Another problematic decision is that of the Court of Appeal in *Callender (1998)* where the Court, following a concession by counsel for the appellant, held, contrary to earlier authority, that the *Andrews (1987)* requirement of lack of opportunity for concoction or distortion applied in all the categories of *res gestae*, and not only to excited utterances.

Roberts and Zuckerman have criticised the 2003 Act on the basis that it creates 'a judicial discretion jamboree'.[5] Sections 116(4) and 117(7) create particular discretions. Section 114(1)(d) introduces a radical new inclusionary discretion. This is elaborated in s 114(2) by a list of nine factors to structure its exercise. However, in *Singh (2006)* the Court of Appeal held that although all these must be considered, a judge does not have to reach a decision on any one of them. Section 121(1)(c) establishes an additional leave requirement applicable to multiple hearsay, apart from business documents. Section 126 creates a new overriding discretion to exclude hearsay of marginal probative value where its admission would result in undue waste of time. The Act preserves the discretion contained in s 78 of PACE, and the common law discretion to exclude prosecution evidence is also untouched.

It can be argued in favour of so many discretions that they will enable a court to regulate the admissibility of hearsay evidence in a way that takes into account justice and common sense. On the other hand, experience of operating the discretions in ss 25 and 26 of the CJA 1988 showed, as the Law Commission noted, such a wide variety of judicial approaches that consistency suffered. Balancing the benefits of being able to do justice in the instant case against the dangers of inconsistency will always be difficult. The 2003 Act, in this respect, probably achieves as satisfactory a compromise as could be made.

## References

1 D. Birch, 'Hearsay: Same Old Story, Same Old Song?' [2004] *Criminal Law Review* 564.
2 See also *Lilley* [2003] EWCA 1789, and D. Birch, 'Hearsay-logic and Hearsay-fiddles: *Blastland* Revisited', in Peter Smith, ed., *Criminal Law: Essays in Honour of JC Smith* (London: Butterworths, 1987).
3 Paul Roberts and Adrian Zuckerman, *Criminal Evidence* (Oxford: OUP, 2004) p 625.
4 See, for example, *PS v Germany* [2002] Crim LR 312.
5 Roberts and Zuckerman, *Criminal Evidence*, p 641.

# Chapter 6

# Hazardous Evidence

## INTRODUCTION

All evidence, without exception, is hazardous. There are several reasons for this.

The first is that all evidence emerges as the result of some sort of selection. One kind may be loosely described as 'natural selection'. Not all the evidence that is relevant to a particular inquiry will have survived. Witnesses may have died; documents may have been destroyed; the physical features of a building may have been altered. Another sort of selection is human selection. In any investigation, someone has to gather the evidence that has survived. But to gather evidence effectively, you have to be intelligent enough to recognise what may be significant, and honest enough to do the job without pre-conceived ideas of what the outcome of the investigation should be. Natural selection and human frailty between them ensure that no jury ever sees more than a part of the whole picture, and that part may be a very small and misleading one.[1]

Another reason for the hazardous nature of evidence is that too much has to be taken on trust. It is not always appreciated that the only direct experience upon which a tribunal of fact can depend in a legal inquiry is its perception of witnesses testifying in the witness box, and perhaps also the perceptions that it experiences from its own examination of an item of real evidence. In relation to a testifying witness, two difficulties arise. The first comes from uncertainty as to whether the witness can trust the evidence of his own senses. He may believe that he saw the defendant stab the victim, but what guarantee has he that things were not otherwise? The second difficulty comes from the fact that the jury has to rely on the witness for an insight into what happened on the occasion under investigation. But all the jury can perceive is the witness in the box giving evidence. What is their justification for inferring from the witness's testimony that the defendant did in fact stab the victim?

A third reason for the hazardous nature of evidence is that, save for some items of real evidence, it is presented through the medium of language. But language is notoriously ambiguous. 'Words . . . may easily be misunderstood by a dull man. They may easily be misconstrued by a knave. What was spoken metaphorically may be apprehended literally. What was spoken ludicrously may be apprehended seriously. A particle, a tense, a mood, an emphasis may make the whole difference between guilt and innocence.'[2] But more than this, the very adversary system adopted in our courts tends to perpetuate ambiguity. One of the earliest lessons learned by a student of advocacy is how to avoid giving a witness whom he is cross-examining a chance to explain his testimony. Closed, leading questions which require a 'yes' or 'no' answer are recommended. These may be good trial tactics, but they are ill designed for the discovery of the truth.[3]

Politicians and lawyers have generally turned a blind eye to these fundamental defects. Attempts to make verdicts a little more reliable have been made only erratically and on a piecemeal basis. This chapter deals with attempts that have been made to control the way in which juries think about evidence which at various times has been thought to be particularly unreliable. These gave rise to law which compelled judges to warn juries in a particular way when they had to consider certain types of evidence, or evidence from certain types of witness.

*Mandatory warnings to the jury*

In the 18th century, when the beginnings of our modern law of evidence can be perceived, both prosecution and defence were often unrepresented by counsel, and the judge played a much larger part in criminal cases than he did in the 19th century and later. In particular, judges had a greater control over juries' deliberations. Summings up could contain much more of the judge's opinion than would now be thought proper. Where it appeared that a deliberation was likely to be short, the jury would often not leave the jury box, and this could provide an opportunity for informal dialogue with the judge about the evidence. Even if a jury returned a verdict with which the judge disagreed, he could persuade them to reconsider.

In time, this informal procedure gave way to a system more like the one we are used to today, though there was one major difference: until 1898, there was no general right for a defendant to testify in his own defence. Prosecution and defence came increasingly to be represented by counsel, possibly because of an increase in the size of the Bar, and the judge's control over the jury's deliberations slackened. But because jurors were free to weigh the evidence without judicial intervention, it became more necessary to warn them in a formal way during summing up about the weight to be attached to certain types of witness and testimony, and of the danger in convicting on the basis of such evidence without some independent support. Warnings were thought to be necessary in three main cases: those involving the evidence of children, of accomplices, and of complainants in cases where a sexual crime was alleged.

For a long time, the manner in which a warning was given, and even whether a warning was given at all, was a matter solely for the trial judge's discretion. But when the Court of Criminal Appeal was set up in 1907, discretionary practices tended to harden into rigid rules of law. Before long, a highly complex law of corroboration had developed. Eventually, it was thought to be so unsatisfactory that Parliament very largely abolished it in s 34(2) of the Criminal Justice Act (CJA) 1988 and in s 32 of the Criminal Justice and Public Order Act (CJPOA) 1994.

Alongside the strict law of corroboration, there had also developed a less formal body of law about warnings that should be given to a jury where a witness might be unreliable even though he did not fall within the limited classes to which corroboration law applied. Thus, it was held that an informal warning should be given where witnesses had a purpose of their own to serve in giving evidence, or suffered from mental disorder (*Beck (1982)*; *Spencer (1986)*). In *Stone (2005)* the Court of Appeal held that this body of law had not survived the abolition of the former rules of corroboration. In *Makanjuola (1995)*, the Court of Appeal emphasised the wide discretion possessed by trial judges to adapt warnings about the testimony of any particular witness to the circumstances of the case. The exercise of that discretion will only exceptionally be reviewed by the Court of Appeal. *Makanjuola* has also been helpful in killing the notion that the old law about corroboration might still somehow apply once the judge had decided to give a discretionary warning.

There remains one common type of evidence where a warning is required which is still governed by a rule based rather than a discretionary system. Identification evidence which falls within the principles set out in *Turnbull (1977)* and subsequent cases must be the subject of a particular type of judicial warning in the summing up. A body of case law has also developed about warnings that should be given to the jury where a defendant's lies, whether told inside or outside court, could be taken to support the prosecution case. See *Lucas (1981)* and *Burge (1996)*.

Code D of the current (2004) Codes of Practice made under the Police and Criminal Evidence Act 1984 (PACE) is likely to be relevant in any problem involving identification. The whole of the Code is important, but you should pay special attention to Annex A (video identification), Annex B (identification parades), and Annex E (showing photographs).

If there has been a breach of the Code, you must be able to advise on the likely consequences. Remember the following:

- what allows the court to look at the provisions of the Code and what makes them relevant. See s 67(11) of PACE;
- if the quality of the identification evidence is poor and there is no other evidence to support it, the jury should be directed to acquit (*Turnbull (1977)*). Thus, the Code breach may so weaken the identification evidence that a submission of no case to answer will be successful;
- the evidence may be excluded under s 78 of PACE. (See Chapter 7 for further details.)

## References

1 This is perhaps more obviously true of a historian's work. See Carr, EH, *What Is History?*, 2nd edn, 1987, Chapter 1. But a little reflection should be enough to show that the same is true of the investigation that precedes a criminal or civil trial.

2 Macaulay (Lord), *The History of England from the Accession of James the Second*, 1848–1861, reprinted 1880, Vol 2, Chapter 5, p 161. Even more hazardous is evidence of statements alleged to have been made on an earlier occasion by a defendant.

3 See, for example, Stone, M, *Cross-Examination in Criminal Trials*, 1988, p 107; Boon, A, *Advocacy*, 2nd edn, 1999, pp 113–114; cf McEwan, J, *Evidence and the Adversarial Process: The Modern Law*, 1992, pp 16–19.

## Checklist

Students should be familiar with the following areas:

- the abolition of corroboration law in the CJA 1988 and the CJPOA 1994;
- the effect of this – see *Makanjuola (1995)*;
- the guidelines in *Makanjuola* about discretionary warnings;
- the rules concerning identification in *Turnbull (1977)*;
- Code of Practice D;
- s 62(11) of PACE;
- the possible effects of Code breach;
- warnings where a defendant has lied;
- s 34 of the Criminal Justice and Public Order Act 1994, and the directions that must be given where that section is relied on (see Chapter 7).

# Question 21

Nigel, who has no previous convictions, is charged with raping Millie, whom he knew. The case for the prosecution is that he went with her to a party at Peter's house, that while there, he persuaded her to go into the wine cellar with him, and that there, he raped her on the floor behind a wine rack. Olive saw Millie emerging from the cellar with her hair disordered and dust on her dress. Apart from that, she says, she did not notice anything unusual. Peter says that Millie was initially with other guests in the garden, that he saw her going into the house, and that she was crying when she returned to the garden. He went up to her and said: 'What's the matter? Is it something to do with Nigel?' Millie then said that Nigel had raped her. Later that evening, Millie made a statement to the police in which she repeated her allegation against Nigel. Before making her statement, she was examined by a doctor, who found evidence indicating that she had had sexual intercourse within the previous 12 hours. When Nigel was interviewed by the police, he at first denied going into the wine cellar. Later he admitted that he had been there and that he had had sexual intercourse with Millie behind a wine rack, but said that he had done so with her consent. He has since discovered that last year Millie made separate allegations of rape against Quentin and Richard, which she subsequently withdrew.

Discuss the evidential issues arising.

## Answer plan

You need to consider the following items of evidence:

- Olive's observations;
- Millie's distressed state;
- Millie's statement to Peter (see Chapter 10);
- the medical evidence;
- Nigel's initial lie;
- his previous good character (see Chapter 9);
- Millie's earlier complaints of rape (see Chapter 10);
- the possibility of a *Makanjuola* warning in relation to Millie's evidence;
- admissibility of her previous false complaints.

# Answer

Olive's observations will not assist the prosecution case because they are as consistent with consensual intercourse as with rape, and Nigel now admits that intercourse took place, albeit with Millie's consent. The same is true of the medical evidence. To some extent, Olive's evidence supports the defence, for, apparently, she observed no signs of distress when Millie emerged from the wine cellar.

Millie's statement to Peter is possibly admissible as a 'recent complaint'. By s 120(4) of the Criminal Justice Act (CJA) 2003, a previous statement by a witness is admissible as evidence of any matter stated of which oral evidence by him would be admissible if any one of three conditions is satisfied and, while giving evidence, the witness indicates that to the best of his belief he made the statement and that to the best of his belief it states the truth. The relevant condition here is in s 120(7), which is really a cluster of conditions ranging from s 120(7)(a) to (f). It seems likely that they will all be satisfied in this case. Millie claims to be a person against whom an offence has been committed; the offence is one to which the proceedings relate; the statement consists of a complaint about conduct which would, if proved, constitute the offence (conditions (a) to (c)). The defence might argue that the complaint was not made as soon as could reasonably be expected, as required by condition (d). Millie said nothing to Olive, but Olive might not have been someone in whom she felt that she could confide. The complaint was not made as the result of a threat or promise (condition (e)). By sub-s (8), the fact that the complaint was elicited (eg, by a leading question) is irrelevant unless a threat or promise was involved. (The fact that Peter said, 'Is it something to do with Nigel?' might affect the weight to be attached by the jury to Millie's complaint.)

According to *Islam (1999)*, the judge would have to warn the jury that Millie's distressed state, observed by Peter, is admissible to show consistency with the description of the incident given in evidence by Millie, but cannot be regarded as confirming that evidence from an independent source. Similarly, according to *Islam*, the complaint cannot be treated as independent confirmation of her evidence, but by s 120(4) it is now evidence of the truth of its contents.

A *Makanjuola* warning will not be given in relation to Millie's evidence merely because the allegation is of a sexual offence. But if the defence relies on specific matters in support of its contention that she is lying, the judge could in his discretion give a warning. He might well be persuaded to do so in this case if there is evidence that she is in the habit of making false allegations of rape. The incidents involving Quentin and Richard suggest that this might be the case. She can be cross-examined about these allegations without falling foul of s 41 of the Youth Justice and Criminal Evidence Act 1999. It was held in *T and H (2002)* that such allegations are not of 'sexual behaviour'. If, however, she denies making these allegations, the defence might not be able to call evidence to rebut her denial. These matters could be regarded as collateral, and *AG v Hitchcock (1847)* established that answers to such questions are 'final'. On the other hand, in *Funderburk (1990)*, the Court of Appeal acknowledged that in cases involving allegations of sexual offences it is difficult to draw a line between matters that are relevant only to credibility and matters that are relevant to the facts in issue.

Nigel was caught out in a lie when he denied going into the cellar, and the prosecution can rely on this as evidence of guilt. No hearsay problem arises of course, because his denial is not being relied on for its truth, but for the reverse, as was the case in *Mawaz Khan v R (1967)*. However, if the prosecution does wish to rely on this item of evidence, the judge must give a *Lucas* direction to the jury on the lines indicated in *Burge and Pegg (1996)*. Since Nigel has admitted the lie, it will not be necessary to warn the jury that they must find it proved beyond reasonable doubt. But the judge must warn the jury that the mere fact that the defendant has lied is not in itself evidence of guilt, because defendants may lie for innocent reasons. Only if the jury is sure that Nigel did not lie for an innocent reason can a lie support the prosecution case. In *Lucas (1981)*, Lord Lane CJ said that in appropriate cases, the jury should be reminded that people sometimes lie in an attempt to bolster up a just cause, or out of shame, or out of a wish to conceal disgraceful behaviour from their family. Any or all of these reasons might apply in Nigel's case.

Nigel's previous good character will entitle him to a *Vye (1993)* direction. He has already made a pre-trial statement, and he will almost certainly give evidence at his trial. In such circumstances, the jury should be told that his good character is relevant to his credibility, and also to the likelihood of his having committed the offence.

# Question 22

Rupert and Edward have been committed for trial, charged with burglary. The case for the prosecution is that they broke into a shop in Brighton owned by Rimsky & Romanov, a firm of jewellers, and there stole a quantity of watches.

Evidence for the prosecution will be given by Tabitha, Rupert's former girlfriend. She has made a statement in which she states that on the evening when the burglary took place, she drove Rupert and Edward to a public house. While drinking there, she overheard Rupert and Edward discussing a plan to break into the premises of Rimsky & Romanov. Later, they all left the public house. Tabitha says that she then drove them in the direction of her house but that on the way Rupert asked her to stop, saying that he and Edward needed to relieve themselves. This was near the rear entrance to the shop owned by Rimsky & Romanov. Tabitha states that she waited in the car for about half an hour until Rupert and Edward returned, and that they then drove to Tabitha's house. Tabitha also states that she helped them with some luggage which they had with them, and that the men left the next day. When the police came to ask for Tabitha's help in this matter, they discovered one of the stolen watches in her bathroom.

The prosecution also have a statement from Tabitha's nephew Archie, aged 10, who says that he found the rest of the stolen goods in Edward's garden shed.

When interviewed by the police without a solicitor, Rupert refused to answer any questions. Edward when interviewed denied having any part in the offence. He said that he spent the evening and the night in question at a hotel in Manchester with a woman called Sheila.

Discuss the evidential matters arising.

## Answer plan

There are six topics that need to be discussed in the answer to this question:

- Should there be an informal warning about the reliability of Tabitha's evidence? Note how it is possible to use the old law to argue by analogy, but be careful to avoid any suggestion that it still has any force as binding authority.
- Sheila's previous convictions.
- Look at the content of Tabitha's evidence. She is reporting what she heard other people say quite a lot. Is all this admissible? Why?
- What is the position about Archie's evidence?
- What is the significance now of Rupert's failure to answer police questions? Try to summarise what the Act says accurately. A student who simply said, for example, that Rupert's silence was evidence of his guilt would not get much credit.
- What are the problems arising from Edward's alibi? Have you read the question carefully enough to deal with this point fully?

# Answer

The first question that arises is whether the judge should give an informal warning about the reliability of Tabitha's evidence when summing up to the jury. There are two reasons why such a warning might be desirable. We are told that she is Rupert's former girlfriend. Is there any evidence of antipathy towards him which would make it possible that she is implicating him from a desire for revenge? The rule in *Beck (1982)* was that where a witness might have an 'interest or purpose of his own to serve' in giving evidence, the judge should warn the jury about this. Earlier cases such as *Willis (1916)* and *Evans (1965)* established that where a wife gave evidence in support of an accomplice, the jury should be warned of the danger in relying on her testimony because she had an interest to serve. In earlier cases, warnings in situations analogous to those requiring corroboration had been required. In *Stone (2005)* the Court of Appeal held that this requirement had not survived the abolition of the corroboration rules. Nevertheless, it would seem sensible to warn the jury about the different but perhaps equally strong interest of someone giving evidence against a former boyfriend towards whom she felt animosity.

It is worth noting that under the old law, the jury might have had to be warned that Tabitha was an accomplice and that it would be dangerous for them to convict on her uncorroborated evidence (*Davies v DPP (1954)*). This suggests another reason for an informal warning to be given about Tabitha's evidence. It is possible that, although she was never charged, she was an accomplice. She clearly knew of the plan to break into the shop. She stopped the car near the shop and it is unlikely that she believed that Rupert and Edward took half an hour to relieve themselves in its vicinity. She helped them with their 'luggage', and later one of the stolen watches was found in her bathroom.

No special difficulties are presented by the content of Tabitha's evidence. Her report of what she heard Rupert and Edward saying about their plans to break into the shop will be admissible as an exception to the rule against hearsay as showing the contemporaneous state of mind and intentions of the accused. In *Moghal (1977)*, a statement of intention to murder made some six months before the commission of the crime was considered admissible. This particular decision was subsequently criticised by Lord Bridge in *Blastland (1986)* on the ground of relevance. However, the House of Lords emphasised in *Blastland* that such a declaration would be admissible if the state of mind evidenced by it was directly in issue at the trial, or was of direct and immediate relevance to an issue arising in the trial. Clearly, those conditions are satisfied here.

Section 118(1) of the Criminal Justice Act (CJA) 2003 preserves, *inter alia*, the common law relating to *res gestae* exceptions to the rule against hearsay, including declarations about contemporaneous mental states, such as intention.

It might also be possible to argue that what was said amounted to a confession by both defendants. A confession is another exception to the rule against hearsay preserved by s 118. By s 82(1) of the Police and Criminal Evidence Act 1984, a confession includes any statement wholly or partly adverse to the person who made it, whether made to a person in authority or not. It may be, despite apparent oddity, that things said before the commission of an offence can amount to confessions if the offence is subsequently committed.

Tabitha will be able to report the excuse given by Rupert for stopping the car near the shop because the prosecution will be relying on its falsity, as in *Mawaz Khan (1967)*, rather than its truth.

It is just conceivable that the judge would think it appropriate to comment on the weight to be attached to Archie's evidence in view of his relationship to Tabitha if the defence makes a point of this. By s 53(1) of the Youth Justice and Criminal Evidence Act 1999, at every stage in criminal proceedings all persons are (whatever their age) competent to give evidence. By sub-s (3), a person is not competent to give evidence in criminal proceedings if it appears to the court that he is not a person who is able to understand questions put to him as a witness and give answers to them that can be understood. There is no suggestion that Archie falls into this category and he will therefore be competent to give evidence. However, his evidence will be unsworn. By s 55(2) of the 1999 Act, a witness may not be sworn unless he has attained the age of 14.

Rupert's failure to answer police questions is now governed by s 34 of the Criminal Justice and Public Order Act 1994. The failure of an accused in such circumstances to mention any fact relied on later in his defence, if it was a fact which in the circumstances existing at the time the accused could reasonably have been expected to mention, will allow the jury in determining whether the accused is guilty of the offence charged to draw such inferences as appear proper. But it is important to know if Rupert was offered a solicitor. Sub-section (2A) of s 34 provides that where the accused was at an authorised place of detention at the time of his failure to mention any fact relied on in his defence, no inferences may be drawn unless he was allowed an opportunity to consult a solicitor before being questioned.

If it is an appropriate case for a s 34 direction, the judge should follow the guidelines set out in *Petkar (2004)*. He must identify the facts on which Rupert relies and which were not mentioned on questioning. He must identify the inferences which it is suggested might be drawn from failure to mention such facts, to the extent that they may go beyond the standard inference of late fabrication. The jury should be told that, if an inference is drawn, they should not convict wholly or mainly on the strength of it. They should be told that an inference should be drawn only if they think it is fair and proper, and it should be drawn only if the only sensible explanation for failure to mention facts relied on is that Rupert had no answers, or none that would stand up to scrutiny. Moreover, an inference should be drawn only if, apart from Rupert's failure to mention facts relied on, the prosecution case is so strong that it clearly calls for an answer by him. The jury should be reminded of the evidence on the basis of which they are invited not to draw any inferences from Rupert's silence.

The trial judge should tell the jury that it is for the prosecution to disprove the alibi beyond reasonable doubt (*Johnson (1995)*). In *Burge and Pegg (1996)*, it was said that a *Lucas (1981)* direction should be given where, among other cases, the defendant relies on an alibi. However, it is clear that a *Lucas* direction does not have to be given in every case where an alibi is raised by a defendant. For example, in *Patrick (1999)* the Court of Appeal held that there is no need for a direction where the only possible basis for rejecting a defendant's alibi would be acceptance by the jury of the prosecution's identification evidence. A rather similar situation arises on these facts. In effect, the members of the jury have to be satisfied beyond reasonable doubt that Tabitha's account is reliable. If they decide that it is, Edward's alibi must be false. In *Middleton (2001)*, the Court of Appeal said that a Lucas direction should not be given where it would only confuse the jury, and probably that would be its effect here.

# Question 23

Augustus, Bertram and Claude have been charged with affray, contrary to s 3(1) of the Public Order Act 1986. The case for the prosecution is that all three made a concerted attack on the staff of a nightclub after they had been told to leave the premises.

Donald, a barman, says that he was wounded by one of the men involved. Donald did not recognise him at the time but thought that he would be able to recognise him if he saw him again, despite the fact that the lighting in the club was dim. Eddie, another barman who had seen the attack on Donald, also thought he could recognise the culprit if he saw him again. At the police station, DS Dapper showed both of them several sets of photographs, each containing 10 pictures of men with convictions for violence. After some discussion, Donald and Eddie picked out a photograph of Augustus. Augustus was then arrested and put on an identification parade where Donald and Eddie both picked him out without hesitation.

Fergus, another barman, says that he also was wounded by one of those causing the affray. He was unable to identify anyone from police photographs, but he was able to give information to the police as a result of which a photofit image of his attacker was created, on the basis of which Bertram was later arrested. Fergus failed to pick out Bertram on a subsequent identification parade. Bertram, however, has made several damaging admissions in recorded interviews with the police, and the photofit bears a strong resemblance to him.

Gina, a waitress, was struck by one of those involved in the affray. Her attacker immediately rushed from the club and Gina, who was not seriously hurt, ran after him. The man escaped, but Gina was able to stop a passing police car and explain what had happened. The officers then drove with her round neighbouring streets to see if she could find her attacker. She saw a man standing in a doorway and asked the police to stop. One of the officers went up to the man with her and said 'Is that him?'. She replied 'Yes, I'm positive'. The man, who identified himself as Claude, was then arrested. Claude later asked to be put on an identification parade but was told that this was unnecessary and impracticable because he had already been positively identified.

Gina was later invited to the police station to see if she could identify any others involved in the affray. She was shown a selection of photographs, including one of Augustus. She identified him then, and she subsequently picked out Augustus on an identification parade. Advise the prosecution on the evidential issues that arise in relation to identification.

### Answer plan

This question mainly concerns identifications where there may have been breaches of Code D. One of the problems is how to order the rather scattered information which you have been given. The following is a suggestion.

*The evidence against Augustus*

- Start with the identification parades involving Augustus at which the witnesses were: (a) Donald and Eddie; (b) Gina. Make the point that such evidence is in principle admissible.
- Introduce the relevant Code and, because you are referring to it for the first time, explain its status and relevance.
- Look at what happened prior to the identification parades and explain what breaches have occurred.

*The evidence against Bertram*

- Deal briefly with the admissibility of admissions (for further details about s 76 of the Police and Criminal Evidence Act 1984 (PACE), see Chapter 7).
- Deal with the evidential value of the photofit.

*The evidence against Claude*

There are two points here:
- Gina's 'on the spot' identification;
- the refusal of an identification parade.

*General point*

- *Turnbull* warnings in relation to all identification witnesses.

*Final check*

- If there have been breaches of the Code, what will be the effect on the items of evidence to which they relate?

# Answer

The facts given do not reveal anything of the circumstances in which the identification parades involving Augustus were conducted. Ordinarily, if the parades had been properly conducted, Donald, Eddie and Gina would give evidence of the assault committed by Augustus in the club and of their subsequent identification of him in the parade. Evidence of pre-trial identification is admissible by virtue of s 120(1), (4) and (5) of the Criminal Justice Act (CJA) 2003. But there is a difficulty with the identification evidence in this case because it may have been affected by breaches of the relevant Code of Practice before the parades took place.

Procedures for the pre-trial identification of suspects are laid down by Code D of the Codes of Practice issued pursuant to s 66 of PACE. By s 67(11) of the Act, if any provision of a Code appears to the court to be relevant to any question arising in the proceedings, it shall be taken into account in determining that question. The court is not obliged to exclude the evidence where there has been breach of a Code; the Court of Appeal in *Grannell (1990)* stated that it is necessary to establish whether the breach has caused unfairness.

Paragraph 3.3 of Code D permits photographs to be shown to a witness where the identity of the suspect is not known. Thus, in principle, it was proper to show photographs to Donald, and if he could not have made an identification from them, it would have been proper to show them to Eddie, or vice versa. However, the showing of any photographs must be done in accordance with Annex E of the Code. Paragraph 3 of Annex D states that only one witness shall be shown photographs at any one time. He is to be given as much privacy as practicable and not allowed to communicate with any other witness in the case. By para 4, the witness shall be shown not less than 12 photographs at a time. The police infringed the provisions of both paragraphs when showing photographs to Donald and Eddie. Since a person who picks out a photograph may later pick out someone on a parade with the photograph in mind rather than the original incident, particular care is needed in showing photographs to a witness to ensure that the provisions of Code D are followed. In this case, a strong defence argument could be presented that the evidence of the identification parades involving identifications by Donald and Eddie should be excluded under s 78 of the Act (see Chapter 7) because the reliability of the identifications was significantly weakened by the procedures adopted in relation to the photographs.

Gina should not have been shown photographs at all. Paragraph 3.3 of Code D provides that a witness must not be shown photographs if the identity of the suspect is known to the police and he is available to take part in a video identification, an identification parade or a group identification. By the time Gina was invited to look at photographs the identity of Augustus was known to the police, and he was presumably available to take part in an identification procedure. It seems likely, therefore, that her identification of him will be excluded also.

Subject to anything that the defence might argue, the admissions made by Bertram will be admissible evidence against him under s 76(1) of PACE. The photofit image that closely resembles Bertram is excluded in principle by the rule against hearsay. By s 115(2) of the CJA 2003, a 'statement' is a representation of fact or opinion made by a person by whatever means, and the sub-section expressly includes a representation made in a sketch, photofit or other pictorial form. Fergus could give evidence describing his attacker, however, and could use the photofit to refresh his memory under s 139 of the CJA 2003. The photofit could itself be put in evidence under s 120(1), (4) and (5). It is a 'previous statement' within s 120(4), and it describes a person, so falling within s 120(5).

In *Kelly (1992)*, the Court of Appeal suggested that when a suspect was found within minutes of the crime, and close to the scene, it might well be that the provisions of the Code did not apply and that the best course was for the police to see if the witness thought that the suspect was the offender. This was a case where a woman complained of attempted rape and, as she was talking to police in the street, saw the accused and pointed him out. One of the officers questioned, but did not arrest, him. The complainant was then brought nearer, she confirmed her identification, and the suspect was then arrested. On appeal it was argued unsuccessfully that an identification ought not to have been permitted in those circumstances, but that an identification parade should have been arranged instead.[1]

Alternatively, it could be argued that the Code was followed. By Code D, para 3.2, where a suspect's identity is not known, a witness may be taken to a particular neighbourhood or place to see whether he can identify the person he saw. The principles applicable to formal identification procedures are to be followed as far as practicable.

Gina's identification of Claude is therefore likely to be admissible in principle. But was Claude entitled to an identification parade? Code D, para 3.2 sets out the circumstances in which an identification procedure must be held. It provides, *inter alia*, that where a witness has identified a suspect prior to a formal identification procedure and the suspect disputes the accuracy of the identification, a procedure shall be held unless it is not practicable or it would serve no useful purpose in proving or disproving whether the suspect was involved in committing the offence. An example, given in the Code, is a situation where the suspect is already well known to the identifying witness. In *Forbes (2001)* the House of Lords held that under a previous version of Code D an identification parade was mandatory where identification was in dispute, save in the circumstances mentioned in the Code or in a case of pure recognition of someone well known to the witness. A prior identification, however complete, did not mean that a parade could be refused.

It is unclear whether this is still the law in the light of subsequent amendments to the Code. In particular, Code D, para 3.2(d) provides that after a witness has made a positive identification it is not necessary, subject to paras 3.12 and 3.13, for that witness to take part in a further identification procedure. Although opinion is divided, the better view is probably that Code D, para 3.12 has not reversed *Forbes*; the 'no useful purpose' exception is limited to the most exceptional cases.[2] So it may well be that Claude has been wrongfully denied a formal identification procedure, and his counsel could argue that to rely on Gina's street identification alone would so adversely affect the fairness of the proceedings that her evidence on this matter ought to be excluded under s 78(1) of PACE.

But, as was emphasised in *Forbes*, exclusion under this provision is only discretionary. A judge might very well admit the evidence of Gina's identification, and merely point out to the jury that there had been a breach of Code D and invite the jury to consider the possible effect of that breach.[3]

In relation to the admissible evidence of all the identification witnesses, the judge will have to direct the jury in accordance with the principles set out in *Turnbull (1977)*. That case requires a judge to do three things when the prosecution case depends wholly or substantially (as it does here) on the correctness of one or more identifications, and the defendant alleges that the identifying witnesses are mistaken. The judge must warn the jury of the special need for caution before convicting the accused in reliance on identification evidence. He must tell the jury the reason why such a warning is needed. Some reference should be made to the possibility that a mistaken witness can be a convincing one, and that a number of such witnesses can all be mistaken. In *Pattinson and Exley (1996)*, the Court of Appeal allowed appeals and criticised a direction on identification evidence for failing to make adequate reference to the risk of miscarriages of justice resulting from mistaken identification evidence. See also *Nash (2005)*. The judge must also direct the jury to examine closely the circumstances in which each identification came to be made. Having warned the jury in accordance with these guidelines, the judge should go on to direct the jury to consider if the identification evidence is supported by any other evidence. At this stage he should identify what is, and what is not, capable of providing such support. Although in some earlier cases the Court of Appeal said that it is not always necessary for the judge to summarise specific weaknesses in the identification evidence that has been given, more recent decisions, such as *Donald (2004)*, show that this is now likely to be treated as an essential requirement of a *Turnbull* direction. It was said in *Turnbull* that where the quality of the identification evidence is good, the jury can safely be left to assess it, even without any supporting evidence, subject to an adequate warning. But where the quality is poor, the judge should withdraw the case from the jury at the end of the prosecution case in the absence of any supporting evidence.

### References

1. See also *Hickin and Others (1996)*; *Malashev (1997)*; *Anastasiou (1998)*.
2. See May and Powles, *Criminal Evidence*, 5th edn, 2004, paras 14–17; Allen, *Practical Guide to Evidence*, 3rd edn, 2004, pp 195–196.
3. *Forbes* [2001] 1 All ER 686, p 698.

## Question 24

Harold and Jamie have been charged with burglary. The prosecution allege that they broke into Lily's flat intending to steal her collection of silver. When Lily returned home and disturbed them Harold gagged her and tied her to a bed. Harold and Jamie then left the flat with Lily's silver, leaving her tied to the bed.

Lily was asked by police to describe the men she had seen. She was able to describe only the man who had tied her to the bed. On the strength of this, she was then shown a selection of police photographs and she picked out one of Harold. She was asked if she would be willing to attend an identification parade but she refused, saying that she was too frightened. The police later arrested Harold and asked Lily if she would be able to identify the man who had tied her to the bed if she saw him from a position where he would be unable to see her. Lily agreed. At the police station, she was taken to a corridor outside Harold's cell and invited to look through a spyhole in the door. The officer who was with her said only, 'Is that the man who tied you up and gagged you?'. Lily said that it was.

After Lily had left the police station, Mick, the porter at the block of flats where Lily lived, was interviewed by the police. He told them that he had seen two men on the premises at about the time of the burglary. He was shown a selection of police photographs and picked out Harold and Jamie as the men he had seen. Harold and Jamie were later put together on an identification parade with eight other men who were volunteers from a nearby health club. At this parade, Mick picked them out without hesitation.

Discuss the evidential issues that arise.

### Answer plan

Not a very difficult question; you need to recognise breaches of Code D. A good way to deal with the problem would be to tackle the points in this order:

- Lily's identification of Harold (a) by photographs, and (b) at the police station;
- Mick's identification of Harold and Jamie (a) by photographs, and (b) by identification parade.

Remember to discuss the results that are likely to follow a finding that there has been a breach of the Code in each case.

### Answer

No details are given of the way in which the police photographs were shown to Lily and it is assumed that the provisions of Annex E of Code D were followed.

However, Lily's subsequent identification of Harold was not in accordance with Code D. By Code D, para 3.14 the suspect shall initially be offered a video identification unless it is not practicable, or an identification parade is both practicable and more suitable than a video identification, or (Code D, para 3.16) a group identification is considered more suitable than either. Nothing suggests that a video identification was impracticable, and in the light of Lily's fear it was the obvious choice. By Code D, para 3.23 the identification officer may arrange for the suspect to be confronted by the witness, but only if it not practicable to follow any other identification procedure.

In any case, the confrontation was improperly conducted. Annex D, para 1 provides that before the confrontation takes place, the witness must be told, *inter alia*, that the person he saw may or may not be the person he is to confront. This warning does not appear to have been given to Lily. By para 2, the suspect or his solicitor must be provided with details of the first description of the suspect given by the witness. It is not clear that the police recorded Lily's description of her attacker, or that she was even asked to give one. In either case there would have been an additional breach of Code D, para 3.1. By para 4, confrontation must take place in the presence of the suspect's solicitor, interpreter or friend, unless this would cause unreasonable delay. It is not clear that either of these rules has been observed, and para 5 has clearly not been observed. Further, the confrontation did not take place in the circumstances laid down in para 6. To carry out a confrontation when Harold was in a cell might have suggested to Lily that the police were satisfied they had the right man, and this might have encouraged her to be more positive in her identification than she would otherwise have been. In this connection, failure to tell Lily that the person she saw might or might not be the person she was going to confront could have been particularly damaging.

In the light of all these breaches Lily's identification of Harold at the police station is likely to be excluded under s 78(1) of the **Police and Criminal Evidence Act 1984 (PACE)**. The question that then arises is whether Lily's picking out the photograph of Harold might be admissible as being, presumably, the only untainted identification evidence left. It is unlikely that the court would permit this. There is an obvious danger of prejudice if the jury hear this evidence because it would inevitably reveal that Harold had a criminal record. In *Wright (1934)*, the Court of Criminal Appeal held that an irregularity had occurred where a witness volunteered in examination-in-chief that he had seen a photograph of the defendant in the 'rogues' gallery' at New Scotland Yard. More recently, in *Lamb (1980)*, the Court of Appeal condemned the production of an album of police photographs as part of the prosecution case on the basis that it was tantamount to adducing evidence that the accused had a criminal record. Lawton LJ said that generally the prosecution should make no reference to such photographs; they should merely inform the defence of their existence and the use to which they were put, and leave it to the defence to decide whether the jury should be informed of those facts. To involve Harold in this prejudice because the police failed to adopt proper identification procedures at a later stage is unlikely to commend itself to any judge as a fair course of action.

Mick should not have been shown the photograph of Harold because Lily had already picked it out. Code D, para 3.3 provides that a witness must not be shown photographs, etc, if the identity of the suspect is known to the police and the suspect is available to take part in an identification procedure. There also appears to have been a breach of para 3.1 of Code D; it appears that Mick was not even asked for a description of the suspects. The subsequent identification parade was improperly conducted. Code D, Annex B, para 9 provides that one suspect only shall be included in a parade unless there are two suspects of roughly similar appearance, in which case, they may be paraded together but with at least 12 other persons. Paragraph 9 also provides that the parade shall consist of persons who so far as possible resemble the suspect in age, height, general appearance and position in life. Did the volunteers from the health club satisfy these conditions? If, for example, they were all young, with good muscular development, and the defendants did not fit this description, the parade would not have been properly conducted.

For these reasons the identification evidence of Mick might also be excluded under s 78. No information has been given about the existence of other evidence that might incriminate these defendants. In the absence of any such evidence the defence would be likely to submit, on the basis of the *Turnbull (1977)* guidelines, that the case should be withdrawn from the jury. Such a submission would be likely to succeed, in view of the many breaches of Code D and the consequent reduction in probative value of the identification evidence.

# Question 25

'We regard mistaken identification as by far the greatest cause of actual or possible wrong conviction' (Criminal Law Revision Committee, 11th Report, 1972).

Has enough been done to reduce this risk?

> ### Answer plan
>
> Start by identifying the modes of protection: *Turnbull (1977)* warnings and Code D. Then deal with the adequacy of *Turnbull* warnings; some reference to voice identification and to 'evidence of description' would be appropriate here. The problems with the application of Code D should then be considered.
>
> In summary, therefore, the essay is constructed as follows:
>
> - outline of the two ways of protecting against mistaken identification;
> - the *Turnbull (1977)* guidelines: *Thornton (1995)*; *Slater (1995)*; *Pattinson and Exley (1996)*; *Qadir (1998)*;

- distinction between evidence of identity and evidence of description: *Gayle (1999)*;
- voice identification: *Hersey (1998); Gummerson and Steadman (1999)*;
- Code D: *Kelly (1992)*; use of s 78(1) of the **Police and Criminal Evidence Act 1984 (PACE)**; Code D, para 3.12; *Forbes (2001)*.

# Answer

English law tries to protect defendants from wrongful convictions that are based on mistaken identification evidence in two ways: by a system of judicial warnings to juries, and by a Code of Practice that governs identification procedures.

In *Turnbull (1977)*, the Court of Appeal established guidelines that were to apply where the prosecution case depended 'wholly or substantially' on the correctness of one or more identifications of the defendant. The words 'wholly or substantially' have not in practice limited the range of cases in which the guidelines have been considered appropriate. A *Turnbull* direction has to be given in cases where identification is based on recognition as well as in cases where the risk of misidentification might seem greater: for example, where identification is based on a fleeting glimpse. The need for a direction will usually arise when the defendant denies that he was present at a particular place. But the direction may also be necessary where the defendant admits being present at a relevant place but denies involvement in the criminal activity taking place there. So, for example, it was held in *Thornton (1995)*, where the defendant was charged with causing grievous bodily harm at a wedding reception, that the *Turnbull* warning ought to have been given because, where others present were similarly dressed, a mistake was clearly possible. As Rose LJ emphasised in *Slater (1995)*, the key question is whether there was, in the particular circumstances, the possibility of mistake. Thus, the circumstances in which the warning is required are probably adequate.

Is the nature of the warning adequate? According to *Turnbull*, several stages have to be followed. First, the judge must warn the jury of the special need for caution before convicting on the basis of identification evidence. Secondly, he must tell the jury why such a warning is needed. Some reference should be made to the fact that a mistaken witness can be a convincing one, and that a number of convincing witnesses can all be mistaken. Thirdly, he must direct the jury to examine closely the circumstances in which each identification was made. In *Turnbull*, the court gave examples of topics for comment, such as the light and the length of the period of observation, but in *Pattinson and Exley (1996)*, the Court of Appeal said that it was not necessary in every case for the judge to summarise all the weaknesses in the identification evidence. The court added that where the judge does summarise the identification evidence, he should point out strengths as well as weaknesses. In later cases, however, such as *Popat (No 2) (2000)*, *Stanton (2004)*, and *Nash (2005)*, failure to mention weaknesses has given rise to a successful appeal. Fourthly, the judge should direct the jury to consider whether the identification evidence is supported by any other evidence. Fifthly, he should identify the evidence that is capable, and incapable, of providing such support. Not surprisingly, the Court of Appeal has deprecated rigid formulas for the fulfilment of *Turnbull* requirements. Thus, in *Qadir (1998)*, it was said that the form and contents of the summing up should, even when identification is in issue, be tailored to the circumstances of the individual case. Nevertheless, the *Turnbull* procedure appears to provide a strong protection for defendants who challenge identification evidence. Further, it was said in *Turnbull* that cases should be withdrawn from the jury where the identification evidence is poor and there is no supporting evidence.

*Turnbull* almost certainly does not extend to evidence from a witness who says that he would be unable to recognise the person he saw if he were to see him again, but who remembers some identifying features of that person. But there seems to be no reason why it should be extended in this way to such 'evidence of description'. As Henry LJ pointed out in *Gayle (1999)*, the danger of an honest witness's being mistaken as to distinctive clothing, or the general description of the person he saw, are minimal.

But *Turnbull* assumes that most identifications are visual. That is so, but sometimes identification may be by the sound of the human voice. On this topic, the law is undeveloped. In *Hersey (1998)*, the Court of Appeal showed support for the equivalent of identification parades for voices, and said that juries should be directed as in cases of visual identification, with appropriate modifications. But, in *Gummerson and Steadman (1999)*, the Court of Appeal disapproved of 'voice identification parades', and the content of any warning in the summing up remains unclear.

The protection given by Code D is less satisfactory. Failure to comply with the appropriate procedure will not lead inevitably to the exclusion of identification evidence (*Kelly (1992)*). What has to be shown is that the breach is sufficiently grave to bring the evidence within the scope of s 78(1) of PACE.

Code D, para 3.12 provides that, except in certain stated circumstances, whenever a suspect disputes, an identification procedure shall be held unless it is not practicable, or it would serve no useful purpose in proving or disproving whether the suspect was involved in committing the offence. It has been suggested that the effect is to reverse the decision of the House of Lords in *Forbes (2001)*, which held that the identification procedure was mandatory save in very limited circumstances, and to revive the Court of Appeal decision in *Popat (1998)*, to the effect that the provision did not apply where a suspect had previously been 'properly and adequately' identified by the witness, or where there had already been an 'actual and complete' identification by the witness. But it is unlikely that Code D, para 3.12 has this effect. If it were otherwise, the problems perceived by the House of Lords in *Forbes* would arise again. First, the police would have to make difficult decisions about the adequacy of earlier identifications. Secondly, to have to make such decisions would be at odds with their primary duty to investigate and prosecute crime. Thirdly, the *Popat* approach overlooked the fact that miscarriages of justice had resulted from identifications that were thought at the time to be satisfactory, but were later proved to be wrong.

It has been argued that the new primacy of video procedures puts a suspect in a more vulnerable position than was the case when identification parades were the primary identification procedure. When a suspect agrees to take part in a parade, he can withdraw his consent if he raises a reasonable objection to its composition or to some other element of unfairness. But once an image has been provided for video procedures, he has no control over the use to which it might be put.[1]

It is too early to say whether enough has been done to reduce the risk of mistaken identification. The contents of a *Turnbull* warning remain uncertain so far as identifying weakness in the identification evidence is concerned, although current authority suggests that this is now an essential feature of the direction. The law relating to voice identification has yet to be developed. The interpretation of Code D, para 3.12 is open to argument. Subject to this, however, much has been done to allay the fears of the Criminal Law Revision Committee.

It seems clear that the Code does not apply to identifications made only a short time after the commission of the offence. Thus, in *Kelly (1992)*, the defendant was charged with attempted rape. The offence took place in a street, and the attacker was distracted before he could commit the full offence. The police arrived soon afterwards, and the victim, while talking to the police, saw the defendant, and told the police that she had seen her attacker. An officer questioned, but did not arrest, the defendant. Meanwhile, the victim was brought closer to him in a police car. She then said that she was sure the man she had seen had been her attacker, and the defendant was arrested. The Court of Appeal rejected the argument that this procedure had denied the defendant the benefit of an identification parade. It added that where a suspect is found within minutes of the crime and close to the scene, it might well be that Code D did not apply. Later decisions such as *Hickin and Others (1996)* and *Malashev (1997)* have confirmed this view.

## Reference

1  See the commentary on *Marcus* [2005] Crim LR 384.

# CHAPTER 7

# CONFESSIONS AND ILL–GOTTEN EVIDENCE

## INTRODUCTION

One of the most important of defence counsel's objectives at trial is to ensure that as little of the prosecution evidence as possible reaches the jury – unless, of course, it happens to favour the defendant. This chapter deals with two important statutory weapons in the defence's armoury: ss 76 and 78 of the **Police and Criminal Evidence Act 1984 (PACE)**. These deal with confessions, and with a discretion to exclude for reasons of fairness evidence on which the prosecution proposes to rely. The sections are very often relied on in the alternative; it was decided in *Mason (1988)* that s 78 applies to confessions just as much as to any other evidence.

Students of this topic need an important warning. In reading cases where evidence has been excluded under either section, but particularly under s 78, you are almost never reading precedents which will have to be followed in later cases. The reason for this is that no situation is ever exactly repeated, defendants are not all alike, and the effect of acts or omissions by the police is likely to vary greatly from case to case. Knowledge of previous decisions cannot be a substitute for rigorous thought about the facts of your own particular case, facts which of course include the personal characteristics of the defendant. This is plain enough from looking at the basic law. Sub-section (2)(b) of s 76 – probably the provision in that section which is most relied on – has the effect of requiring the court to attend to the particular circumstances of the individual defendant who relies on the provision. And, in *Jelen and Katz (1990)*, the Court of Appeal emphasised that the application of s 78 was 'not an apt field for hard case law and well founded distinctions between cases'.[1]

It is, of course, in relation to a confession that an argument for exclusion will very often have to be made. When a confession appears in a set of prosecution statements or in an examination question, you need to be able to do three things. You must be able to recognise it when you see it, assess its impact on the case as a whole, and work out what arguments are available to you to get it excluded.

## Recognising the confession

You may think a confession would be easy to spot: 'OK guv; it's a fair cop. You've got me bang to rights.' Perhaps in real life that sort of thing is said more often than we might expect. But because examiners are interested in grey areas, you are not likely to have to deal with anything so simple in the examination. Your starting point is the partial definition contained in s 82(1) of PACE. With that in mind, you must interpret what has been said. Remember that a favourite topic for questions is the extent to which an accused person can, by something other than an oral statement, *adopt* an allegation against him. Consider some possibilities: he begins to weep; he hangs his head; he blushes violently; he runs away; he says nothing; he attacks the accuser. For a vivid example, see *Batt (1995)*.

## Impact on the case as a whole

The obvious impact is that of something said by an accused person which inculpates the maker of the statement in relation to the offence in question. But remember to make the point, where appropriate, that an inculpatory statement made by one accused about another outside court, and not in the presence of the co-accused,[2] will not be evidence against the co-accused,[3] and will be admissible only to the extent that it also implicates the person who makes the statement.[4]

There is a very widespread misapprehension that wherever defendants have embarked on a joint endeavour, anything said at any time by any of them, even after arrest, will be admissible evidence against any of the other absent defendants. The case of *Blake and Tye (1844)* is often cited in this connection. This is a totally false understanding of the law, as a reading of *Blake and Tye* would show. Probably because the report is an old one and not readily available, not many students have read it. Fortunately, to understand the law on this point you do not have to read this case because the matter was dealt with more recently by the Court of Appeal in *Gray and Others (1995)*. In that case, the court cited and adopted as an accurate exposition of the law a passage from the judgment of Dixon CJ in the Australian case of *Tripodi v R (1961)*. In the course of his judgment, in the passage cited and adopted by the English Court of Appeal, Dixon CJ said that the reason for admitting the evidence of the acts or words of one defendant in a joint enterprise against the others was that the agreement to commit the crime was considered as implying an authority to each to act or speak *in furtherance of the common purpose* on behalf of the others. But from the nature of the case, it could seldom happen that anything said by one of the defendants which was no more than a *narrative or account of events that had already taken place* could be admissible against his companions in the common enterprise, though it might be admissible as a confession against the speaker. Usually, Dixon CJ said the question of admissibility would relate to directions, instructions or arrangements, or to utterances accompanying acts.[5]

# Confessions and Ill-Gotten Evidence

Another favourite topic for questions is the evidential worth of the exculpatory parts of a mixed statement.[6]

## Excluding the confession

In practice, this will involve the operation of s 76(2) of PACE and, as a subsidiary argument in case the first should fail, s 78. Many candidates lose marks because they fail to construct sensible *arguments* at this point in answering a question. The examiner does not want a string of cases; he wants an argument based on the facts of the particular problem. Note particularly that it is foolish to say much in relation to s 76(2)(a) unless there is a proper factual basis for suggesting that there may have been oppression.[7]

In very many cases, you will be relying on breaches of Code C. Remember that even though there may have been a breach, you still need to put an argument on paper about why this is relevant to exclusion. Remember also that this is an area where decisions in other cases are of limited use.[8] This has an advantage for you because it means that you don't have to learn lists of 'authorities'; on the other hand, you will be required to think creatively in the examination about the facts.

Particular attention should be paid to the extent to which the provisions of Code C apply to persons who are at a police station 'assisting the police with their inquiries' but who, technically, are there voluntarily because they have not been arrested.

## References

1. See also *Roberts (1997)*.
2. If made in the presence of the co-accused, you would have to consider whether the latter had adopted what was said.
3. Because of the rule against hearsay.
4. *Gunewardene (1951)*. But cf evidence from a co-accused in a joint trial. This, of course, will be given as part of his own defence case, but it may nevertheless implicate another defendant in the commission of the offence. If it does so, it will be evidence which can be used by the jury against that defendant just as much as the evidence from prosecution witnesses. See *Rudd (1948)*. Problems arise where one accused makes a statement outside court which implicates both himself and a co-accused. The judge has no discretion to exclude relevant evidence on which a *defendant* proposes to rely (*Lobban v R (1995)*), and a co-defendant will have to make do with a warning to the jury in the summing up that what is said outside court by one defendant is not evidence against another.
5. [1995] 2 Criminal Appeal Reports 100, pp 128–129. But it has been said that an account of events narrated by one of the parties to another while the

common enterprise was continuing, in order to bring that other up to date, might be regarded as in furtherance of the enterprise, and so admissible against all the parties referred to in it: see *Jones and Others (1997)*.
6  See *Sharp (1988)*; *Grayson (1993)*.
7  See s 76(8) and look at what was said about the definition of oppression in *Fulling (1987)* and *Parker (1995)*.
8  See, for example, observations to this effect in *Jelen and Katz (1990)* and in *Grannell (1990)*.

## Checklist

Students should be familiar with the following areas:

- the definition of 'confession';
- the adoption by an accused person of allegations made against him;
- the distinction between *Gunewardene (1951)* and *Rudd (1948)*;
- the principle in *Sharp (1988)*;
- s 76 of PACE;
- s 78 of PACE;
- the provisions of Code C;
- the extent to which Code C provisions apply to persons who have not been arrested;
- ss 34, 35, 36, 37 and 38 of the Criminal Justice and Public Order Act (CJPOA) 1994.

# Question 26

'The reforms made by the Criminal Justice and Public Order Act (CJPOA) 1994 to the right of silence in the police station are more extensive and more difficult to defend than those relating to the accused's failure to testify at trial.'

Discuss.

## Answer plan

The question itself contrasts the two different situations where a right to silence has to be considered. In each case, it is necessary to look at the old law to see how much change has been effected by the 1994 Act. It is probably better to take the right to silence at trial first, as the change in this respect seems, in view of the way the common law was developing, far less radical than the provisions affecting the right to silence in pre-trial proceedings. A good summary of arguments for and against the changes that were being debated before the 1994 Act can be found in Greer, S, 'The right to silence: a review of the current debate' (1990) 53 MLR 709, pp 709–730.

In summary, therefore, the essay is constructed as follows:

- comments on failure to testify at common law: *Bathurst (1968)*; *Brigden (1973)*; *Martinez-Tobon (1993)*;
- effect of s 35 of the CJPOA 1994: *Murray v DPP (1993)*;
- s 35 and the burden of proof;
- justification of s 35;
- effect of s 34 of the CJPOA 1994;
- arguments in favour of s 34;
- counter-arguments;
- conclusions on ss 34, 36 and 37.

# Answer

At common law, the trial judge was permitted to comment on the failure of an accused person to testify at his trial, but he was required by *Bathurst (1968)* to emphasise that the jury must not assume guilt from such a failure. In certain cases, provided this basic point had been made, some criticism was regarded as acceptable. For example, in *Brigden (1973)*, the accused's case, put to the appropriate witnesses in cross-examination, was that the police had planted incriminating evidence on him. The accused himself did not testify. The Court of Appeal approved the trial judge's comment to the effect that the jury had not heard from the accused, and that this might help them in deciding whether there was any truth in the allegation against the police. The same sort of criticism could be made where the accused did not testify, but relied on facts which must have been within his knowledge. Thus, in *Martinez-Tobon (1993)*, the accused was charged with the illegal importation of cocaine in a packet. The defence was that he had thought the packet contained emeralds, but the accused did not testify. The trial judge commented in his summing up that if the defendant had thought the drugs were emeralds, one might have thought that he would be very anxious to say so. On appeal against conviction, it was argued that the judge's comment had gone beyond what was permissible, but the Court of Appeal disagreed. Provided the *Bathurst* essentials were complied with, a judge might think it appropriate to make a stronger comment where the defence case involved alleged facts which (a) were at variance with the Crown's evidence or additional to it and exculpatory, and (b) must, if true, be within the defendant's knowledge.

By s 35 of the CJPOA 1994, the court or jury, in determining whether the accused is guilty of the offence charged, may draw such inferences as appear proper from the failure of the accused to give evidence or his refusal, without good cause, to answer any question once he has chosen to testify. However, the section does not make the accused a compellable witness.

How far does this go beyond the common law? It is likely that the section involves a significant change by making it permissible to infer guilt from failure to testify. In *Murray v DPP (1993)*, the House of Lords had to interpret a provision in similar terms to s 35 in the law of Northern Ireland. It was held that the inferences that could be drawn were not limited to specific inferences from specific facts, but included an inference that the accused was guilty of the offence charged. As Lord Slynn put it, if the evidence clearly calls for an explanation which the accused ought to be in a position to give if an explanation exists, then a failure to give any explanation may as a matter of common sense allow the drawing of an inference that there is no explanation, and that the accused is guilty. This looks very much like the law as it was being developed in *Martinez-Tobon*, minus the protection afforded by the *Bathurst* direction. The effect of *Martinez-Tobon* was to create a situation only too familiar to students of evidence law, where a judge follows an approved formula to save himself from the strictures of the Court of Appeal, gives the defendant protection with one hand, promptly takes it away with the other, and thoroughly confuses any thinking members of the jury.

It was sometimes argued that to change the law in this respect would shift the burden of proof. But, there is no reason why changes in evidence law to help the prosecution *discharge* its burden should have the effect of *shifting* it. Even before the 1994 Act, it was not the case that the prosecution's obligation was to establish the accused's guilt beyond reasonable doubt *without any help from the accused*. If it had been so, evidence of such matters as breath tests, fingerprints and handwriting would have had to be excluded, and s 62(10) of the Police and Criminal Evidence Act 1984 provided that such inferences as appeared proper might be drawn from refusal to provide an intimate sample.

Section 35 can be defended on the basis that it makes sense out of a confusing situation at common law and does not affect the burden of proof.

The change in law affecting the right to silence at the police station is both more radical and far less easy to defend.

At common law, no inference was permitted from the exercise of the right to silence in the face of questioning by the police or others charged with the investigation of offences. By s 34 of the 1994 Act, the failure of an accused in such circumstances to mention any fact relied on later in his defence, if it was a fact which in the circumstances existing at the time the accused could reasonably have been expected to mention, will allow the jury in determining whether the accused is guilty of the offence charged to draw such inferences from the failure as appear proper.

The essence of the argument in favour of this change was twofold. First, there was a gut reaction that anyone who was innocent would trust the police and would want to explain things to them as soon as possible. Secondly, although in the past a very few police had misbehaved, the protection given in PACE of access to legal advice and recorded interviews meant that no suspect who was innocent now had anything to fear.

Unfortunately, recent research suggests that this protection is insufficient. It has been proved that the police use a number of devices to discourage access to legal advisers, such as reading the suspect's rights too quickly or failing to mention that legal advice is free. There have been routine breaches of the Codes of Practice, such as the holding of improper 'informal' interviews before the recorded interview. The style of questioning in at least one interview was so bullying as to be branded oppressive by the Court of Appeal. Legal advisers may be not only unqualified, but inexperienced and passive, providing no protection at all for the suspect.[1]

Police do not have to be corrupt for the innocent suspect to fear for his safety. They need only to have made some assumptions about the guilt of their suspect and be prepared to use guile to establish what they believe to be the truth. The innocent citizen probably sees the possibility of making a false confession as remote and so, perhaps, it may be. What is far more likely is that he will give an ambiguous answer which will add to the case against him. And how can he avoid giving ambiguous answers? Not only is language riddled by its very nature with ambiguity, but all the circumstances surrounding a police interrogation conspire to increase the risk. The suspect may be in a highly emotional state. He may feel guilty even though he has committed no offence – for example, feelings of anger or guilt are well established reactions to bereavement. He may be ignorant of a vital fact that explains away suspicious circumstances. He may be frightened, confused or forgetful.

Nor does the innocent suspect have to fear anything so horrific as a miscarriage of justice at trial, though past experience has shown that this is all too possible. A mistake or ambiguity in something said to the police can suggest that there is at least a reason for charging the suspect and a case to answer. That may mean a remand in custody. At the very least it is likely to mean months of anxiety whilst on bail awaiting trial. Much is made of the high standard of proof that is required before a court may convict on a criminal charge. But no such standard applies to other decisions made during the pre-trial stages. Yet these decisions may have terrible implications for an innocent suspect's liberty and for his own and his family's financial security and peace of mind.

At the pre-trial stage, a right to silence is, as things stand now in this country, an essential protection for the innocent. The innovations brought about by ss 34, 36 and 37 of the 1994 Act are indeed *defensible*, but only on the most shortsighted and crudely utilitarian basis, which accepts that it is expedient that innocent people should suffer for the sake of the majority.

### Reference

1 Greer, S, 'The right to silence: a review of the current debate' (1990) 53 MLR 709, pp 721–722; Sanders, A and Bridges, L, 'Access to legal advice and police malpractice' [1990] *Criminal Law Review* 494, pp 494–509; Hodgson, J, 'Tipping the scales of justice: the suspect's right to legal advice' [1992] *Criminal Law Review* 854, pp 854–862. For a particularly gross example of police oppression, see *Paris (1993)*.

# Question 27

To what extent does s 78(1) of the Police and Criminal Evidence Act 1984 provide a protection for defendants against the use of improperly obtained evidence?

### Answer plan

Your starting point is the concept of fairness embodied in s 78. In order to discuss the scope of this provision, it is essential to clarify this concept for the examiner. The points can be made that not all unfairness is relevant for the operation of the sub-section, and that exclusion is, in any case, a matter only of discretion. The next step is to ask how unfairness can arise. Obviously, unreliable evidence can lead to unfairness, and you can show how the sub-section is used to exclude such evidence, with particular reference to unfairness resulting from the way in which evidence has been obtained. Move on then to examples of s 78(1) where factors other than reliability have been taken into account. The object of your argument will be to show that this provision can be used to protect process values as well as reliability. A study of Ian Dennis's article, referred to in the footnote, will be particularly helpful here. You have to face up to the decision in *Chalkley and Jeffries (1998)*, and that involves showing, by reference to other appellate decisions, that the limited view of s 78(1) taken in that decision was wrong. Of particular importance is the article by Choo, A and Nash, S, 'What's the matter with section 78?' [1999] Crim LR 929. Finally, however, it is necessary to point out that although in principle, s 78(1) can be used to protect process values without regard to reliability, in practice it is unlikely to be used very often to do so, and the protection afforded to defendants is therefore limited.

In summary, therefore, the essay is constructed as follows:

- the concept of fairness in s 78(1): *Mason (1988)*; *DPP v Marshall (1988)*; *Walsh (1990)*; *Christou (1992)*;
- unreliable evidence as a source of unfairness: *O'Connor (1987)*; *Keenan (1990)*; *Smurthwaite and Gill (1994)*;
- process values relied on in *Smurthwaite and Gill (1994)*;
- the problem presented by *Chalkley and Jeffries (1998)*;
- decisions at odds with *Chalkley and Jeffries*: *Matto v Wolverhampton Crown Court (1987)*; dicta in *Walsh (1990)*; *Alladice (1988)*; *Khan (1997)*; and *Looseley (2001)*;
- argument based on s 82(3) of PACE;
- reliability of evidence as a determining factor in practice: *Stewart (1995)*;
- conclusion: the limited protection of s 78(1).

# Answer

At the root of s 78(1) is the idea that the admission of certain evidence is capable of adversely affecting the fairness of proceedings, but it is clear from cases such as *Mason (1988)* and *DPP v Marshall (1988)* that 'proceedings' refers only to proceedings before a court. It is also clear from the sub-section that fairness is not an all or nothing affair. The exclusionary discretion is to be exercised only if the admission of the evidence in question would have 'such an adverse effect on the fairness of the proceedings that the court ought not to admit it'. Thus, in *Walsh (1990)*, it was said that even if evidence had been obtained in breach of the Codes, the breach had to be 'significant and substantial' to lead to exclusion. It follows that the protection afforded by s 78(1) is a limited one. It is limited still further by the fact that the section does not make exclusion mandatory; the judge has merely a discretion to exclude, and the Court of Appeal does not readily upset exercises of judicial discretion. It was said in *Christou (1992)* that exercise of a discretion under this provision can be faulted only for '*Wednesbury* unreasonableness'.

One obvious way in which the fairness of proceedings can be adversely affected is by inviting the jury to convict on the basis of unreliable evidence. We accept that one of the objects of a criminal trial is to secure rectitude of decision, and a criminal trial will therefore cease to be fair to the extent that the likelihood of attaining this end diminishes. Many decisions show the significance of reliability in considering this discretion. In *O'Connor (1987)*, for example, the Court of Appeal held that the trial judge ought to have excluded under s 78(1) evidence of a former co-accused's conviction for conspiracy with the defendant. The reason was that the effect of admitting this evidence had been to enable the prosecution to put before the jury a statement made by the co-accused in the absence of the defendant, without having the former co-accused present for cross-examination.

Evidence which might ordinarily be reliable may be rendered unreliable by the way in which it has been obtained, and s 78(1) has been used to exclude it where this has been so. Thus, in *Keenan (1990)*, it was said that the provisions of Code C that were designed to ensure that interviews were fully recorded and the suspect given an opportunity to check the record should be strictly followed, and that courts should not be slow to exclude evidence following substantial breaches.

Where evidence has been obtained by entrapment, admissibility has in part depended on reliability. In *Smurthwaite and Gill (1994)*, Lord Taylor CJ set out some factors which a judge might take into account. These included whether there was an unassailable record of what had occurred and whether it was strongly corroborated. Other factors were not relevant to reliability, but to the degree of impropriety involved in obtaining the evidence in question. Had the police enticed a defendant to commit an offence which he would not otherwise have committed? Had the police abused their role by asking questions which ought properly to have been asked only at a police station and in accordance with the Codes? This at least suggested that evidence could be excluded under s 78(1) if, although reliable, it had been obtained in a way that showed contempt for what can broadly be referred to as 'process values'. In other words, as Ian Dennis has argued, 'apparently reliable evidence may need to be excluded if it carries significant risks of impairing the moral authority of the verdict'.[1]

An obstacle in the way of this approach was the decision of the Court of Appeal in *Chalkley and Jeffries (1998)*, in which the court said that the reference to 'the circumstances in which the evidence was obtained' in s 78(1) was not intended to widen the common law rule stated by Lord Diplock in *Sang (1980)*; namely, that save in the case of admissions and confessions and generally as to evidence obtained after the commission of the offence, there was no discretion to exclude evidence unless its quality was or might have been affected by the way in which it was obtained.

Shortly after s 78(1) had become law, there were suggestions that it had not altered the common law as stated in *Sang*, but this narrow construction was rejected in other decisions and quite a number of appellate decisions suggest that the Court of Appeal in *Chalkley and Jeffries* was wrong on this point. It has already been shown that *Smurthwaite and Gill* took into account factors that had nothing to do with reliability. In *Matto v Wolverhampton Crown Court (1987)*, the Divisional Court held that evidence of breath specimens should have been excluded under s 78(1) because they had been obtained in bad faith and as the result of oppression. The Court of Appeal has frequently emphasised the importance of bad faith on the part of police in connection with s 78(1). For example, in *Walsh (1990)*, it was said that bad faith might make 'substantial or significant' a breach of the Code that would not otherwise have been so. And in *Alladice (1988)*, the Court of Appeal said that a distinction was to be drawn when considering the effect of refusing access to a solicitor between cases where the police had acted in good faith and those where they had acted in bad faith. However, bad faith is irrelevant if the court is concerned solely with reliability.

More recently, the House of Lords in *Khan (1996)* accepted that a breach of a defendant's right to privacy under Art 8 of the European Convention on Human Rights was at least a relevant consideration under s 78(1). Yet how could it be so if the sole concern of a court is with the reliability of evidence, however improperly obtained? Further, in *Looseley (2001)*, there are several suggestions in speeches of the Law Lords that the s 78(1) discretion is wide enough to exclude evidence on the basis of unfairness, even though the way in which it was obtained had no effect on its reliability. For example, Lord Hoffmann, with whom Lord Hutton agreed on this point, said that an application to exclude evidence under s 78(1) may in substance be a belated application for a stay of proceedings. If so, it should be treated as such and decided according to the principles appropriate to the grant of a stay (which do take into account breach of process values). But to be able to use s 78(1) in this way, its potential scope must be wider than was suggested in *Chalkley and Jeffries*. A final consideration is that in saying that s 78(1) merely restated the common law, the Court of Appeal in *Chalkley* failed to account for s 82(3) of the 1984 Act, which expressly preserves the common law discretion to exclude evidence.

In principle, therefore, s 78(1) appears to be available to protect process values as well as reliability, and so to provide substantial protection for defendants. In practice, however, judges are often reluctant to use it in this way, and reliability will often be the determining factor. For example, in *Stewart (1995)*, the defendant was convicted of abstracting electricity and stealing gas. Electricity company officials, accompanied by police, entered the defendant's house in circumstances that were arguably unlawful. There they found a mechanical apparatus used to bypass the meters. The Court of Appeal held that it was unnecessary to decide about the lawfulness of the entry. Even assuming the entry had been unlawful, the admission of the evidence had not had any effect on the fairness of the proceedings because the apparatus had been there for all to see. It was quite a different case from one involving evidence of admissions where there had been a breach of Code C. The basis of the distinction was clearly that in this case, unlike a case where Code C had been breached, there was no doubt about the reliability of the evidence.

Thus, the protection afforded by s 78(1) is a limited one. Not all unfairness comes within its scope; it confers only a discretion and, although it is likely that in principle, the provision is available for the protection of process values regardless of reliability, in practice, if evidence is reliable, it is unlikely to be excluded under s 78(1).

Q&A EVIDENCE 2007–2008

### Reference

1 See Dennis, IH, 'Reconstructing the law of criminal evidence' (1989) Current Legal Problems 21, pp 35–44.

# Question 28

Nigel is arrested on suspicion of murdering Olive. At the police station, he is told of his right to a solicitor but says he does not want one because 'they cost too much and waste a lot of time'. His watch and other personal possessions are taken away from him and he is then locked in a cell for five hours. At the end of that time, he is interviewed by DS Lestrade. After three hours of questioning, Lestrade suddenly produces a photograph. 'Just look at that', he says: 'Now, will you tell me the truth, or do I have to get my box of tricks out?' The photograph, which is in colour, shows Olive's mutilated body. Nigel screams and says: 'For God's sake, my nerves can't stand it. I killed her but I never meant to. She drove me to it.' The next day, he is interviewed again by DS Lestrade, but this time in the presence of a solicitor. He again confesses to the murder.

Discuss the evidential issues that arise.

### Answer plan

Here, we have two confessions and the admissibility of each has to be considered.

*The first confession*

- Application of s 82(1) of the **Police and Criminal Evidence Act 1984 (PACE)**.
- The possibility of oppression.
- Causation – always vital when considering s 76.
- Note the use made of the information about the watch.
- Breaches of Code C.

*The second confession*

- The continuing effect of the first confession – *McGovern (1991)*; *Neil (1994)*.
- Finally, remember the point based on *Sharp (1988)*.

# CONFESSIONS AND ILL–GOTTEN EVIDENCE

> A useful case to remember when dealing with any breach of the Codes is *Elson (1994)*, where the Court of Appeal said that the Codes of Practice were there to protect the individual against the might of the State. The individual, the court said, was at a great disadvantage when arrested by the police, and that was so whether or not the police behaved with the utmost propriety.

# Answer

Two main questions have to be considered: the admissibility of Nigel's first confession and that of the second confession, made in the presence of a solicitor.

In relation to the first confession, there are two problems: (a) is it likely to be excluded under s 76 of PACE?; (b) if not, is it likely to be excluded under s 78? Although the first confession contains exculpatory matter, it is obviously partly adverse to the maker, and so falls within the definition of 'confession' in s 82(1).

Might the first confession have been obtained by oppression? Once the question is raised, the burden is on the prosecution to prove beyond doubt that the confession was not so obtained. The court is likely to be interested in two matters: the reference to the 'box of tricks' and the showing of the photograph. Oppression is partly defined in s 76(8) of PACE as including 'torture, inhuman or degrading treatment, and the use or threat of violence (whether or not amounting to torture)'. It is possible that 'box of tricks' could have been understood as a reference to equipment designed for torture, or at least violence, so as to make what was said a threat of violence. However, a causative link has to be established between the threat and the confession and Nigel must be able to confirm that this threat, as well as the shock of seeing the photograph, operated on his mind at the time in question.

Showing the photograph to Nigel does not fall within the partial statutory definition of oppression. However, in *Fulling (1987)*, the Court of Appeal approved the *Shorter Oxford Dictionary* definition of oppression as the 'exercise of authority or power in a burdensome, harsh or wrongful manner; unjust or cruel treatment of subjects, inferiors, etc, or the imposition of unreasonable or unjust burdens'. The court added that it would be hard to envisage any circumstances in which oppression would not entail some impropriety on the part of the interrogator. Showing the photograph appears to be on the borderline of oppression. It could be argued that it was psychologically burdensome to show it. There appears to be a good chance of persuading the court that the confession *may* have been obtained by oppression, and an even chance that the prosecution would be unable to prove beyond reasonable doubt that it was not.

Even if the argument on oppression failed, the matters relied on could be used to support an argument for exclusion based on s 76(2)(b). Other matters may be relevant under this head. Nigel may well have been suffering from disorientation after the time spent first in his cell and then in being questioned. His watch had been removed, and he was therefore very likely to have been without any means to measure the passing of time. It is possible that the police acted improperly in removing the watch. Paragraph 4.2 of Code C says that a detained person may retain clothing and personal effects unless the custody officer considers that he may use them to cause harm to himself or others, interfere with evidence, damage property or effect an escape, or they are needed as evidence. Did any of these reasons apply? The police might also try to argue that the watch was an 'item of value', and so excluded from the definition of personal effects under para 4.3.

The detention for five hours before the interview began may have been a breach of para 1.1 of Code C, which requires that all persons in custody must be dealt with expeditiously. What was the reason for the delay? The three hours of interviewing may have been a breach of para 12.8, which requires breaks at recognised meal times and short breaks for refreshment at intervals of approximately two hours, subject to the interviewing officer's discretion. There may also have been a breach of para 11.2 of Code C, which requires the interviewing officer to remind the suspect immediately before the interview begins of his right to *free* legal advice. One of the reasons given by Nigel for not wanting a solicitor suggests that he was not aware of this right.

Section 78 of PACE applies to evidence of a confession (*Mason (1988)*). Thus, all the matters referred to in connection with s 76 could be used, if submissions under that section fail, to support an argument based on s 78. But, under this section, there is only a discretion to exclude, and, as the Court of Appeal acknowledged in *Anderson (1993)*, it is not entirely clear where the burden of proof lies.[1]

If the first confession is excluded under s 76, the question arises whether the second confession was so tainted by the circumstances in which the first was made that it should be excluded also. In *McGovern (1991)*, the defendant had confessed in two interviews. The first had been without a solicitor and, because of breaches of s 58 of PACE and for other reasons, that confession was excluded. The Court of Appeal emphasised that when an accused person has made admissions at a first interview, the very fact that those admissions have been made is likely to have an effect on the person during the course of the second interview. It was therefore held that the confession in the second interview should have been excluded, as well as that in the first (see also *Ismail (1990)*). In *Neil (1994)*, the Court of Appeal said that where there is a series of two or more interviews, and the court excludes one on the ground of unfairness, the question whether a later interview which itself is unobjectionable should also be excluded is a matter of fact and degree. It is likely to depend on whether the objections leading to the exclusion of the first interview were of a fundamental and continuing nature and, if so, if the arrangements for the later interview gave the accused a sufficient opportunity to exercise an informed and independent choice as to whether he should repeat or retract what he said in the objectionable interview, or say nothing. There is clearly room for argument in Nigel's case. Much may depend on what he says about his state of mind in the second interview (see also *Nelson (1998)*).

If the confession is admitted, the evidential value of the exculpatory part will have to be considered. This may be particularly important if Nigel chooses not to give evidence at trial. The Court of Appeal in *Duncan (1981)* held that the jury should be directed that both incriminating and exculpatory parts of a confession must be considered in deciding where the truth lies, and that it was not helpful to try to explain that the exculpatory parts were something less than evidence of the facts they stated. The judge may, however, comment on the relative weight of the two parts. This approach was approved by the House of Lords in *Sharp (1988)* and also in *Aziz (1995)*.

## Reference

1 However, in *Stagg (1994)*, very experienced prosecuting counsel accepted that it was for the prosecution to show either that there was no unfairness, or that its degree did not warrant the exclusion of the evidence.

# Question 29

Earlier this year, a painting by the well known modernist painter Bruno Hatte was stolen from a public art gallery in Barchester. Acting on information received, DS Proudie arrested two local men, Josh and Luke, in connection with the theft. When they arrived at the police station, they were placed in separate cells.

After about 10 minutes, Josh was taken to an interview room where Proudie was waiting. Josh said at once: 'I want to see a solicitor.' Proudie replied: 'Look, a valuable painting has been stolen. If there should, at present, be any chance of recovering the painting, that chance will cease to exist if we have to wait for a solicitor. Besides, you know the form. You don't need some pimpled trainee to hold your hand.'

After cautioning Josh, he questioned him for 80 minutes, but all Josh would say in answer to questions was 'No comment'. Finally, Proudie said: 'Right. We'll see what your friend Luke has to say. You won't mind waiting in a cell for a few more hours, will you? You won't be lonely; we've just pulled in some skinheads for causing an affray.' Unknown to Proudie, Josh was terrified of skinheads because he had recently been attacked by a group of them. He said to Proudie: 'Look, don't put me with them. Luke and I did it together. But I only got involved because he made me; he's such a bully. We hid the painting in the well in Luke's garden.'

Proudie then visited Luke in his cell. Luke said at once: 'You got nowhere, did you?' Proudie laughed and said: 'In the well in your garden.' Luke shouted: 'Treacherous bastard!' He then refused to say any more.

The painting was found in the well by the police on the following day. Josh and Luke were then offered access to free legal advice, which they both refused. They were then charged with theft of the painting and cautioned. Neither made any reply.

Discuss the evidential issues that arise.

## Answer plan

### Josh

- Definition of confession.
- Quick reference to ss 76 and 78 – need to refer to Code C.
- Dispose quickly of the possibility of oppression. Don't waste time by going in detail into what is meant by oppression; there are more important things to write about in an answer to this question.
- What exactly was said about a solicitor? Anchor your argument to the facts and ask for further information, as you would in practice.
- Circumstances in which the police can refuse access to legal advice.
- The *Alladice* point.
- The 'special motive' point – *Rennie (1982)*.
- The reliability point – note that the emphasis in s 76(2)(b) is on potentiality; it is irrelevant that evidence obtained afterwards confirms the truth of the confession.
- Old favourites: *Gunewardene (1951)* and *Sharp (1988)*.

### Luke

- Discovery of evidence via an inadmissible confession.
- Is what Luke said a confession within the Police and Criminal Evidence Act 1984 (PACE) definition?
- Arguments for exclusion.
- Both defendants

Their refusal to answer police questions or to say anything after caution when charged.

# Answer

*The case against Josh*

Josh has made a statement to the police that is partly adverse to him and is therefore a confession within the definition in s 82(1) of PACE.

The first matter that has to be considered is whether the confession is likely to be excluded under either s 76 or s 78. In considering this question, it will be necessary to take into account the extent to which there may have been breaches of Code C of the Codes of Practice. It is important to remember that the Code does not apply as fully to someone who is voluntarily assisting police with their inquiries as to someone who has been arrested. But arguments can to some extent be based on the Code, as the following provisions suggest.

Note 1A of the Notes for Guidance to Code C states that although certain sections of the Code apply specifically to persons in custody at police stations, 'those there voluntarily to assist with an investigation should be treated with no less consideration . . . and enjoy an absolute right to obtain legal advice or communicate with anyone outside the police station'. However, by para 1.3, the Notes for Guidance are not provisions of the Code. Caution therefore has to be used in arguing that there have been breaches of the Code in relation to Josh. But it is likely that the provisions of the Code would be taken to provide guidelines as to what makes for fairness and reliability, so that even if the provisions of the Code do not strictly apply, they might well be taken into account in questions arising under ss 76 and 78. In *Christou (1992)*, the Court of Appeal took the view that Code C protected persons who had not been arrested, but were being questioned by a police officer about an offence. For the sake of convenience, I shall refer hereafter to 'breaches' of the Code, but that expression should be understood as being qualified by what appears above.

It does not appear that any question of oppression arises in relation to Josh and, accordingly, I shall consider those matters that would be relevant in arguments based on s 76(2)(b) and s 78.

The first of these is the refusal to provide an opportunity for Josh to take legal advice. (I assume from the words uttered that this was a refusal and not just discouragement, but I should like to know whether Josh said anything more about having a solicitor after Proudie's remarks.) It is relevant to ask whether Proudie would have been entitled to delay the opportunity for Josh to obtain legal advice if Josh had already been detained. Proudie would have been so entitled if, amongst other things, Josh had been detained for an indictable offence, and an officer of the rank of superintendent or above had reasonable grounds for believing that the exercise of his right to legal advice would, amongst other things, hinder the recovery of property obtained as a result of such an offence.

Theft is an indictable offence. But Proudie would almost certainly not have been justified in refusing Josh access to a solicitor. Annex B of Code C, para 3 provides that authority to delay a detainee' s right to consult privately with a solicitor may be given only if the authorising officer has reasonable grounds to believe that the solicitor whom the detainee wants to consult will, inadvertently or otherwise, pass on a message from the detainee or act in some other way that will have any of the consequences referred to in s 58(8). If this is the case, the detainee must be allowed to choose another solicitor. As Note B3 says, a decision to delay access to a specific solicitor is likely to be a rare occurrence, and on these facts Josh does not appear to have been asking for a specific solicitor. His request could have been met by allowing him access to the duty solicitor.

The question also arises whether, even if delay had not been justified, Josh suffered prejudice as a result. If Josh is experienced in being questioned by the police, the presence of a solicitor might have made no difference. Josh's replies of 'No comment' for 80 minutes suggests that this could well have been the case. In *Alladice (1988)*, the appellant admitted that he could cope with being interviewed and said that he was aware of his legal rights. He had requested legal advice because he had wanted a check on the conduct of the police during the interview. The Court of Appeal held that his confession made in the absence of a solicitor was admissible, but the decision in that case was based on findings that the police had made an honest mistake about the appellant's entitlement to legal advice, and that the interview had been properly conducted. It is not clear on the facts given whether the police acted innocently or not.

There is also the problem caused by the suggestion that Josh might share a cell with some skinheads. Paragraph 3.21 of Code C provides that any person attending a police station voluntarily for the purpose of assisting with an investigation may leave at will unless placed under arrest. The police seem to have ignored, or at least to have obscured, this right. In any case, by para 8.1, it is provided that, so far as practicable, not more than one person should be detained in each cell. Was this practicable? Or was the reference to skinheads intended as a threat? If Proudie was acting in bad faith, a court would be more likely to exclude the confession, either under s 76(2)(b) or under s 78, than if he was not. In *Walsh (1990)*, it was said that bad faith might make substantial or significant a breach which might not otherwise be so.

The position is more difficult if Proudie was acting in good faith. A confession will not be excluded under s 76(2)(b) merely because the accused had a special motive for making it. As Lord Lane CJ said in *Rennie (1982)*, very few confessions are inspired solely by remorse. But what we have here are words uttered by Proudie to Josh which trigger a particular fear, which in turn leads to the confession. Section 76(2)(b) can be used even where there has been no police impropriety (*Fulling (1987)*) and it might therefore be applied here. The fact that the confession is in fact proved reliable by the subsequent discovery of the painting is no bar to the operation of s 76(2)(b).

If the confession is admitted, it will be evidence only against Josh. An extra-judicial confession is generally not admissible evidence against the co-accused of its maker (*Gunewardene (1951)*). The jury will be entitled to treat the exculpatory part as evidence of the facts stated (*Duncan (1981)*; *Sharp (1988)*). This may be important if, for example, Josh raises the defence of duress at trial.

## The case against Luke

Even if Josh's confession is inadmissible, evidence can be given that the painting was found in the well in Luke's garden (s 76(4) of PACE).

Has Luke by his reaction to Proudie's taunt produced a confession? It could be argued that Luke's reaction amounts to a confession on the basis that his guilt could be inferred from the words uttered. They would then fall within the partial definition of a confession in s 82(1) of PACE. However, he does not appear to have been cautioned or offered legal advice, and he was not interviewed and recorded in accordance with Code E. For all these reasons, his confession is likely to be excluded under s 76(2)(b) of the 1984 Act.

The prosecution will be unable to rely on Josh's initial refusal to answer police questions. By s 34(2A) of the Criminal Justice and Public Order Act 1994, inferences cannot be drawn if a suspect has not been allowed an opportunity to consult a solicitor before being questioned. Nor will the prosecution be able to rely on Luke's silence in the face of questions. Not only was no offer of legal advice made, but he does not appear to have been questioned under caution, as is required by s 34. However, the prosecution may be able to rely on the silence of both defendants when they were charged if at trial they rely on some fact which they could reasonably have been expected to mention at that stage. In *Dervish (2002)*, the Court of Appeal held that the 1994 Act does not exclude the possibility of drawing an inference from silence on being charged, even if no inferences can be drawn from a suspect's silence on being questioned. The only question would be whether, on the facts of the particular case, it would be fair to draw inferences. The Court of Appeal added that it might not be fair where the police had acted in bad faith by deliberately breaching the Code in the knowledge that an inference could be drawn from a later silence on being charged.

If s 34 is held to apply, the judge will have to give a careful direction to the jury based on what was said in *Petkar (2004)*. He must identify the facts on which each of the defendants relies and which were not mentioned on questioning. He must identify the inferences which it is suggested might be drawn from failure to mention such facts, to the extent that they may go beyond the standard inference of late fabrication. The jury should be told that, if an inference is drawn, they should not convict wholly or mainly on the strength of it. They should be told that an inference should be drawn only if they think it is fair and proper, and it should be drawn only if the only sensible explanation for failure to mention facts relied on is that the defendant had no answers, or none that would stand up to scrutiny. Moreover, an inference should be drawn only if, apart from a defendant's failure to mention facts relied on, the prosecution case is so strong that it clearly calls for an answer by him. The jury should be reminded of the evidence on the basis of which they are invited not to draw any inferences from silence.

# Question 30

Benson is charged with obtaining property by deception. The case for the prosecution is that he deceived Miss Prism into agreeing that he should repair some of the windows in her house by falsely telling her that they were in an unsafe condition and that £7,000 was a reasonable price for the work that he did.

After receiving a complaint from Miss Prism's brother, DS Japp went to an address in Anglebury where he saw Benson, who was smelling strongly of alcohol. Japp told him that he wanted to ask some questions about work that Benson had done for Miss Prism. At that moment, Mrs Benson entered the room and shouted at her husband: 'Tell the copper how you cheated the old girl, you bastard! Tell him you'd cheat your own mother for a fiver!' Benson began to weep and said: 'All right. I'll tell you the truth. I cheated her. I told her she couldn't get a cheaper job anywhere else and it wasn't true.'

Benson was then arrested and cautioned and taken to Anglebury police station. He was offered legal advice but said that he did not need any. He was interviewed shortly afterwards.

When the interview began, Benson said: 'I must get a drink soon. I've got the shakes and I'm feeling sick. If I make a statement will I get bail?' DS Japp replied: 'You know I can't make any promises, but it costs a lot to keep someone in custody.' Benson then fully admitted the offence.

Discuss the evidential issues that arise.

## Answer plan

The two confessions should be dealt with separately. Some comment is needed on the content of the first confession – it is certainly not a full one but is clearly adverse to Benson. The following points should then be made:

- the importance of whether Japp should have cautioned Benson at an earlier stage;
- a quick dismissal of the possibility of oppression;

> - the application of s 76(2)(b). Points need to be made about the fact that Benson was prompted to confess by his wife, and about the significance of alcohol consumption.
>
> In relation to the second confession, you should make these points:
> - the significance of inadequate legal representation;
> - the possibility that if the first confession is excluded, the second one might be also, on the principle in *McGovern (1991)* (see also Question 28);
> - the effect of Benson's need for more alcohol – see *Goldenberg (1988)*;
> - the conversation about bail.

# Answer

In relation to the charge against Benson, his words 'I cheated her . . . and it wasn't true' appear to be at least partly adverse to him, although they do not amount to an admission of the whole of the prosecution case. They therefore constitute a confession under s 82(1) of the **Police and Criminal Evidence Act 1984**, and the question of admissibility arises.

Presumably, the prosecution will submit that when Japp went to make inquiries of Benson, he did so only to obtain information or his explanation of the facts, and that he did not at that stage have grounds to suspect him of an offence. By Code C, para 10.1, a person whom there are grounds to suspect of an offence must be cautioned before any questions about an offence are put to him, if either his answers or silence are to be given in evidence in a prosecution.

On the facts given, the complaint was not made by Miss Prism, but by her brother, who presumably related his sister's account of what Benson had said and how much she had paid. Had Japp obtained this information directly from Miss Prism, and had he perhaps had this substantiated by a receipt or bank statement to show the sum paid, it is likely that a court would find that he did suspect a crime to have occurred, and Benson to have committed it. Is the position likely to be different where the information came second hand through Miss Prism's brother, apparently without any supporting evidence? This might well change the view a court would take of Japp's state of mind. What may also be of significance is the reason for the complaint's coming from Miss Prism's brother rather than from herself. Was it because Miss Prism was too old or ill to be able to make a complaint herself? If so, might she have been muddled about what happened? This possibility, and the difficulty of assessing the weight to be attached to an account related on behalf of someone else, make it likely that an initial caution was not required.

On that assumption, is the confession admissible? This is not a case where oppression could be relied on, but would a submission under s 76(2)(b) of PACE be likely to succeed? The words uttered by Mrs Benson might have amounted to something said which was likely, in the circumstances existing at the time, to render unreliable any confession that Mr Benson might have made in consequence. The words or action do not have to come from the police. In *Harvey (1988)*, a woman heard her lover confess to a murder. As this may have led her to make a false confession to protect him, her statement was excluded. In Benson's case, part of the circumstances existing at the time included the fact that he had, probably recently, consumed alcohol. There appears to be no question of his having done so to such an extent that he was unable to appreciate the significance of questions, or of his own answers. But the probability that alcohol had recently been consumed might be thought to add to the likelihood of unreliability. It seems clear that the accused's own mental state may be part of the circumstances under s 76(2)(b) of PACE. Thus, in *McGovern (1991)*, the physical condition and particular vulnerability of the defendant, who was six months pregnant and of low intelligence, were held to have been part of the background against which a submission should have been considered.[1]

If a submission under s 76(2)(b) fails, it is possible that one under s 78 might succeed. *Mason (1988)* establishes that this section as well as s 76 is applicable to evidence of confessions.

If the first confession is excluded, the second confession at the police station may be excluded also on the basis that it is tainted by the defects attaching to the first, as was the case in *McGovern (1991)*. But in *Neil (1994)*, the Court of Appeal said that whether a later interview, which is in itself unobjectionable, should be excluded is a matter of fact and degree. Exclusion is likely to depend on whether the arrangements for the second interview gave the suspect sufficient opportunity to exercise an informed and independent choice about what, if anything, to say.

Benson's need for another drink is not by itself likely to be of assistance. Under s 76(2)(b), unreliability must come from something said or done by someone other than the defendant. Thus, in *Goldenberg (1988)*, where it was argued that admissions were unreliable because the defendant was a heroin addict with withdrawal symptoms who would have done anything to be able to get more heroin, the Court of Appeal held that the unreliability of the confession had nothing to do with anything said or done by someone else, and so was beyond the scope of the provision.[2]

But might Japp's response to the question about bail bring s 76(2)(b) into play? It is arguable that it would. Paragraph 11.5 of Code C provides that if the person being interviewed asks the officer directly what action will be taken in the event of his making a statement, the officer may inform the person what action the police propose to take in that event. That is what Japp did. He implied that bail would probably be granted. But *this* was something said or done by someone other than the suspect. It was not improper, but it does not have to be to trigger s 76(2)(b) (*Fulling (1987)*; *Harvey (1988)*). Once s 76(2)(b) has been triggered, all the circumstances can be taken into account *(Everett (1988)*; *McGovern (1991)*), and these would include Benson's alcohol withdrawal symptoms. It is therefore possible that for this reason the second confession would be excluded under s 76(2)(b).

> ### References
>
> 1  See also *Everett (1988)*.
> 2  So, according to *Goldenberg (1988)*, s 76(2)(b) requires something that was external to the person making the confession and which was likely to have had some effect on him. Benson's earlier confession was prompted by his wife's remarks. Once these had brought s 76(2)(b) into play, the fact that Benson was affected by alcohol became part of the relevant circumstances. But it appears that without the trigger provided by Mrs Benson's remarks, the defence could not have relied on his condition under s 76(2)(b). But see *Walker (1998)*.

# Question 31

Simon and Tim are jointly charged with the burglary of a valuable collection of paintings belonging to Ulrica. Simon was the first to be arrested and interviewed by the police. Vivian, a senior police officer, refused his request for a solicitor on the ground that to allow it would hinder recovery of the paintings. He then forced Simon to remain standing while he interviewed him, after cautioning him, between 11 am and 4 pm without a break. Finally, Simon said: 'I'll tell you what you want to know. I was involved in the burglary, but it was only because Tim threatened to kill me if I didn't help him. You'll find the paintings in the house where Wanda, Tim's girlfriend, lives.' Acting on this information, Vivian went to Wanda's house. When he discovered that she had gone away, he broke in unlawfully, ransacked the house, and recovered the paintings.

Tim was later arrested and taken to the police station. When interviewed by the police, he refused to answer any questions. He later instructed solicitors, and told them that he had not been involved in the burglary and that he had no knowledge of the paintings that were found in Wanda's house. He said that he now believed that they had been 'planted' there by Simon, who had a grudge against him because of an affair that Tim had had during the previous year with Simon's wife.

Discuss the evidential issues arising.

## Answer plan

Take the defendants separately.

*Simon*

The first thing to do is to try to get his confession excluded. Try s 76(2)(a) of the police and Criminal Evidence Act 1984, alternatively s 76(2)(b). There's no point in discussing s 78; you are better off with s 76 because of the burden placed on the prosecution by that section, and because it makes exclusion mandatory rather than discretionary. On these facts, any arguments available under s 78 can be used equally well under s 76. Look for breaches of Code C and think about how you can use them to support arguments under s 76. On the assumption that the confession might not be excluded, you need to say something about its evidential status. You might add something about the burden of proof where a defence of duress is raised. Section 76(4) will be important for the discovery of the paintings. A brief discussion of s 78 is appropriate to cover the unlawful entry that led to their discovery.

*Tim*

You need to discuss the effect of Tim's silence at the police station. Note the importance of discovering if he was offered legal advice. On the assumption that he was, you need to describe how the judge will direct the jury in relation to s 34 of the Criminal Justice and Public Order Act 1994. Another point to consider is whether Tim's theory about planting the paintings is something caught by s 34.

# Answer

Although what Simon said to Vivian was partly exculpatory, it was also partly adverse because he admitted taking part in the burglary. It therefore comes within the definition of a confession in s 82(1) of the Police and Criminal Evidence Act 1984 (PACE). The first question to be considered is whether it could be excluded under s 76. Although s 78 is theoretically available also, all the arguments for exclusion are relevant to s 76, and it is better for the defence to rely on s 76 because of the burden of proof that it imposes on the prosecution, and because exclusion under that section is mandatory if the circumstances are appropriate, whereas under s 78(1), exclusion is only discretionary.

By s 76(8), oppression includes, among other things, 'inhuman or degrading treatment'. In *Fulling (1987)*, Lord Lane CJ relied on a dictionary definition that included 'exercise of authority or power in a burdensome, harsh or wrongful manner ... the imposition of unreasonable or unjust burdens'. He also emphasised the seriousness of the conduct needed to constitute oppression. This seems to be a borderline case. No violence was involved, although *Paris (1993)* shows that this is not an essential element. It is arguable that it was oppressive to question somebody forced to stand for five hours. There was clearly bad faith; Vivian must have known that by para 12.6 of Code C, persons being questioned shall not be required to stand, and that by para 12.8, breaks from interviewing shall be made at recognised meal times and that short breaks for refreshment shall be provided at intervals of approximately two hours. There is nothing to suggest that the exceptional conditions referred to in that paragraph apply here.

If an argument under s 76(2)(a) fails, the same facts can be relied on under s 76(2)(b). In addition, Simon could rely on the fact that he was wrongly refused access to a solicitor. Under s 58 of PACE, delay is only permitted for limited reasons where someone has been arrested for an indictable offence and where the authorisation of an officer of at least the rank of superintendent has been obtained. Burglary is an indictable offence. We do not, however, know Vivian's rank. If he was not at least a superintendent, was the delay in access to legal advice authorised by someone who was? Even if the delay was authorised by an officer of appropriate rank, it is most unlikely that the s 58(8) condition applied. Section 58(8)(c) does indeed authorise delay where the exercise of the right will hinder the recovery of any property obtained as a result of the offence. But the Court of Appeal stated in *Samuel (1988)* that the right of access to legal advice was one of the most important and fundamental rights of a citizen. The court also said that where the police try to justify denial of access to a solicitor, that can be done only by reference to specific circumstances, including evidence about the person detained or the actual solicitor involved. The officer has to believe, inadvertent or unwitting conduct apart, that if allowed to consult with Simon, the solicitor would commit a criminal offence. The effect of this decision was summarised in Annex B of Code C, para 3. There is no evidence whatsoever to support such a belief by Vivian. Provided causation can be shown, there is no reason why an argument based on s 76(2)(b) and relying on the denial of access to a solicitor as well as the matters relied on under s 76(2)(a) should not succeed.[1]

If, by a remote chance, the confession is not excluded, its evidential status will have to be considered. It is evidence only against its maker (see the wording of s 76(1) and *Gunewardene (1951)*), but, following *Lobban v R (1995)*, the references to Tim will not be edited out unless Simon agrees. He is unlikely to do so because he will want to show that he raised his defence of duress at an early stage. He does not have the legal burden of proving this defence, but he has an evidential burden in respect of it (*Gill (1963)*).

Even if the confession is inadmissible, the discovery of the paintings will be admissible under s 76(4) of PACE. It would be possible to argue that this evidence should be excluded under s 78 because of the unlawful way in which the paintings were discovered. But although s 78 is probably in principle available to protect process values regardless of reliability, in practice, where the reliability of evidence has not been affected by the impropriety of the way in which it was obtained, it is unlikely to be excluded. For example, in *Cooke (1995)*, a case where rape and kidnapping were alleged, the question arose whether s 78(1) should be used to exclude evidence of a sample of hair that might have been improperly taken from the defendant. The Court of Appeal agreed with the trial judge's decision to admit the evidence, regardless of any possible assault. The fact of an assault on the defendant would have cast no doubt on the accuracy or strength of the evidence.

Tim faces the possibility of a direction to the jury under s 34 of the Criminal Justice and Public Order Act 1994 in respect of his silence at the police station. However, if he was not offered legal advice before being questioned no inferences from silence can be made: see s 34(2A). If he was offered legal advice, and he relies at trial on facts that he did not mention to the police, it is possible that a direction would be given. His lack of involvement in the burglary and ignorance of the paintings are facts that might be caught. The defence could argue, following *Mountford (1999)* and *Gill (2001)*, that the truth of these facts was the central issue in his trial, and that accordingly, a s 34 direction should not be given. In *Gowland-Wynn (2002)*, however, another division of the Court of Appeal rejected this approach and the law is therefore uncertain.[2] Tim's suggestion that Simon planted the paintings is a theory and not a fact and, as such, following *Nickolson (1999)*, would not be caught by s 34 unless he could reasonably have been expected to tell the police about the fact of Simon's grudge. If a s 34 direction is given, the judge would have to follow the guidelines based on *Petkar (2004)*. He must identify the facts on which Tim relies and which were not mentioned on questioning. He must identify the inferences which it is suggested might be drawn from failure to mention such facts, to the extent that they may go beyond the standard inference of late fabrication. The jury should be told that, if an inference is drawn, they should not convict wholly or mainly on the strength of it. They should be told that an inference should be drawn only if they think it is fair and proper, and it should be drawn only if the only sensible explanation for failure to mention facts relied on is that the defendant had no answers, or none that would stand up to scrutiny. Moreover, an inference should be drawn only if, apart from a defendant's failure to mention facts relied on, the prosecution case is so strong that it clearly calls for an answer by him. The jury should be reminded of the evidence on the basis of which they are invited not to draw any inferences from silence.

### References

1 See also Code C, Annex B.
2 See also *Chenia (2003)*.

# Question 32

The police suspected that George and Harry were dealing in drugs. Without a warrant, they broke into a house occupied by the two men solely in order to look for evidence while George and Harry were away. They discovered a large quantity of cocaine. As a result of their discovery, George and Harry were arrested several days later and taken to the police station for questioning. Both men refused to answer any questions until they had received legal advice. When their solicitor arrived, she advised them to remain silent and accordingly they continued to refuse to answer any police questions. The police later placed them together in a cell in which a listening device had been secretly installed which recorded all their conversation. At one stage, George was overheard saying to Harry: 'One thing's for sure, they can never prove we didn't have the stuff for our own use.' Harry replied: 'I wish I'd made as much out of it as you. I'd be in the south of France by now.' Then came the sound of two men laughing. Nothing further of significance was overheard.

## Answer plan

The first point should be a familiar one – improperly obtained evidence and the use of s 78(1) of the **Police and Criminal Evidence Act 1984 (PACE)**. After that, you need to refer to a problem that has occurred recently on several occasions. Is evidence of possession of cash admissible or even relevant on a charge of drug dealing? This is the sort of point which you could deal with perfectly well in an exam if you did not know the cases but thought clearly about basic ideas of relevance and admissibility. It quite often happens that a question will be based, at least in part, on recent decisions. But the examiner looks primarily for an intelligent answer. You are not expected to be an encyclopedia of case law in this subject. Of course, if you have actually read the cases because you read *The Times* or subscribe to the Criminal Law Review or Criminal Appeal Reports, that is a bonus.

You need to consider the exercise of the right to silence on legal advice, and the special direction that has to be given to the jury in such cases. Then we come to evidence obtained by bugging. You ought to be able to deal with this if you've studied the law relating to s 78 efficiently. Finally, some thought is needed about the content of the conversation. Are there any confessions there? If so, how many? And by whom? Note yet again that the examiner is looking to see if you can *analyse* the information you are given.

# Answer

The first question that arises is whether the cocaine discovered during the unlawful search will be admissible. The trial judge will have to consider whether, in view of the circumstances in which this evidence was obtained, he should exercise the discretion which he has under s 78 of PACE to exclude evidence of what was found on the ground that its admission would so adversely affect the fairness of the proceedings that it ought not to be admitted.

It is implicit in s 78(1) that it is possible for the way in which evidence is obtained to result in its exclusion. This is particularly likely where the police have acted in bad faith. In *Matto v Wolverhampton Crown Court (1987)*, the defendant was convicted of driving with excess alcohol. Police officers had requested a specimen of breath when they were on the defendant's property. This was unlawful and they knew it to be so. The specimen proved positive. The defendant was then arrested. At the police station, he provided another positive specimen. The appeal was allowed on the ground that because the police had acted in bad faith and oppressively, the Crown Court could have decided to exclude the evidence under s 78 if it had directed itself properly.

However, in cases where improperly obtained real evidence has been considered by the Crown Court in a s 78 application, it is usually admitted because any impropriety in obtaining it is far less likely to have affected its reliability than evidence of an improperly obtained confession. Thus, in *Cooke (1995)*, the Court of Appeal pointed out that the vast majority of cases under s 78 had concerned alleged confessions obtained in breach of the Codes. In that case, where a sample of hair had been obtained from the defendant in circumstances that may have been improper, the court held that the trial judge had properly decided to admit the evidence, despite the possibility that there might have been a technical assault on the defendant. This did not cast doubt on the accuracy or strength of the evidence.

Two features might make an application to exclude slightly more likely to succeed in this case. It seems very likely that the police were acting in bad faith, and it is clear that their entry was unlawful. But the offence is regarded as such a serious one that the discretion is still not likely to be exercised in the defendants' favour.

By s 34 of the **Criminal Justice and Public Order Act 1994**, if either George or Harry failed to mention when questioned by the police any fact relied on as his defence in subsequent proceedings, and that fact was one which in the circumstances existing at the time he could reasonably have been expected to mention, the jury may draw such inferences from the failure as appear proper.

In *Argent (1997)*, the Court of Appeal said that when considering whether a fact was one that a defendant could reasonably have been expected to mention, the court must take into account all relevant circumstances at the time of questioning, including the personal characteristics of the defendant. It was also said that legal advice is something the court might have to consider as one of those circumstances. Its significance was more fully considered in *Condron (1997)*. In giving guidance, the Court of Appeal said that where a defendant says he failed to answer questions on legal advice, that bare assertion is unlikely to be regarded as a sufficient reason for failure to mention matters relevant to the defence. In practice, a defendant will have to go further and provide, either through his own testimony or that of his solicitor, the reasons for the advice.

If a direction is given under s 34, the judge should follow the guidelines based on *Petkar (2004)*. He must identify the facts on which each of the defendants relies and which were not mentioned on questioning. He must identify the inferences which it is suggested might be drawn from failure to mention such facts, to the extent that they may go beyond the standard inference of late fabrication. The jury should be told that, if an inference is drawn, they should not convict wholly or mainly on the strength of it. They should be told that an inference should be drawn only if they think it is fair and proper, and it should be drawn only if the only sensible explanation for failure to mention facts relied on is that the defendant had no answers, or none that would stand up to scrutiny. Moreover, an inference should be drawn only if, apart from a defendant's failure to mention facts relied on, the prosecution case is so strong that it clearly calls for an answer by him. The jury should be reminded of the evidence on the basis of which they are invited not to draw any inferences from silence.

A special direction must be given, because the defendants' silence was on legal advice. In *Betts and Hall (2001)* the Court of Appeal held that adverse inferences could not be drawn from silence where the defendant had honestly relied on legal advice in his refusal to answer questions, and was not simply using the advice as a cloak behind which to hide. But in *Howell (2003)* the Court of Appeal held that genuine reliance on legal advice was not of itself enough to avoid the application of s 34. The Court said that what was reasonable depended on all the circumstances. Even where silence was advised, there must always be soundly based objective reasons for that advice. In *Knight (2003)* the Court of Appeal observed, *obiter*, that if there was any conflict between *Betts and Hall* and *Howell*, *Howell* was to be preferred. Although in *Robinson (2003)* another division of the Court of Appeal seemed to prefer the approach taken in *Betts and Hall*, it was later confirmed in *Hoare (2004)* and *Beckles (2004)* that *reasonable* reliance on legal advice is necessary to prevent the drawing of adverse inferences, and this is reflected in the amended Judicial Studies Board specimen direction on s 34.

In theory, the admissibility of evidence obtained by a trick can be challenged under s 78(1) of PACE but, for a long time, evidence obtained by eavesdropping has been admitted. In *Maqsud Ali (1966)*, for example, a tape recorder was used to eavesdrop on a conversation between two suspects, and the evidence obtained was admitted. More recently, in *Bailey and Smith (1993)*, the judge admitted evidence of confessions made by the two defendants and tape recorded during conversations between them while they were sharing a bugged cell at a police station after being arrested, charged and remanded in custody. The Court of Appeal upheld the decision to admit the evidence but said that this was a device to be used only in grave cases. Drug dealing for commercial gain is regarded as a grave offence, as was shown recently in *Khan (1996)* where the decision to admit evidence of drug dealing obtained by bugging private property was upheld by the House of Lords. The legality of bugging the cell will now depend on the provisions of the Regulation of **Investigatory Powers Act 2000**, and the Code of Practice issued under it. Clearly, if no provisions of the Act or its Code have been infringed, there will be no room for argument under s 78.

The exchange between Harry and George is ambiguous. Does it amount to a confession by either defendant? 'They can never prove we didn't have the stuff for our own use' is an observation which is at least partly adverse to both defendants in that it is capable of being interpreted as an admission that the drugs were in the possession of both Harry and George. Harry did not dissociate himself in any way from George's remark and may therefore be taken to have adopted it. On similar principles, a confession was admitted against both defendants in *Batt (1995)*. Ashley and Kerry were convicted of robbery. One of them had appeared to be holding a gun which was partly concealed by material. While on remand in custody, they were sharing a cell. A police officer gave evidence that on one occasion Kerry had said to Ashley: 'They'll fuck themselves if they show that gun in court. It's not the one used.' The Court of Appeal held that this was evidence against Ashley as well as Kerry. Ashley had said nothing, but he had not dissociated himself from his companion's remark.

Harry's remark to George, 'I wish I'd made as much out of it as you', is capable of being interpreted as a confession to dealing and, on the principle just outlined, George's failure to dissociate himself from what was said is capable of being interpreted as an adoption of it.

# Chapter 8

# Character Evidence I

## INTRODUCTION

Character evidence is relevant mainly in criminal trials. Before the Criminal Justice Act (CJA) 2003, the common law recognised two ways in which such evidence could be relevant. It could be relevant to any witness's credibility, and it could also be relevant to the likelihood of a defendant's guilt. Whether an item of character evidence was relevant to one or both of these matters depended on the circumstances. Broadly speaking, evidence of a defendant's good character was relevant to both matters, and under *Vye (1993)* a direction to this effect became compulsory. The question whether a good character direction should be given or not, or given only in a qualified way, can arise either where the defendant has one or more previous convictions that can be regarded as not amounting to serious criminal behaviour, or where he has no convictions, but his evidence at trial discloses some criminal behaviour, though not that alleged by the prosecution. Students should note particularly the decisions in *Gray (2004)*, *Goss (2005)*, *Teeluck and John (2005)* and *Payton (2006)*. Evidence of bad character was primarily relevant to guilt where the prosecution was allowed to introduce it as part of its case against a defendant under the rules relating to similar fact evidence. Where such evidence was admitted only because of the way in which the defence was conducted, under rules contained in the Criminal Evidence Act 1898, it was generally meant to be relevant only to credibility. This distinction was not always easy to maintain in practice, and the CJA 2003 does not preserve it. In former editions of this book it was easy to deal with these topics separately, because the sources of law for each were quite distinct. This is no longer the case, as the law relating to evidence of bad character is now governed by the provisions of Part 11, Chapter 1 of the CJA 2003. To some extent, therefore, there is overlapping of the subject matter of Chapters 8 and 9 in this book, although the emphasis in Chapter 8 is on what used to be called similar fact evidence, and the emphasis in Chapter 9 is on evidence of bad character that becomes admissible by virtue of the way in which the defence is conducted. What is said here should be treated as an introduction to both chapters.

The relevant provisions where the prosecution wishes to adduce evidence of bad character as part of its case against a defendant are s 101(1)(c) and (d). Sub-section (1)(c) has to be read with s 102. Very broadly speaking, it covers the sort of evidence that was admissible before the CJA 2003 as 'background' evidence. Examples can be found in *Fulcher (1995)* and *M(T) and Others (2000)*. Section 101(1)(d) has to be read in conjunction with s 103.

The provisions that can be used to admit evidence of bad character by virtue of the way in which the defence is conducted are s 101(1)(e),(f) and (g). These provisions must be read with ss 104, 105 and 106 respectively.

Where evidence of a defendant's bad character is not admitted by agreement under s 101(1)(a) or elicited on behalf of the defendant himself under s 101(1)(b), it is necessary to consider arguments that may be available to exclude it. You should note particularly s 101(3) and (4), and s 103(3) and (4). You should also consider the possibility of using the common law discretion, confirmed by *Sang (1980)*, to exclude prosecution evidence where its prejudicial effect exceeds its probative value. This discretion appears to have been unaffected by the CJA 2003. Save in relation to s 101(1)(d) and (g), which are covered by sub-s (3), it may also be useful to consider the application of s 78(1) of the **Police and Criminal Evidence Act 1984 (PACE)**, but it should be remembered that this provision applies only to evidence on which the prosecution proposes to rely.

The Court of Appeal has considered the new legislation on evidence of bad character on frequent occasions. Guidelines have been given in some cases to help trial judges to apply the statutory rules. Those laid down in *Hanson (2005)* are particularly important. There are several consolidated appeals where application of the legislation in particular cases can be studied; for example, *Edwards (2006)*, *Renda (2006)* and *Weir (2006)*. These are useful to read in order to get the 'feel' of the way in which the legislation is being applied, but it must be remembered that cases are likely to be decided very much on their own facts. It would be a mistake to regard these decisions as precedents in the strict sense.

One of the most important of the guidelines in *Hanson* concerns the direction that a judge should give to a jury where evidence of previous convictions has been admitted. For reasons of space, and to avoid too much repetition, I have not included this in all the model answers. However, in your examination you should remember to set it out in full if there is any possibility that previous convictions will be admitted. It will show the examiners that you have at least some familiarity with the *Hanson* guidelines, and that you recognise the growing importance in evidence law of the content of judicial directions in a summing-up. The judge in summing up should make these points to the jury:

(i) they should not place undue reliance on previous convictions. In particular, they should not conclude that the defendant has been untruthful or has committed the offence with which he has been charged merely because he has these convictions;

(ii) whether the convictions do in fact show propensity is for them to decide;

(iii) if they do find propensity, they are entitled to take this into account when determining guilt. But it is only one relevant factor, and they assess its significance in the light of all the other evidence in the case.

## Checklist

Students should be familiar with the following areas:

- relevance;
- Part 11, Chapter 1 of the CJA 2003;
- *Sang (1980)*;
- s 78(1) of PACE;
- s 27(3) of the Theft Act 1968;
- evidence of good character; note particularly the guidelines set out in *Gray (2004)* for cases where a defendant does not have an absolutely good character;
- the guidelines in *Hanson (2005)*.

# Question 33

James is charged with indecently assaulting Kate in a large department store during the January sales. The case for the prosecution is that he approached her from behind and whispered in her ear, 'You look sexy. What about a drink?' It is alleged that he then fondled one of her breasts. James denies that he said anything to Kate, whom he had never met before. He admits that he might have touched her breast, but says that if he did, it was an accident. A crowd of shoppers had suddenly pushed him forward, and he had instinctively clutched at the person standing in front of him to ensure that he did not lose his balance and fall to the ground. James was carrying a briefcase at the time. When this was lawfully searched by the police after his arrest it was found to contain several magazines devoted to heterosexual pornography. James was convicted three months ago of a public order offence in connection with a political demonstration and was fined £50.

Q&A Evidence 2007–2008

Discuss the evidential issues arising.

> ### Answer plan
>
> This appears to be a relatively simple set of facts, but in order to answer the question well you must analyse them carefully. There are two potential problems to be considered: the discovery of the magazines, and the significance of the previous conviction.
>
> *The magazines*
>
> The first question to consider is relevance. Remember how to construct an argument for relevance by finding an appropriate generalisation. Why is relevance so important? Note the dictum of Lawton LJ in *Turner (1975)*. Take into account the possibility that, while logically relevant, the evidence may not be weighty enough to be legally relevant. Don't be satisfied with reaching the conclusion that the evidence is irrelevant and leaving the matter there. What if the judge decides it *is* relevant? What law will be applicable? It might be the common law, because the Criminal Justice Act (CJA) 2003 applies only to evidence of 'bad character' within the meaning of s 98 and s 112. Look at those sections. Do you think the discovery of the magazines might count as evidence of bad character for the purposes of the 2003 Act? Can you get any guidance from some of the principles in *Hanson (2005)*? (You should memorise a summary of these.) The distinction drawn in *Weir* may be helpful. What opportunities for exclusion are there, (a) assuming the Act does not apply; (b) assuming that it does?
>
> *The previous conviction*
>
> Note the missing information that may well determine what happens at trial. Can the defence argue that James should be treated effectively as a man of good character? If so, what is the position about a *Vye* direction? (Don't forget to spell out for the examiner the contents of such a direction.) Could the prosecution make use of the previous conviction? Obviously it wasn't for a similar offence. How, then, could they use it? Have you studied the 2003 Act sufficiently well to remember s 103(1)(b)?

# Answer

The first question is whether the prosecution can rely on the magazines to support the case against James. Are they relevant at all? If they are, does their discovery amount to evidence of bad character within s 98 of CJA 2003?

It could be argued that they are relevant on the basis that a man with an interest in heterosexual pornography is more likely than a man without such an interest to commit an indecent assault on a woman. But the success of such an argument must be doubtful. Obviously, if a judge is not persuaded of the truth of the generalisation that would make the magazines relevant, they will be excluded. Relevance, as Lawton LJ said in *Turner (1975)* is a condition precedent to admissibility. A judge might decide that the evidence was logically relevant, but of insufficient weight to give it legal relevance. In those circumstances also it would be excluded. If a judge decides that it has both logical and legal relevance, it will have to be decided if it is evidence of 'bad character' within s 98 of CJA 2003.

By s 98, evidence of a person's 'bad character' is evidence of, or of a disposition towards, misconduct on his part. (It does not appear that the evidence has anything to do with the alleged facts of the offence, or that it is evidence of misconduct in connection with the investigation or prosecution of the offence.) 'Misconduct' is defined in s 112 as 'the commission of an offence or other reprehensible behaviour.' Possession of the magazines presumably does not constitute an offence in itself. Might it count as reprehensible behaviour? In *Weir (2006)* a contrast was drawn between behaviour that was 'reprehensible' and that which was merely 'unattractive'. The distinction might well be drawn here. If possession of the magazines does not count as reprehensible behaviour, it will not amount to evidence of bad character within the meaning of s 98. In that case, the 2003 Act will have no application and admissibility will be decided on ordinary principles. (It is assumed that a judge has decided it to be relevant.) The first of these is the common law principle, established in *Sang (1980)*, that allows a judge to exclude prosecution evidence where its probative value is exceeded by its prejudicial effect. Reliance could also be placed on the discretion contained in s 78 of the Police and Criminal Evidence Act 1984.

If it is thought that possession of the magazines does amount to reprehensible behaviour, the prosecution will argue that it is an evidence of bad character that is admissible under s 101(1)(d) of CJA 2003, on the basis that it is relevant to an important matter in issue between the defendant and the prosecution, because it shows a propensity in the defendant to commit offences of the kind with which he is charged (see s 103(1)(a)). At this stage it will be important for the court to consider some of the principles laid down by the Court of Appeal in *Hanson (2005)*.

The starting point should be to bear in mind that Parliament's purpose in the legislation was 'to assist in the evidence-based conviction of the guilty, without putting those who are not guilty at risk of conviction by prejudice'. Where propensity to commit the offence is relied on as the basis for admitting evidence of bad character under s 101(1)(d), it has to be considered whether the proceedings will be unfair if the evidence is admitted. The court has a duty, not merely a discretion, under s 101(3) to exclude evidence that is in principle admissible under s 101(1)(d) if it appears to the court that the admission of the evidence would have such an adverse effect on the fairness of the proceedings that the court ought not to admit it. If the evidence is admitted, the judge when summing up should tell the jury that whether possession of the magazines does show propensity is for them to decide. If they do find propensity, they are entitled to take this into account when determining guilt. But it is only one relevant factor, and they must assess its significance in the light of all the other evidence in the case.

The next consideration is James's previous conviction. The crucial question here seems to be whether he pleaded guilty or not guilty, and whether he gave evidence or not. If he pleaded guilty, or at least gave no evidence but merely tested the strength of the prosecution case in cross-examination, there would be a good argument for treating him as a person of good character for the purposes of this trial. In *Gray (2004)* the Court of Appeal discussed what should be done where a defendant does not have an absolutely good character. Among guidelines laid down was one stating that if a defendant has a previous conviction which, because of its age *or nature*, may entitle him to be treated as being effectively of good character, the trial judge has a discretion to treat him in this way. Another guideline stated that where the previous conviction is irrelevant in relation to the offence charged, the judge's discretion ought to be exercised in favour of the defendant. The conviction for the public order offence clearly falls into this category. If a defendant is treated as being effectively of good character, the judge must then give a full direction in accordance with the rules laid down in *Vye (1993)*. That is to say, he must tell the jury that good character is relevant to a defendant's credibility and also to the likelihood of his having behaved as alleged by the prosecution. In James's case there may be a slight difficulty if it is decided that evidence of the magazines should be admitted as evidence of disposition. A judge might decide to qualify the *Vye* direction in some way. On the other hand, he might choose to refer to the evidence of the magazines but balance that reference by giving a full *Vye* direction.

The position is likely to be different, however, if the defendant pleaded not guilty at the earlier trial and gave evidence in his own defence, especially if he denied that he committed the action constituting the public order offence. The prosecution might then be able to rely on his conviction as evidence of a propensity to be untruthful, under s 103(1)(b) of CJA 2003, because his evidence on oath had been disbelieved. The nature of the offence would then be unimportant. The Court of Appeal in *Hanson*, when referring to evidence of propensity to commit the kind of offence with which he is charged, said that a single previous conviction for an offence of the same description or category will often not show propensity. But the Court was not considering propensity to be untruthful. Perhaps a judge might be prepared to apply the same principle and say that one incident involving unsuccessful testimony is not enough to establish a disposition to be untruthful. But it is by no means certain that that would be the outcome, especially as the trial for the public order offence was only a few months ago.

# Question 34

Leo is charged with indecently assaulting Mike on a coach journey between York and London. The case for the prosecution is that they had not met before, but were sitting next to each other, and that after a while Leo began a conversation by asking Mike if he had been to a recent exhibition of 19th century Russian paintings. It is alleged that during the following conversation Leo fondled Mike's thigh. Leo denies the charge. He admits touching Mike's thigh, but says that he did so only by accident when the coach swerved suddenly and he was thrown across his seat. Last year Leo was convicted of indecently assaulting Nigel, who had been sitting next to him in a railway carriage on a journey between Bristol and Exeter. On that occasion Leo had begun a conversation with Nigel, whom he had not met before, about a current exhibition of 20th century French sculpture. A little later he had fondled Nigel's thigh. His defence, in support of which he gave evidence, was that he had not touched Nigel, and that Nigel had invented the whole incident.

Discuss the evidential issues arising.

## Answer plan

You have to consider the relevance and admissibility of the earlier convictions, and of the circumstances leading to it. Note the two possible arguments for admissibility under the Criminal Justice Act (CJA) 2003:

- under s 101(1)(c);
- under s 101(1)(d).

Note the arguments for exclusion, and how use is made by the *Hanson* guidelines.

# Answer

The question is whether the prosecution case can be supported by evidence of Leo's previous conviction and the circumstances leading to it. It can plausibly be argued that a person with a recent conviction for indecently assaulting another man is more likely to be guilty of a further indecent assault on a man than someone without such a previous conviction. It can also be argued that where features of the current allegations resemble features of the earlier offence, the likelihood of the defendant's guilt is increased. There can be little doubt that a judge would find that the earlier incident was relevant to the current charge. The previous conviction obviously falls within the meaning of misconduct in s 112(1) of the CJA 2003. It is therefore evidence of bad character within s 98, and so its admissibility is governed by Part 11, Chapter 1 of the Act.

There are two possible arguments for admissibility. The first is that the evidence is admissible under s 101(1)(c) on the basis that it is important explanatory evidence as defined by s 102. In other words, without this evidence the court or jury would find it impossible or difficult to understand properly other evidence in the case, and its value for understanding the case as a whole is substantial. The idea of important explanatory evidence is based on the former common law relating to 'background evidence'. According to the Law Commission, such evidence could be admissible, *inter alia*, where it was close in time, place or circumstances to the facts or circumstances of the offence charged, and where it helped to establish motive. It is arguable that both considerations apply on these facts. Although only one earlier incident is relied on, it is fairly close in time, and there are common features in the two sets of circumstances, although there are dissimilarities also. However, it could be argued that the former law is less than helpful because an explicit statutory test has replaced a test that was confusing and potentially too wide. In *Pettman (1985)*, it was stated that background evidence was admissible either where the account placed before the jury would be incomprehensible without it, or where without it the account would be merely incomplete. It is difficult to see how, without evidence of the previous conviction, the court or jury would find it impossible or difficult to *understand* other evidence in the case, as s 102 of the CJA 2003 requires, unless understanding evidence is taken to include assessing its weight, which seems to stretch the meaning of 'to understand' too far.

The second argument for admissibility would be based on s 101(1)(d) of the Act. The prosecution would say that evidence of the earlier conviction is relevant to an important matter in issue between the defendant and the prosecution. On the facts, there are two principal matters in issue. The first is whether Leo 'fondled' Mike's thigh or merely touched it. The second is whether he came into physical contact with Mike deliberately or by accident. To support its case in relation to both issues the prosecution will allege that Leo has a disposition, or propensity, towards indecency with other men, and that in giving expression to that propensity he follows a similar method of procedure, whereby he engages male fellow passengers on public transport in a conversation begun by a remark on a broadly artistic subject, and subsequently fondles their thighs. On that basis, the evidence would fall within s 103(1)(a) of CJA 2003. The prosecution will also say that the recent conviction rebuts Leo's defence of accident, and that in relation to such incidents he has a propensity to be untruthful. On that basis, the evidence would fall within s 103(1)(b) of CJA 2003. Reliance will be placed on the fact that on the earlier occasion he pleaded not guilty and gave evidence that was disbelieved. The Explanatory Notes issued with the CJA 2003 suggest that s 103(1)(b) is intended to admit only a limited range of evidence, such as convictions for perjury or other offences involving deception. But this may be over-optimistic.

Under s 101(1)(d), there is no requirement that the probative value of the bad character evidence should be substantial. But by s 101(3), the court must not admit evidence under sub-s (1)(d) if, on an application by the defendant to exclude it, it appears to the court that the admission of the evidence would have such an adverse effect on the fairness of the proceedings that the court ought not to admit it. Moreover, by s 103(3), proof of propensity to commit offences of the kind with which a defendant is charged by reference to a previous conviction is not permissible if the court is satisfied 'by reason of the length of time since the conviction *or for any other reason*' that it would be unfair to prove the conviction. Further, the common law discretion to exclude prosecution evidence, confirmed by the House of Lords in *Sang (1980)*, has almost certainly survived the CJA 2003. On any of these bases the judge could be invited to look again at the weight and prejudicial effect of the previous conviction and exclude the evidence.

The trial judge, in considering whether to admit or exclude evidence of the earlier convictions, would no doubt take into account the guidelines laid down in *Hanson (2005)*. In that case, the Court of Appeal emphasised the intention of Parliament 'to assist in the evidence-based conviction of the guilty, without putting those who are not guilty at risk of conviction by prejudice.' The Court said that where propensity to commit the offence is relied on as the basis for admitting evidence under s 101(1)(d), there are three questions to be considered:

(i) Does the history of convictions establish a propensity to commit offences of the kind charged?
(ii) Does that propensity make it more likely that the defendant committed the offence charged?
(iii) Is it unjust to rely on the convictions, and, in any event, will the proceedings be unfair if they are admitted?

Importantly for this case, the Court in *Hanson* said that although there was no minimum number of events necessary to demonstrate propensity, a single previous conviction for an offence of the same description or category would often not be enough. But it might be enough if it showed a tendency to unusual behaviour, or where its circumstances demonstrated probative force in relation to the offence charged. Such circumstances were not to be confined to those sharing striking similarity.

It could be argued convincingly on the facts given that both these conditions are satisfied. The mode of commission of both offences shows a tendency to unusual behaviour, and the circumstances of the earlier offence have a special probative value because they tend to rebut the defence of accident raised in the current case. It would be necessary, however, for the prosecution to prove the circumstances of the earlier offence by admissible evidence, and not rely simply on information provided via the Police National Computer. The Court of Appeal in *Ainscough (2006)* emphasised the need for proper proof of method and any other relevant information that is required in addition to the mere fact of conviction. If a written statement under s 9 of the Criminal Justice Act 1967 by the earlier complainant is unacceptable, it will be necessary for him to give oral evidence of the relevant matters.

# Question 35

Edgar is charged with indecently assaulting Fergus. Fergus, aged 15, was flying his kite at dusk in a public park when he was approached by a man who said that he had a collection of kites and invited Fergus to his house, which he said was nearby, to see them. Fergus agreed to go with him, but while they were walking together, the man made indecent suggestions to him and then indecently assaulted him. Fergus, somewhat hesitantly, picked out Edgar in an identification parade. Garry, aged 17, has made a statement to the police in which he says that he was in another public park in the same town shortly before the date of the assault on Edgar. He said that he was flying his kite when he was approached by a man who said that he had a collection of kites and invited him to his house to see them. Garry agreed to go with him, but while they were walking together the man made indecent suggestions to him. At this, Garry knocked him down and then ran away. Garry identified Edgar in an identification parade as the man who had approached him. Garry and Fergus attend the same school and know each other slightly. Rumours have been circulating at the school about a man who molests boys. When Edgar's house is lawfully searched, no kites are found, but the police find a collection of homosexual videos, some leather masks and several pairs of handcuffs.

Edgar denies meeting Fergus and Garry and claims to have been mistakenly identified by them.

Advise the prosecution on the evidential issues arising.

## Answer plan

First, you need to determine the relevance of Garry's evidence, ie, the probative job that it is intended to do. It is clearly evidence of the defendant's bad character; what argument for admissibility does the *Criminal Justice Act (CJA) 2003* provide? What are the possibilities for exclusion? Don't forget to deal with the possibility of some form of collusion, and with the problems of relevance arising from the search.

# Answer

The primary question is whether the rather weak evidence that Fergus is able to give can be supported by the evidence of Garry. It is important that it should be supported because of the special danger that attaches to evidence of identification, and the consequent need for directions to be given to the jury in accordance with *Turnbull (1977)*. According to the decision of the Court of Appeal in that case, a judge must warn the jury of the special need for caution before convicting on identification evidence. He must tell the jury the reason for having to give such a warning. Some reference should be made to the possibility that a mistaken witness can be a convincing one, and that a number of convincing witnesses can all be mistaken. He should direct the jury to examine the circumstances in which each identification was made. Although the Court of Appeal has not always been consistent, recent decisions such as *Donald (2004)* suggest that another essential ingredient of a *Turnbull* direction is that the judge should point out to the jury the weaknesses in any identification evidence. The judge should also direct the jury to consider whether the identification evidence is supported by any other evidence, and should identify for them the evidence that is capable of providing such support.

Garry's evidence is clearly evidence of Edgar's bad character within ss 98 and 112(1) of the CJA 2003. Although the events narrated by Garry were close in time, place, and in some circumstances to those narrated by Fergus, it seems unlikely that it will qualify as important explanatory evidence under s 101(1)(c); it can hardly be said that without it the jury would find Fergus's evidence impossible or difficult to understand properly, as required by s 102.

But Garry's evidence could be relevant to an important matter in issue between the defendant and the prosecution – namely, the identity of the assailant – and therefore admissible under s 101(1)(d). By s 101(3) the court must not admit evidence under s 101(1)(d) if, on an application by the defendant to exclude it, it appears to the court that its admission would have such an adverse effect on the fairness of the proceedings that the court ought not to admit it. This test is the same as that contained in s 78(1) of the **Police and Criminal Evidence Act 1984 (PACE)**, and the decisions under that sub-section show that the test can be satisfied where the prejudicial effect of an item of evidence exceeds its probative value. For example, in *Boyson (1991)* and in *Lee (1996)* this argument led to the exclusion of convictions tendered under s 74 of PACE. Either under s 101(3), therefore, or under the common law discretion confirmed by *Sang* (1980), it will be open to the defence to argue that Garry's evidence ought to be excluded.

So far as the weight of Garry's evidence is concerned, everything depends on the extent to which collusion is a likely danger, and on the improbability of similar features in the incidents being due merely to coincidence.

The relevant similarities are as follows:

(i) both the victims were teenage boys;
(ii) both were in public parks in the same town;
(iii) both events took place at dusk;
(iv) both events took place within a short time of each other;
(v) both boys were flying kites when they were approached;
(vi) both boys were told of a collection of kites and invited to view them;
(vii) both boys were subjected to indecent suggestions.

However, only Fergus was indecently assaulted. This may have some significance. In cases decided under the former law of similar fact evidence, such as *Johnson (1995)*, the Court of Appeal said that a judge who has to decide whether each incident bears the signature of the accused should look at the nature and quality of any disparities that exist. But it was also said that the presence of some dissimilarities will not lead inevitably to exclusion. Item (vii) would be significant if the suggestions were sufficiently unusual.

It should be observed, though, that in *Somanathan (2005)* the Court of Appeal held that evidence admitted under s 101(1)(d) does not have to satisfy the former test for admissibility of similar fact evidence, which is now to be regarded as obsolete. Dissimilarities may therefore be less significant under the new law. The guidelines laid down by the Court of Appeal in *Hanson (2005)* included one to the effect that a single conviction will often not show propensity, but that it may do so where it shows a tendency to commit unusual behaviour, or where its circumstances demonstrate probative force in relation to the offence charged. Although the incident in relation to Garry did not result in a conviction, the same principle is likely to be applied, with the court taking the view that it does show a tendency to unusual behaviour on the part of the defendant. Further, the earlier incident has probative value in relation to the offence charged because it is evidence that tends to support the complainant's identification of the defendant. On the other hand, it was also said in *Hanson* that the judge must consider the strength of the prosecution case. If there is no, or very little, other evidence against a defendant, it is unlikely to be just to admit a defendant's previous convictions. Presumably the same principle applies where an earlier incident did not give rise to criminal proceedings.

There seems to be little risk of collusion in the ordinary sense because although the boys attend the same school, they know each other only slightly. However, in *DPP v Boardman (1975)*, Lord Wilberforce referred also to a risk of falsity arising from 'a process of infection from media or publicity or simply from fashion', and in *Ryder (1993)* the Court of Appeal recognised the possibility of collusion in the sense of a witness's being unconsciously influenced by another. What is present on these facts is a common source of rumour that might have tainted the accounts of both boys and increased their similarity. However, by s 109 of the CJA 2003, in the assessment of the probative value of evidence, the assumption must be made that it is true, unless it appears on the basis of any material before the court that no court of jury could reasonably find it to be true. It is very likely that the assumption of truth will be made in this case and that the possibility of even indirect collusion will be disregarded.

The absence of kites when Edgar's house was searched is ambiguous. It may show that the police have got the wrong man; on the other hand, the account of a kite collection may have been no more than a ploy to entice the defendant's victims to his house. Unless the leather masks and handcuffs can be connected with the indecent suggestions, their discovery will be irrelevant, and so inadmissible. The discovery of the videos is more difficult. If they are in Edgar's possession, they are capable of showing that he has a homosexual inclination. The probative value of this is that that it tends to confirm the identification by Fergus. What a coincidence it would be if the man *misidentified* by Fergus also had a homosexual inclination. A case that may support this argument is *Thompson v R (1918)*, where a defence of mistaken identity was rebutted by proof of facts tending to show that the defendant was a homosexual with a taste for boys. For the defence, it could be argued that the possibility of coincidence is greater than was realised in 1918, since homosexuality is recognised now to be a more frequent phenomenon. It might also be argued that proof of a general homosexual tendency has little or no probative worth where a sexual assault on a boy under the age of 16 is alleged. The interesting question also arises whether possession of homosexual videos counts as evidence of bad character under ss 98 and 112(1) of the CJA 2003. If it does, the prosecution would have to establish that this evidence is admissible under s 101(1) of the Act.

# Question 36

Hector is charged on an indictment containing two counts of handling stolen goods. Count 1 alleges that on 1 February last year, he received 50 bottles of gin, knowing or believing them to have been stolen. Count 2 alleges that on 1 March last year, he received 500 cigars, knowing or believing them to have been stolen. Hector's defence to count 1 is that he purchased the gin honestly from a teetotal friend in the belief that his friend had received it as a gift. His defence to count 2 is that it was not he who had received the cigars, but his identical twin brother. Four years ago, Hector was convicted of handling 500 bottles of stolen whisky. His defence on that occasion, which he supported by giving evidence, was that he had purchased the whisky honestly from a teetotal friend in the belief that his friend had won it as a prize in a raffle. Hector continues to maintain that he received the whisky innocently and says that he was wrongly convicted by the jury.

Advise the prosecution on the evidential issues that arise.

> **Answer plan**
>
> This question is based on the special provisions of s 27(3) of the **Theft Act 1968**. Note particularly:
> - the limited purpose for which evidence can be adduced under s 27(3);
> - the discretion to exclude, even though the section is available;
> - the notice provision and time limit;
> - limits on what can be given in evidence: *Fowler (1988)*;
> - s 74(3) of the Police and **Criminal Evidence Act 1984 (PACE)**;
> - the direction that should be given to the jury where there are several counts in the indictment.

# Answer

The first matter that has to be considered is whether and to what extent the prosecution can rely upon Hector's conviction for handling whisky to support the present case against him. Section 27(3) of the Theft Act 1968 provides, amongst other things, that where a person is being proceeded against for handling stolen goods, if evidence has been given of his having in his possession the goods which are the subject of the charge, evidence of a previous conviction for handling shall be admissible for the purpose of proving that he knew or believed the goods to have been stolen. In the present case, therefore, evidence of Hector's previous conviction will be admissible in relation to count 1, because on that count receiving is admitted and the only issue is guilty knowledge. Evidence of the previous conviction would not, however, be admissible in relation to count 2 where the live issue is whether it was Hector or his identical twin brother who received the goods. By s 27(3)(b), the conviction must have been within the five years preceding the date of the offence charged. This condition is satisfied. There is also a further condition requiring that seven days' notice in writing be given to the defendant of intention to prove the conviction.

The judge has power to exclude s 27(3) evidence on the ground that its prejudicial effect outweighs its probative value (*Smith (1976)*; *Perry (1984)*). Because the conviction will be relevant on one count only, the judge may very well exercise this discretion in Hector's favour. If he does admit the evidence, he will have to explain carefully to the jury the extent to which it is relevant (*Wilkins (1975)*).

The sub-section does not permit details of the earlier conviction to be given; a bare recital of the conviction is all that is allowed. If the prosecution wants to adduce evidence of the details of the previous offence they must rely on s 101(1)(d) of the Criminal Justice Act (CJA) 2003. However, the effect of s 73(2) of PACE is that any certificate of conviction following trial on indictment must state the substance and effect of the indictment and conviction, including the type of property involved. In *Hacker (1994)*, such a certificate was held by the House of Lords to be admissible in evidence, subject only to the judge's discretion to exclude it if its admission would prejudice the fairness of the proceedings.

It is possible that the prosecution would be permitted to adduce evidence of the circumstances of the previous offence under s 101(1)(d) because of the defence raised on that occasion. It could be argued with some force that the jury ought to know about the earlier defence which failed because it makes it most unlikely that, remembering his earlier experience, this defendant would have accepted a very similar story had he indeed been told it. It would be possible to argue more generally that the earlier offence shows a propensity to commit offences of the kind with which the defendant is currently charged, and also that the defendant has a propensity to be untruthful, since on the earlier occasion he pleaded not guilty and gave evidence in his defence that must have been disbelieved. This would make the earlier offence relevant to both counts. The defence could argue that, just as one swallow does not make a summer, so one conviction is not enough to establish a disposition. Such a submission could be supported by reference to the guidelines in *Hanson (2005)*, one of which states that a single conviction will often not show propensity, but that it may do so where it shows a tendency to unusual behaviour, or where its circumstances demonstrate probative force in relation to the offence charged. On these facts a judge might well find that the circumstances of the previous conviction do have probative force, because they tend to make improbable the defendant's account of the innocent circumstances in which he received the gin. It could also be argued, relying on s 103(3), that by reason of the length of time since the conviction it would be unjust to admit it in this case. But it seems that this argument is available only in relation to the use of a conviction under CJA 2003 to establish disposition to commit offences of the kind currently charged. It does not appear to be available if the conviction is relevant to some other matter that assists the prosecution, such as the significance on these facts of the earlier defence, or the defendant's propensity to be untruthful. The defence could, however, rely on s 101(3), or on the common law discretion, confirmed in *Sang (1980)*, to exclude prosecution evidence on the basis that its prejudicial effect outweighs it probative value.

It appears that if evidence of the earlier conviction is given, Hector will insist that it was wrongful. The ordinary rule, provided by s 74(3) of PACE, is that where it is proved that the accused has been convicted, he shall be taken to have committed the offence in question unless he proves the contrary. This raises the interesting possibility that the defendant might try to use the current trial to try to establish his contention in relation to the earlier conviction. Such an issue would clearly be collateral to the issue being tried, but to prevent the defendant from adducing evidence relating to matters considered at the earlier trial would turn the presumption contained in s 74(3) of PACE into a conclusive one for the purposes of the current trial, which, according to s 74(3), it is not.

A final argument for the admissibility of Hector's previous conviction would be based on s 101(1)(g) of the CJA 2003: by putting the blame on his twin brother in relation to count 2 he has made an attack on another person's character. Under the former law, a defendant was free to attack the character of persons who were not co-defendants, witnesses for the prosecution, or deceased victims of the alleged crime without having his own bad character revealed. But the reference in s 101(1)(g) to 'another person's character' seems wide enough to include anybody. If this argument is accepted, the defence could argue that the evidence should be excluded, either under s 101(3) or under the common law discretion.

In *Highton (2006)* the Court of Appeal held that where evidence of bad character was admitted under any of the gateways established by s 101(1), it was admissible for any purpose relevant to the case, and could therefore go to both credibility and propensity.

# Question 37

Steven, aged 18, has been charged with murder. The case for the prosecution is that on 3 May he raped and strangled Lynne, a classmate, after taking her in his car to an area known as Coppett's Wood where her body was afterwards found. Steven told the police that at Lynne's request he had given her a lift to a nearby railway station, had left her there, and had never seen her again. The prosecution have a statement from Jocelyne, another classmate of the accused. She said that she and Steven had made an arrangement to go bird watching on 3 May in Coppett's Wood. Jocelyne said that Steven had asked her to keep the arrangement secret. On the day in question, Jocelyne had changed her mind and had decided to go shopping with some other classmates instead. There is also police evidence that when they searched Steven's locker at school they found a collection of heterosexual pornographic magazines. Two weeks before the murder, Steven had been arrested for indecently exposing himself to two women in Coppett's Wood.

Advise the prosecution on the evidential issues that arise.

### Answer plan

This question requires consideration of three items of evidence:
- Jocelyne's statement. You need to discuss its relevance. Remember the need to determine what probative job the disputed evidence is expected to do.

# CHARACTER EVIDENCE I

> Note the discussion of the generalisation on which the prosecution would need to rely. *Rodley (1913)* is a useful case to bring in by way of illustration. Don't forget to reach a conclusion, with reasons, for admissibility or inadmissibility.
>
> - The magazines. Note the importance of the initial assumption that they had no special bearing on what had been done to Lynne. In practice, you would need to know the exact nature of these magazines, and you should indicate this to the examiner. Again, relevance is all important, and finding an appropriate generalisation which would establish this forms a significant part of the discussion.
> - Indecent exposure. You will have to consider the relevance of these events in relation to ss 101(1)(d) and 103(3) of **Criminal Justice Act (CJA) 2003**, and also in relation to the relevant guidelines in *Hanson (2005)*.
>
> The final paragraph is an important one. Thinking in general is 'not to be conceived to "form a chain which is no stronger than its weakest link"', but as 'a cable whose fibres may be ever so slender provided they are sufficiently numerous and intimately connected' (Peirce, CS, *Collected Papers* 5, p 265). Much defence advocacy works on the assumption that this is *not* the case.

# Answer

With regard to Jocelyne's statement, the main problem is one of relevance. Does the arrangement with Jocelyne tend to show that the accused was not telling the truth to the police about his encounter with Lynne? It might do so if it indicated that Steven had determined to take *some* girl, regardless of who it was, to Coppett's Wood that day for the purpose of sexual intercourse, to be obtained by force if necessary. It would then appear that when Jocelyne dropped out, Lynne was substituted as the victim.

It is useful to consider whether Jocelyne's statement would be thought to have significance if she had said nothing about a request for secrecy. Almost certainly it would not. But a person who asks another to keep an assignation secret usually does so because he does not wish others to know about it. One reason, but only one, why he might wish this is because he intends to do something unlawful, or at least improper, with his companion. But there might be innocent reasons for not wanting to be disturbed by others. Thus, if a bird watching exercise were planned, stillness and silence would be wanted.

On the assumption that Steven said nothing else to throw light on his request, the position would be that if Jocelyne were to testify, the jury would have before them a piece of evidence with very little probative value but which might easily mislead because of its tendency to invite speculation. Perhaps a similar problem arose in *Rodley (1913)*. The appellant was charged with housebreaking with intent to rape. The prosecution called evidence to show that he had entered a house by climbing down the chimney and had been met by the father of his supposed victim. The appellant said that he had indeed intended to have intercourse with the daughter, but only with her consent. The prosecution also called evidence to show that later that night he had climbed down the chimney of another house and had had consensual intercourse with a woman living there. It was held that this evidence should have been excluded. It proved nothing at all about the real issue of the appellant's willingness to commit rape. On the other hand, it certainly showed a lustful disposition which may well have prejudiced the appellant in the eyes of the jury.

So here, Jocelyne's testimony would prove nothing about Steven's willingness to commit rape and murder, but it might prejudice him because it would leave the jury guessing and without the means to advance beyond that stage to a reasoned conclusion. It is likely, therefore, that her evidence would be excluded.[1]

In considering the pornographic magazines, it is assumed that the pornography has no marked resemblance to what was done to Lynne. Apart from this, the finding of these magazines will be relevant if, and only if, an appropriate generalisation can be found about the way things are in the world that makes them so. We must discard at once something like 'Most persons who rape and murder girls take an interest in pornography'. (This generalisation will be referred to as 'G1'.) While it might be the case that most persons who rape and murder girls do in fact take an interest in pornography, it is not the case that most persons who take an interest in pornography rape and murder girls. If G1 is used to establish relevance, you attain it only by assuming the truth of the very thing that the pornography is meant to prove – that Steven is a rapist and murderer.

Might a more useful generalisation be that people who take an interest in pornography are more likely to rape and murder girls than those who do not ('G2')? In the first place, although this *may* be true, it is not obviously so, and if the prosecution is going to rely on its truth to establish guilt they must be prepared to adduce expert evidence on the matter, for it would almost certainly be challenged by the defence.

But, supposing that G2 can be established, what is the probative value of the discovery? It must be almost nothing. The police evidence will have put Steven in a class of persons who are more likely to rape and murder girls than those not in that class. However, that class will certainly be a large one, and the question in relation to any individual in it will be how much greater his membership makes the likelihood of his having raped and murdered a particular victim. The possession of pornography is unlikely to increase significantly the probability that Steven committed this crime. Unless there is a resemblance between what appears in the magazines and what was done to Lynne, its discovery, even if relevant, is likely to be far more prejudicial than probative, and it will be excluded, either under *Sang (1980)* or under s 78(1) of Police and Criminal Evidence Act (PACE) 1984.

The prosecution might wish to adduce evidence of the earlier incidents of indecent exposure. Again, relevance would seem to present difficulties. Is it the case that a man who indecently exposes himself to women is more likely than someone who does not do so to rape and murder a woman? It is far from obvious that this is so. If this evidence is regarded as relevant, it will certainly be evidence of Steven's bad character within ss 98 and 112(1) CJA 2003. But the guidelines in *Hanson (2005)* suggest that the evidence is unlikely to be admitted under s 101(1)(d). If they are held to be relevant, the judge will have decided that they tend to establish a propensity to commit offences of the kind charged, and circumstances demonstrating probative force are not confined to those sharing striking similarity with the incident that is the subject of the charge. But there is little, if any, similarity between the current offences and the earlier incidents, and this is something that a judge may take into consideration when considering the fairness of the proceedings and s 103(3). He may also take into account the respective gravity of the past and present offences. Further, it was said in *Hanson* that a judge must always consider the strength of the prosecution case. If there is no, or very little, other evidence against a defendant, which is the case here, it is unlikely to be just to admit previous convictions. On these facts, of course, there are as yet no convictions in respect of the earlier incidents, which Steven may well deny on the basis of mistaken identity.

In relation to all three items of evidence – Jocelyne's statement, the pornographic magazines, and whatever may be the evidence of indecent exposure – the prosecution might argue that all are items of circumstantial evidence and that they operate cumulatively. Like the strands in a cord, one might be insufficient to sustain the weight of the prosecution case, but three woven together may be of sufficient strength.[2] The answer to this is that circumstantial evidence must be evidence of relevant facts, and the objection in all three cases has been that the evidence in question is of irrelevant facts. Something that you have already decided to be irrelevant will not be made relevant by being added to something else that is irrelevant, although it is sometimes the case that what initially appears to be irrelevant may later be seen to be relevant in the light of some later discovery of relevant matter. Suppose, for example, that the magazines, contrary to the supposition in this answer, contained material that resembled what had been done to Lynne. They would then acquire more significance and would stand a greater chance of being considered relevant, and so admissible. The position would also change if it were discovered that Steven had no interest in bird watching, so that he would appear to have been lying to Jocelyne and to have had some hidden purpose in persuading her to accompany him to Coppett's Wood.

## References

1 Cf the Canadian case *Reference re R v Truscott (1967)*; Le Bordais, I, *The Trial of Steven Truscott*, 1966.
2 Cf Pollock *CB in Exall (1866)*.

# Chapter 9

# Character Evidence II

## INTRODUCTION

This chapter continues the topic begun in Chapter 8, and you are referred to the introduction to that chapter for the background to the new law on this subject. This chapter concentrates, though not exclusively, on the ways in which a defendant's bad character can emerge as a result of the way in which the defence is conducted.

### Checklist

Students should be familiar with the following areas:

- relevance;
- spent convictions;
- Part 11, Chapter 1 of the Criminal Justice Act 2003;
- *Sang* (1980).

# Question 38

Edna and Mavis are being tried in the Crown Court for theft. The case for the prosecution is that they are both guilty of shoplifting in the Ealing branch of Bromides, the well known chain of chemists. A store detective gives evidence and states that Edna and Mavis were together in the store. She says that Mavis was carrying a holdall and that she opened it to allow Edna to conceal in it a bottle of shampoo and a tin of talcum powder, the property of Bromides, for which neither defendant paid. Edna gives no evidence, but her counsel cross-examines the manager of the store, who is one of the prosecution witnesses, about a conviction which he had for indecent exposure when he was a student at university. Mavis gives evidence in her own defence and states that she was with Edna in the store, but was not herself involved in any shoplifting. She admits that when stopped outside the store she was carrying the holdall, but says that it belonged to Edna, who alone had been carrying it in the store. She said that Edna had given it to her to hold outside the store so that she, Edna, could more easily look for her season ticket, which she thought she had lost. Edna has a number of recent convictions for theft and for offences involving prostitution. Mavis has several recent convictions for theft. They all involved similar items stolen from other branches of Bromides.

Edna and Mavis are separately represented. Discuss the evidential issues that arise.

### Answer plan

The following points need to be considered:
- the effect of Edna's failure to give evidence;
- the legitimacy of the cross-examination of the manager;
- the effect of the cross-examination of the manager on Edna;
- the possible prosecution argument about Edna's previous convictions;
- the effect of Mavis's denial of the store detective's evidence about the holdall;
- the effect of Mavis's evidence on Edna;
- the possible prosecution argument about Mavis's previous convictions.

# Answer

Edna has chosen not to give evidence and the first question that arises concerns the extent to which comment can be made on this. By s 35(3) of the **Criminal Justice and Public Order Act 1994**, the court or jury, in determining whether the accused is guilty of the offence charged, may draw such inferences as appear proper from the failure of the accused to give evidence. Further, under the pre-1994 law, counsel for a co-defendant always had a right to comment on a defendant's failure to give evidence, and the judge had no discretion to prevent this (*Wickham (1971)*). The 1994 Act has not altered this. Thus, Edna's failure to testify is likely to be the subject of comment by both the judge and counsel for Mavis.

The Court of Appeal emphasised in *Napper (1996)* the general rule that it should be open to a jury to draw adverse inferences when a defendant fails to testify, and said that attempts to marginalise the section are contrary to the spirit of its provisions. The judge, in any direction under the section, must tell the jury that: (1) the defendant is entitled to remain silent; (2) an inference from silence cannot prove guilt on its own; and (3) they must be satisfied that there is a case to answer before drawing any inferences from silence. (The judge must have thought there was, or the case would have already been stopped. But the jury may not believe the witnesses whose evidence was considered by the judge to raise a *prima facie* case.) The judge must also tell the jury that if they conclude that the silence can only sensibly be attributed to the defendant's having no answer, or none that would stand up to cross-examination, they may draw an adverse inference. The effect of this appears to be that the jury must not draw such an inference unless sure that there is no other explanation, consistent with innocence, to account for it. However, the defence will not be able to suggest innocent reasons for the defendant's silence that are unsupported by evidence at trial (*Cowan (1996)*).

The cross-examination of the manager by Edna's counsel may well have been improper. If the conviction was spent, it should not have been referred to without leave of the judge, who should not have given leave unless he was satisfied that the interests of justice required that this matter be put. Further, cross-examination of the manager is now governed by provisions relating to the bad character of non-defendants in s 100 of the Criminal Justice Act (CJA) 2003. By sub-s (1), such evidence is admissible, if not agreed, if, and only if, it is important explanatory evidence, or has substantial probative value in relation to a matter which is in issue in the proceedings and is of substantial importance in the context of the case as a whole. Even then, the leave of the court is required by sub-s (4). On the facts, the conditions in s 100(1) are not satisfied, and the question should not have been put. Having put it, however, Edna is in the position of having made an attack on another person's character. Accordingly, evidence of her bad character is in principle admissible under s 101(1)(g) of the CJA 2003. The Court of Appeal held in *Highton (2006)* that wherever evidence of bad character is admitted, it is admissible for any purpose that is relevant in the case; the particular 'gateway' that allows admission does not affect this. Accordingly, evidence of Edna's previous convictions can go to propensity as well as credibility.

However, by s 101(3), such evidence must be excluded if it appears to the court that its admission would have such an adverse effect on the fairness of the proceedings that it ought not to be admitted. The onus is on the defendant to raise the issue. In determining whether evidence of Edna's previous convictions should be admitted, the court will take into account the prejudice likely to follow from disclosure of the convictions for prostitution, and these may be excluded. The recent convictions for theft are in a different category. It might be objected that these convictions are likely to prejudice Ellen because the jury will jump to the conclusion that if she has committed theft before, she is likely to have done so again. However, even under the pre-2003 law the fact that a defendant's previous convictions were for the same or similar offences to that being currently tried was not inevitably a bar to adducing them. And under the new law it would have been possible for the prosecution to argue that Edna's convictions for theft were admissible under s 101(1)(d), though it is difficult to predict the likelihood of success in such an application.

Mavis's evidence that she was carrying the holdall only outside the store contradicts the store detective's evidence, but this is not likely to be construed as an attack on the store detective's character under s 101(1)(g) because it is probably a matter about which the store detective could have made an honest mistake. However, Mavis's evidence is likely to have substantial probative value in relation to an important matter in issue between her and her co-defendant, Edna. It is not wholly clear what Edna's defence is, because she does not give evidence. But the evidence of Mavis clearly has the effect of placing the blame for any theft that took place on Edna. Edna will therefore be able to cross-examine Mavis about her previous convictions under s 101(1)(e) of the CJA 2003. There is no judicial discretion to exclude such cross-examination either under the Act or by virtue of the common law. The discretion confirmed in *Sang (1980)* applies only to prosecution evidence. Cross-examination of Mavis in these circumstances is very likely to be held relevant to guilt, not merely to credibility, and could therefore extend to the circumstances in which the earlier offences were committed.

It would have been open to the prosecution to rely on Mavis's previous convictions under s 101(1)(d). Section 103 expressly states that for the purposes of this provision, the matters in issue between the defendant and the prosecution include the question whether the defendant has a propensity to commit offences of the kind with which he is charged. Had the prosecution done so, it is unlikely, in view of the substantial similarity of the previous offences and the fact that they were recent, that a court, bearing in mind the guidelines in *Hanson (2005)*, would have excluded them under s 101(3) or 103(3).

If the court had disallowed a prosecution application to adduce evidence of Mavis's convictions, the question would then arise whether the jury would be entitled to consider them in relation to the prosecution case against Mavis as well as in relation to Edna's defence. The Court of Appeal is at present divided on problems of this kind. In *Price (2005)* and *B(C) (2004)* it was held that there was no need to warn a jury not to consider, when dealing with the prosecution case against D1, evidence of D1's bad character adduced by D2 rather than by the prosecution. But the contrary was held in *Mertens (2005)* and in *Murrell (2005)*. In *Robinson (Dennis) (2006)*, which was concerned with a similar situation, the Court of Appeal said that a direction should not needlessly perplex the jury, and certified a point of law of general public importance: where evidence of the propensity of D1 is a fact in issue between the prosecution and D2, but was not admissible against D1 on the prosecution's application, whether the judge should direct the jury that the evidence was inadmissible and to be ignored when considering the case of D1.

# Character Evidence II

# Question 39

Ian and Jason are both aged 26 and are charged with committing an act of gross indecency in a public place, the case for the prosecution being that they were seen engaging in fellatio on Hampstead Heath by PC Plod. Both plead not guilty. Ian wishes to call Katie as a defence witness. She is prepared to say that she has known Ian since they were at university together seven years ago, and that during that period she and Ian have had regular, normal sexual intercourse. Ian plays football most weekends and he also wishes to call Larry, a fellow member of his football club, to say that Ian is well known among members for his dislike of homosexuals. Ian has a letter from his local vicar which states that Ian has sung in the church choir for the last five years. The vicar also writes that from his knowledge of Ian he is sure the allegation must be false. Ian has no previous convictions of any kind, but Jason has two recent convictions for persistently importuning for immoral purposes.

(a) Discuss the evidential issues that arise in relation to admissibility.
(b) On the assumption that Ian and Jason both testify in their own defence, how should the judge direct the jury about their characters?

## Answer plan

The first part of this question requires you to consider what is admissible as evidence of good character. You should refer to the restriction imposed by *Rowton (1865)* and point out that the sort of evidence permitted in *Redgrave (1982)* is heard because of a concession only.

You should then consider generally the impact of Jason's previous convictions and conclude by referring to the ruling of the Court of Appeal in the case of *Vye (1993)*.

# Answer

The defence may call witnesses to testify as to the accused's good character. However, the right to adduce such evidence is restricted by the rule in *Rowton (1865)* that evidence of specific acts, or of the opinions of specific persons, is inadmissible to establish either good or bad character. In strictness, the only way in which character evidence can be given is by getting a witness to speak of the reputation of the accused among those who know him. In practice, this rule tends to be loosely applied.

However, so far as Katie's evidence is concerned, the court would have to take into account the decision of the Court of Appeal in *Redgrave (1982)*. In that case, the appellant had been charged with persistently importuning for immoral purposes in a public lavatory. The trial judge refused to allow him to call evidence of his relationships with a number of girlfriends which would, the defence hoped, establish that the accused had heterosexual rather than homosexual inclinations. The Court of Appeal acknowledged that in that sort of case, indulgence was sometimes shown to accused persons, but said that it was only an indulgence and not a right. Failure to extend it to any particular defendant could not form the basis of a successful appeal.

Lawton LJ said that the court was not trying to stop defence counsel from putting questions designed to show that the accused was happily married and had a normal sexual relationship with his wife. He went on to suggest that evidence of a sexual relationship with one woman, even though she was not married to the defendant, might be unobjectionable. But he emphasised that questions on such matters could be asked only with the indulgence of the court. Katie's evidence will not, therefore, be heard as of right, but only with the goodwill of the judge. It should be added that it is not clear on the facts that the relationship with Katie has the substantial quality that Lawton LJ seems to presuppose. If, when the facts were more fully investigated, it turned out, for example, that she was merely one regular sexual partner among several and that Ian had no special emotional ties to her, it is doubtful whether her evidence would be admitted.

By contrast, Larry's evidence does appear to be evidence of reputation and so is admissible under the rule in *Rowton*.

It seems clear that the evidence of the vicar, even if he were willing to attend court and give oral testimony, would be inadmissible under *Rowton (1865)*. The fact that Ian sings in the church choir is today likely to be thought irrelevant to any question of character. In any case, testimony to this effect would not be testimony of Ian's reputation. The vicar's own opinion of Ian's innocence would certainly not be admitted.

Ian's counsel will, of course, be able to bring out the fact that his client is of previous good character in the sense of having no previous convictions recorded against him.

A zealous prosecutor might argue that Jason's previous convictions are admissible under s 101(1)(d) of the CJA 2003 and in the light of the guidelines in *Hanson (2005)*. It could be argued that the evidence is relevant because a man with such convictions is more likely to have a sexual encounter with another man in a public place than a man without such convictions. In reply, it could be argued that even if the evidence is admissible, it ought to be excluded under s 101(3) because of the prejudice that would be caused to Ian; his guilt could be seen as more likely if his co-defendant's history is revealed. If Jason pleaded not guilty and gave evidence in his defence on the earlier occasions, the prosecution could also argue that his convictions are admissible as being relevant to the question whether he has a propensity to be untruthful. The same argument for exclusion of the convictions under s 101(3) would apply.

Rules for the proper direction of the jury where good character is relevant were laid down by Lord Taylor CJ in the judgment of the Court of Appeal in the case of *Vye (1993)*. They are as follows:

- A direction as to the relevance of good character to a defendant's credibility should be given where he has testified or made pre-trial answers or statements. Such a direction will clearly be appropriate in Ian's case, assuming that he testifies or has at least made some admissible pre-trial statement.
- A direction as to the relevance of good character to the likelihood of the defendant's having committed the offence charged is to be given, regardless of whether he has testified or made any pre-trial answers or statements. Again, such a direction will obviously be appropriate in Ian's case.
- Where there are two defendants, one of good character and the other not, the first two principles still apply. The trial judge should either say nothing at all about the character of the defendant with previous convictions, or he should direct the jury that they have heard nothing about this and should not speculate.

Ian's position is therefore unaffected by the fact that Jason has previous convictions.

# Question 40

Alex and Bess are charged with the robbery of Philip. Philip testifies that he was attacked in a car park one evening by Alex and Bess, one of whom grabbed a gold watch from his wrist. Alex, wearing the uniform of a security company, testifies in his defence that Philip attacked him and Bess without warning, and that he hit back to defend himself and Bess. He says that the strap of Philip's watch probably broke in the struggle and denies stealing it. Bess gives no evidence. Alex has one recent conviction for robbery of a man whom he attacked in a car park. Bess has no previous convictions.

Discuss the evidential issues arising.

## Answer plan

You should deal with the defendants separately. In relation to Alex, you need to consider whether evidence of his previous conviction can be given, either under s 101(1)(f) or 101(1)(g). You should also mention the possibility of an application under s 101(1)(d). Don't forget to deal with arguments for exclusion as well, and remember that you may have to consider how far the evidence of the previous conviction can go. In this connection you have to consider the evidential value of the conviction. Is it relevant to credibility and to guilt, or only to credibility?

When you deal with Bess's failure to testify, remember to set out at least the most important directions, based on *Cowan (1996)*, that have to be given. How much of the *Vye* direction will it be proper to give?

# Answer

There appear to be several opportunities for cross-examination of Alex under Part 11, Chapter 1 of the Criminal Justice Act (CJA) 2003. First, it may be argued that he has given evidence of his own good character, either by his testimony that he hit back to defend himself *and Bess*, or by appearing in the witness box in the uniform of a security company.

On this basis the prosecution could submit that evidence of his bad character (the recent conviction for robbery) should be given under s 101(1)(f) to correct a false impression given by Alex. By s 105(1), a defendant gives a false impression if he is responsible for the making of an express or implied assertion which is apt to give the court or jury a false or misleading impression about the defendant. Section 105(2) lists the circumstances in which a defendant is to be treated as being responsible for an assertion. An obvious instance is where the assertion is made by the defendant while giving evidence in the proceedings: see s 105(2)(a).

A problem may occur where a defendant gives evidence as a necessary part of his defence that incidentally has the effect of showing good character. The same problem arose under s 1(f)(ii) of the Criminal Evidence Act 1898, which allowed cross-examination of a defendant about previous convictions where he had given evidence of his good character. The provision was held to apply only where the defendant went beyond what was necessary to meet the prosecution case about the facts in issue.

For example, in *Malindi v R (1967)*, the defendant was charged with conspiracy involving the use of violence against property. He gave evidence that at a meeting in his house at which violence was discussed, and which the prosecution relied on as part of its case, he had disapproved of violent action and advised against it. It was held by the Privy Council that this should not have brought s 1(f)(ii) into play: the defendant had restricted his evidence to his own account of an incident relied on by the prosecution. He had not asserted his own good character as an independent reason for making it unlikely that he had done what the prosecution alleged.

On this basis, Alex's evidence that he hit back to defend Bess, as well as himself, will not amount to giving evidence of his own good character. However, it may be that his wearing the security company's uniform would be so regarded. because it suggests that his employers regard him as a person of integrity. Section 101(1)(f) makes it clear that an assertion in this context can be implied, and this is confirmed by s 105(4), which includes false impressions given by conduct other than the giving of evidence. By sub-s (5), 'conduct' includes appearance or dress. The legitimacy of the conduct need not be challenged. It is the claim to good character associated, rightly or not, with certain occupations at which sub-s (4) and (5) are aimed.

By s 105(3), a defendant may withdraw an assertion, but this may not be easy on the facts. If he does not, the defence might argue that the judge should exercise his discretion to exclude evidence of the previous conviction, either under s 78(1) of the **Police and Criminal Evidence Act 1984 (PACE)** or under the common law confirmed in *Sang*.

If the judge allows cross-examination about the conviction, can questions extend to the similarities with the present charge? Cross-examination under s 1(f)(ii) of the 1898 Act was relevant only to credibility, not to guilt. But this distinction was condemned by the Law Commission as unworkable in many cases. It was held by the Court of Appeal in *Highton (2006)* that whenever evidence of bad character is admitted, it is admitted for any purpose that is relevant to the case. The particular 'gateway' that allows the evidence to be admitted does not affect the use made of it. Once admitted under s 101(1)(f) of CJA 2003, the evidence of Alex's previous conviction for robbery can be used to assess his guilt as well as his credibility.

In *Hanson (2005)* the Court of Appeal said that there is no minimum number of events necessary to demonstrate propensity, but that a single previous conviction for an offence of the same description or category will often not show propensity. It may do so, however, where it shows a tendency to unusual behaviour, or where its circumstances demonstrate probative force in relation to the offence charged. Circumstances demonstrating probative force are not confined to those showing striking similarity. It is possible, therefore, that an application under s 101(1)(d) would be successful, bearing in mind the recent date of the previous conviction, and the fact that the robbery to which that related also took place in a car park.

Alex's suggestion that the watch strap broke in the struggle does not, in itself, suggest that Philip was lying, as opposed to merely being mistaken in his testimony, and alone would not bring section 101(1)(g) into play. But the evidence that Philip was the aggressor clearly amounts to an attack on his character and would let in Alex's previous conviction, unless excluded by s 101(3) or the common law discretion.

It remains possible that the prosecution might argue that evidence of the conviction is admissible under s 101(1)(d), especially in view of its potential to rebut the defence that Alex was defending himself and Ben from an attack by Philip.

As Bess gives no evidence, the judge will instruct the jury that they may, in determining whether the prosecution has proved its case, draw such inferences as appear proper from her failure to testify. However, the directions based on *Cowan (1996)* will have to be given. In particular, the judge must tell the jury that the defendant is entitled to remain silent; that an inference from silence cannot be the sole or main basis for convicting; and that the jury must be satisfied that there is a *prima facie* case to answer before drawing any inferences.

Assuming that Bess said nothing outside court that was evidence of the truth of its contents, the only limb of the *Vye* direction required (on the significance of her good character) will be that relating to the likelihood of her guilt.

# Question 41

Callum and Daniel are charged with the robbery of Ethan. Ethan testifies that he was attacked in a public park one afternoon by three men, two of whom were Callum and Daniel. The third man got away and was never caught. He says that one of the three men stole his wallet. Callum gives evidence in his defence to the effect that he and Daniel had been joined in the park that day by a third man, whom they did not know. He says that Ethan, who was drunk, attacked all three of them, and that he hit back to defend himself and Daniel. He denies stealing Ethan's wallet, and says that it probably fell from Ethan's pocket in the struggle. Daniel subsequently testifies in his defence that he had stopped to rest some distance behind Callum and the third man and did not see what happened when they met Ethan. When Daniel was interviewed by the police he said that he alone had robbed Ethan. But the trial judge refused to allow the prosecution to adduce this in evidence because it had been made in response to a promise by the police that Daniel would get bail if he confessed. Callum has several previous convictions for robbery. Daniel has previous convictions for indecently assaulting another man and for committing an act of gross indecency in a bus shelter.

Discuss the evidential issues arising.

# Character Evidence II

> ## Answer plan
>
> The best approach is to take each defendant separately and consider the arguments that the prosecution and the co-defendant might wish to use to reveal his previous convictions. These can be summarised as follows:
>
> | *Callum* | | *Daniel* | |
> |---|---|---|---|
> | Prosecution: | s 101(1)(d) | Prosecution: | s 101(1)(d) |
> | | s 101(1)(g) | Callum: | s 101(1)(e) |
> | Daniel: | s 101(1)(e) | | |
>
> In addition, you need to consider whether Callum can adduce evidence of Daniel's confession even though it is not open to the prosecution to do so.

# Answer

The first question is whether the prosecution can adduce evidence under s 101(1)(d) of the Criminal Justice Act (CJA) 2003 of Callum's previous convictions as part of the case against him. By s 103(1)(a), the matters in issue between defendant and prosecution include the question whether the defendant has a propensity to commit offences of the kind with which he is charged, except where having such a propensity makes it no more likely that he is guilty of the offence. By s 103(2), the propensity can be established by evidence that the defendant has been convicted of an offence of the same description as the one with which he is charged. There are no details of idiosyncratic features of Callum's previous robberies, and the question therefore arises whether propensity to commit a commonplace offence in a commonplace way makes it more likely that Callum is guilty on this particular occasion. On one view it does, because the propensity adds weight to Ethan's evidence against him. If this submission is upheld, the defence could argue that evidence of the convictions ought nevertheless to be excluded, either under s 101(3) or under the common law discretion, which *Sang (1980)* confirmed, to exclude prosecution evidence where the probative worth is outweighed by prejudicial effect. An important factor might be whether his convictions are recent or are spent under the Rehabilitation of Offenders Act 1974.

The previous convictions might also be relevant to Callum's propensity to be untruthful, which, by s 103(1)(b), is capable of being a matter in issue between prosecution and defendant. Although the Explanatory Notes issued with the CJA 2003 suggest that only a limited range of convictions, such as convictions for perjury or other offences involving deception, will be relevant to such a propensity, it is doubtful whether s 103(1)(b) can be limited in this way. There seems to be nothing to prevent the prosecution from adducing evidence that a defendant has been found guilty of offences in the past, in relation to which he pleaded not guilty and gave evidence in his defence. Such evidence is likely to be particularly weighty where the defence unsuccessfully raised on an earlier occasion is of the same nature as the one raised in the current trial. Whether reliance is placed on s 103(1)(a) or (b) or both, the court would take into account the relevant guidelines in *Hanson (2005)*. These would include the 'starting point': Parliament's purpose in the legislation was 'to assist evidence-based conviction of the guilty, without putting those who are not guilty at risk of conviction by prejudice.' The age of a previous conviction may be a relevant consideration in deciding whether to admit it. An important factor might therefore be whether Callum's previous convictions are recent, or spent under the Rehabilitation of Offenders Act 1974. If evidence of Callum's bad character is given, the judge in summing up should make these points to the jury:

(i) they should not place undue reliance on previous convictions. In particular, they should not conclude that the defendant has been untruthful or has committed the offence with which he has been charged merely because he has these convictions;
(ii) whether the convictions do in fact show propensity is for them to decide;
(iii) if they do find propensity, they are entitled to take this into account when determining guilt. But it is only one relevant factor, and they assess its significance in the light of all the other evidence in the case.

Another prosecution argument would be that Callum has made an attack on Ethan's character by saying that he was drunk and attacked Callum and his companions. The fact that this is a necessary part of his defence is unlikely to prevent the operation of s 101(1)(g). Even under the Criminal Evidence Act 1898 that would not have been a reason for excluding cross-examination under s 1(f)(ii), as the House of Lords decided in *Selvey v DPP (1970)*. If s 101(1)(g) is held to apply in principle, the defence arguments for exclusion will be the same as those available in relation to s101(1)(d). In *Hanson (2005)* it was said that pre-2003 authorities on what constitutes an attack on another person's character will apply to the extent that they are not incompatible with s 106, which contains provisions supplementing s 101(1)(g).

Daniel may be able to cross-examine Callum about his previous convictions on the strength of s 101(1)(e), on the basis that Callum's bad character has substantial probative value in relation to an important matter in issue between co-defendants. If this test is satisfied, the court has no power to exclude the evidence. Daniel would argue that s 101(1)(e) applies because Callum's evidence contradicts Daniel's case that he was some distance from the incident with Ethan and did not see what happened. On one view, Callum has simply provided the jury with another reason to acquit Daniel, so the matter in issue between the two defendants is not important. But under the former law, a line of authority based on *Crawford (1998)* supported the view that one defendant could give evidence against another for the purposes of s 1(f)(iii) where his testimony varied from that of his co-defendant so as to undermine the co-defendant's credibility, thus making the prosecution case against him more likely to be true. Section 104 CJA 2003, which supplements s 101(1)(e), says that evidence of bad character is admissible only if the nature or conduct of the defence is such as to undermine a co-defendant's defence. It is certainly possible that in interpreting s 101(1)(e) the court will follow the *Crawford* approach. If evidence of Callum's bad character is admitted only under s 101(1)(e), and not under s 101(1)(d), it is unclear whether the jury should be told to take it into account only when considering Daniel's defence, and not when considering the prosecution case against Callum. The Court of Appeal is at present divided on problems of this kind. In *Price (2005)* and *B(C) (2004)* it was held that there was no need to warn a jury not to consider, when dealing with the prosecution case against D1, evidence of D1's bad character adduced by D2 rather than by the prosecution. But the contrary was held in *Mertens (2005)* and in *Murrell (2005)*. In *Robinson (Dennis) (2006)*, which was concerned with a similar situation, the Court of Appeal said that a direction should not needlessly perplex the jury, and certified a point of law of general public importance: where evidence of the propensity of D1 is a fact in issue between the prosecution and D2, but was not admissible against D1 on the prosecution's application, whether the judge should direct the jury that the evidence was inadmissible and to be ignored when considering the case of D1.

Daniel's previous convictions show no propensity to commit robbery, and their admissibility under s 101(1)(d) could be justified only on the basis that they might show a propensity to untruthfulness. Even this is not very likely; someone who has been untruthful about his sexual activity could be entirely reliable where other matters are concerned. If the condition in s 101(1)(d) were found to be satisfied, the likelihood of exclusion under s 101(3) or under the common law discretion would be substantial in view of the possible moral prejudice against Daniel when the nature of his previous convictions is revealed.

Callum might wish to adduce evidence of Daniel's previous convictions under s 101(1)(e) on the basis of the discrepancy between Daniel's evidence and his own. But Daniel's convictions could be relevant only to his credibility. Although at common law any kind of offence was relevant to credibility, the common law rules governing admissibility have been abolished by s 99(1) of the CJA 2003, and the nature of Daniel's convictions is unlikely to be considered to have any bearing on his credibility. The point has already been made that even if he pleaded not guilty and gave evidence at the earlier trials, that is unlikely to have any bearing on his credibility in very different circumstances. While a judge has no *discretion* to exclude evidence of bad character that is admissible under s 101(1)(e), he would have a *duty* to exclude it if he was not satisfied of its relevance.[1]

### Reference

1 Cf *Gadsby (2006)*.

The final question that arises is whether Callum can adduce evidence of Daniel's confession. The relevant law is contained in s 76A(1) of the **Police and Criminal Evidence Act 1984 (PACE)**, which provides in effect that where one defendant proposes to adduce evidence of a co-defendant's confession, the rules about admissibility are the same as those applying to the prosecution, save for the standard of proof. Callum is unlikely to be able to prove on the balance of probabilities that Daniel's confession was not obtained in consequence of anything said or done which was likely, in the circumstances existing at the time, to render unreliable any confession that might be made by him in consequence thereof. Accordingly, he will not be able to adduce evidence of Daniel's confession.

# Question 42

Liza, Mabel and Nellie are charged with committing burglary in a block of flats. Liza chooses not to give evidence in her own defence, but her counsel in cross-examination puts to one of the prosecution witnesses that her evidence against Liza is concocted out of spite because Liza has been having an affair with the witness's husband. Liza has three recent convictions for burglary.

Mabel gives evidence in her own defence and claims to have been elsewhere at the time the burglary was committed. When prosecuting counsel puts it to her in cross-examination that this is a lie, Mabel bursts into tears and shouts, 'I'm an honest woman! I've never told a lie in my life!'. Last year, Mabel was convicted of obtaining property by deception and of assisting in the management of a brothel.

Nellie gives evidence in her own defence. She admits having entered the building and climbed the stairs, but says that she did so because she loves animals and wanted to rescue a kitten which she had seen stranded on a window ledge. Nellie has two spent convictions for burglary.

Discuss the evidential issues that arise.

# Character Evidence II

> ## Answer plan
>
> It does not appear that any of the defendants has undermined another's defence. So, dealing with each defendant separately, the following points should be considered:
>
> *Liza*
>
> s 35 CJPOA 1994
> s 101(1)(d) CJA 2003
> s 101(1)(g) CJA 2003
>
> *Mabel*
>
> s 101(1)(d) CJA 2003
> s 101(1)(f) CJA 2003
>
> *Nellie*
>
> s 101(1)(d) CJA 2003
> s 101(1)(f) CJA 2003

# Answer

Liza's failure to give evidence is likely to bring into operation s 35(3) of the Criminal Justice and Public Order Act 1994. Under this provision the court or jury, in determining whether the accused is guilty of the offence charged, may draw such inferences as appear proper from the failure of the accused to give evidence. In any direction under s 35 the judge must follow the guidelines based on *Cowan (1996)*. He must tell the jury that the defendant is entitled to remain silent; an inference from silence cannot be the sole or main basis for a conviction; and the jury must be satisfied that there is a case to answer before drawing any inferences from silence. The judge must also tell the jury that they may draw an adverse inference only if they conclude that silence can only sensibly be attributed to the defendant's having no answer to the charge, or none that would stand up to cross-examination. However, the defence cannot suggest reasons for silence that are unsupported by evidence.

The prosecution could argue that evidence of Liza's previous convictions should be admitted under s 101(1)(d) as showing a propensity to commit burglary, and perhaps also a propensity to be untruthful if in any of the earlier cases she pleaded not guilty and gave evidence in her own defence. Although Liza gave no evidence on this occasion, a propensity for untruthfulness could still be relevant in light of the allegation made on her behalf against a prosecution witness. It would be open to the defence to argue, under s 101(3), that the admission of this evidence would have such an adverse effect on the fairness of the proceedings that the court ought not to admit it. Alternatively, reliance might be placed on s 103(3). However, such arguments would be likely to fail, as it is a recent history of convictions for the same offence, and, presumably, the prosecution has other cogent evidence to support its case against Liza. In the absence of other evidence, or if there were only weak evidence, the defence, relying on the *Hanson (2005)* guidelines, could argue that the judge has a duty to consider the strength of the prosecution case and, if there is no, or very little, other evidence against a defendant, it is unlikely to be just to admit previous convictions, whatever they are.

Through her counsel, Liza has made an attack on another person's character by suggesting that a prosecution witness's evidence has been concocted out of spite. Evidence of her bad character is therefore admissible in principle under s 101(1)(g) and s 106(1)(b) of the **Criminal Justice Act (CJA) 2003**. The Court of Appeal held in *Highton (2006)* that, if admitted through this 'gateway', the evidence would be relevant to propensity as well as credibility. It would be open to the defence to argue for exclusion under s 101(3).

Could the prosecution adduce evidence of Mabel's previous convictions under s 101(1)(d)? Neither offence is of the same kind as the current offence. The offence of obtaining property by deception almost certainly involved the telling of lies, so this would be admissible in principle to show a propensity to be untruthful, regardless of her plea or whether she gave evidence on that occasion. If she pleaded not guilty to the other offence and gave evidence in her defence that the jury must have disbelieved, those facts also would show a propensity to be untruthful. But in view of the availability of the conviction for deception, and the moral prejudice that might attach to a conviction for assisting in the management of a brothel, a defence argument that this conviction should be excluded, either under s 101(3) or s 103(3) might be successful.

In Mabel's case the question also arises whether evidence of her convictions can be adduced under s 101(1)(f) in order to correct the false impression given when she said that she was an honest woman who had never told a lie. Her best course would be to withdraw the claim, which appears to have been made in the heat of the moment. If she does so, by s 105(3) she will not be treated as responsible for the assertion. If she fails to withdraw, it would be open to her counsel to argue that the evidence of her convictions should be excluded on the basis of the common law discretion confirmed in *Sang (1980)*. At this stage the judge might distinguish between the two convictions and exclude the one for assisting in the management of a brothel because of the moral prejudice to which it might give rise. Arguably, s 78(1) of the Police and Criminal Evidence Act 1984 (PACE) would also be available, but a doubt is created by s 101(3), which confines the s 78 test built into s 101(3) to sub-ss (1)(d) and (1)(g). Further, by s 105(6), evidence is admissible under s 101(1)(f) only if it goes no further than is necessary to correct the false impression. Almost certainly, the conviction for obtaining property by deception would be regarded as sufficient for this purpose. As with 'gateway' (g), evidence of bad character admitted under s 101(1)(f) can be relevant to both credibility and propensity (*Highton, 2006*).

Can Nellie's spent convictions for burglary be admitted under s 101(1)(d)? Depending on whether she gave evidence in her own defence on those occasions, the evidence could fall within s 103(1)(a) and (b). True, both the convictions are spent, and this would invite argument for exclusion under s 101(3) or s 103(3). It was said in *Hanson (2005)* that the age of a previous conviction may be a relevant consideration in deciding whether to admit it, but, as one of the consolidated appeals in *Hanson* showed, this will not be a conclusive argument.

It is unlikely that evidence of Nellie's spent convictions can be given under s 101(1)(f). She has almost certainly not created a false impression by saying that she is an animal lover, for there is no reason why an animal lover should not be criminally inclined. Her explanation that she wanted to rescue the kitten is necessary to account for her presence of the premises. Even if that shows her character in a good light, it does so only incidentally and should not bring s 101(1)(f) into operation if the reasoning adopted under the Criminal Evidence Act 1898 is followed. In *Malindi v R (1967)*, the defendant, charged with conspiracy to use violence against property, testified that he had been present at a meeting during which violence had been discussed, but had disapproved and had advised against it. The Privy Council held that this had not brought s 1(f)(ii) of the 1898 Act into operation because it did not amount to an independent assertion of good character.

# Question 43

Oscar is charged with burglary of Penelope's flat. He gives evidence in his defence and admits being in the flat on the day when the burglary took place. But he says he was there because Penelope had given him a key as they were lovers, and he had called in that evening on his way home in the hope of having sexual intercourse with her. In cross-examination, it is put to him by the prosecution that he entered by a window, not the door. Oscar replies: 'Anyone who says that is a liar.' Oscar has three previous convictions for obtaining property by deception.

Discuss the evidential issues that arise.

## Answer plan

You have to consider the various arguments that could be put forward to admit or exclude evidence of Oscar's previous convictions. Note that the facts do not reveal whether or not they are spent. Take arguments under s 101(1)(d) first, remembering s 103(1)(b). Then consider s 101(1)(g). Note that there are two aspects to this: whether Oscar has attacked Penelope's character, and the significance, if any, of what Oscar has said during cross-examination.

# Answer

On what basis, if any, can the prosecution adduce evidence of Oscar's previous convictions? One approach would be to rely on s 101(1)(d) of the Criminal Justice Act (CJA) 2003, arguing that evidence of the convictions is relevant to two important matters in issue between he defendant and the prosecution: first, the question whether the defendant has a propensity to commit offences of the kind with which he is charged; secondly, whether he has a propensity to be untruthful.

By s 103(2), a defendant's propensity to commit offences of the kind with which he is charged may be established by evidence that he has been convicted of an offence of the same category as the one with which he is charged. Categories of offences can be prescribed by order of the Secretary of State under s 103(4)(b). But by sub-s (5), a category prescribed by order must consist of offences of the same type. Obtaining property by deception is not in the theft category prescribed by the Criminal Justice Act 2003 (Categories of Offences) Order 2004.[1]

However, the defendant has given evidence, and the prosecution may wish to establish a propensity to be untruthful under s 103(1)(b). Convictions for offences of obtaining property by deception could be used for this purpose according to the Explanatory Notes issued with CJA 2003. However, we do not know whether the convictions are spent. The defence might want to rely on s 103(3) to argue that because of the length of time that has passed, it would be unjust to rely on them. Curiously, sub-s (3) applies only to evidence of a defendant's propensity to commit offences of the kind with which he is charged. But the defence could still rely on s 101(3) and on the common law discretion, confirmed by *Sang (1980)*, to exclude prosecution evidence where the probative worth is outweighed by prejudicial effect.

Another argument for admitting the convictions could be based on s 101(1)(g), relying on the fact that the defendant has made an attack on another person's character. By s 106(2), evidence attacking another person's character includes evidence to the effect that the other person has behaved in a reprehensible way. Potentially this creates a problem on these facts. Is it reprehensible for a woman to have a sexual relationship with a person to whom she is not married? Do the personal circumstances and beliefs of Penelope have to be taken into account when deciding if Oscar's allegation is one of reprehensible behaviour? Probably these awkward questions can be avoided by arguing, if Penny denies the relationship, that the allegation necessarily implies that Penelope's evidence is deliberately false. It was established in *Britzman (1983)*, for the purposes of the 1898 Act, that a defendant could make an imputation on a prosecution witness, and so expose himself to cross-examination about his own previous convictions, if what was alleged amounted in effect to an allegation of perjury. It is inconceivable that Penelope could have made an honest mistake by denying her affair with Oscar. His allegation would therefore amount to one of perjury, and so be an attack on Penelope for the purposes of s 101(1)(g). Again, the defence could argue for exclusion under s 101(3). Following the *Hanson* guidelines, as in all cases where evidence of previous convictions is admitted, the judge in summing up should make these points to the jury:

(i) they should not place undue reliance on previous convictions. In particular, they should not conclude that the defendant has been untruthful or has committed the offence with which he has been charged merely because he has these convictions;
(ii) whether the convictions do in fact show propensity is for them to decide;
(iii) if they do find propensity, they are entitled to take this into account when determining guilt. But it is only one relevant factor, and they assess its significance in the light of all the other evidence in the case.

The prosecution might also rely on Oscar's answer in cross-examination to the effect that anyone who says he entered Penelope's flat by a window is a liar. However, it is not clear that in saying this he has attacked another person's character. Unless there is a witness who has given evidence to this effect, the expression seems to amount to no more than a strong denial. Certainly under the 1898 Act a distinction was drawn between using words such as 'lying' or 'liar' simply as strong denials, and using the words to allege perjury. For example, in *Desmond (1999)* a prosecution witness gave an account of events that differed significantly from that in his witness statement and, in doing so, implicated the defendant further. Defence counsel in cross-examination suggested to him that he was lying under oath, but the Court of Appeal held this to be no more than an emphatic denial of the charge.

## Reference

1  SI 3346, Sched Pt 1.

# CHAPTER 10

# THE COURSE OF TESTIMONY

## INTRODUCTION

You are likely to find the sort of problems in this chapter inserted as part of questions dealing with more central topics such as hearsay or character evidence. Another favourite of examiners is a question about a charge of rape, where points on recent complaints can arise as well as on the complexities of ss 41–43 of the Youth Justice and Criminal Evidence Act 1999. It is well worth studying these sections carefully, together with the cases that have been decided about the restrictions they impose on the conduct of the defence.

Most topics concerning the course of testimony are well explained in textbooks, but a warning is needed about the finality of answers to collateral questions. The rule is sometimes expressed in this way, and sometimes by saying that when a witness in cross-examination answers questions on collateral matters, his answers are conclusive. There is quite a common misunderstanding that the effect of this is that once counsel in cross-examination gets a denial of the collateral matter that is being put, he may ask no further questions about it. This is not the case. Counsel may continue to question the witness about the collateral matter if he thinks he is likely to obtain any advantage in doing so. What he cannot do is call evidence in rebuttal if the witness persists in his denial. It is only in this sense that the witness's answers are 'final' or 'conclusive'.

You should note that, by ss 119 and 120 of the Criminal Justice Act (CJA) 2003, where evidence of a witness's previous consistent or inconsistent statement is admitted, it is evidence of any matter stated of which oral evidence by the witness would be admissible. It is no longer relevant to credibility alone, as was the case before the new legislation. Note also the circumstances, set out in s 120, in which evidence of previous consistent statements is now admissible. An important change in the law extends the 'recent complaint' exception, formerly applicable only where the charge related to a sexual offence, to all offences where the person making the complaint is a person against whom the offence has been committed. Further, it is now irrelevant, so far as admissibility is concerned, that the recent complaint was elicited, eg, by a leading question, unless a threat or a promise was involved: see s 120(8).

## Checklist

Students should be familiar with the following areas:
- refreshing memory;
- unfavourable and hostile witnesses;
- previous consistent statements;
- cross-examination of the parties as to credit;
- *Edwards (1991)* and subsequent decisions;
- ss 41–43 of the Youth Justice and Criminal Evidence Act 1999 and *A (2001)*;
- previous inconsistent statements;
- finality of answers to collateral questions.

# Question 44

Len is being prosecuted for assaulting Mick, who had identified Len to the police in a nearby street shortly after the attack and subsequently on an identification parade. At his trial, Len claims that he has been wrongly identified. Mick has a recent conviction for handling stolen goods.

(a) Mick identifies Len in court as the person who attacked him. May he also give evidence of his previous identifications of Len in the street and in the identification parade?

(b) Len tells his counsel that Mick is a heavy drinker and that he can produce a witness, Olive, who will support this and who can say that she saw Mick drinking whisky in a public house on the evening when Mick alleged that he was assaulted by Len, but at a time before the alleged attack took place. In cross-examination, Mick denies being a heavy drinker and says that he had nothing at all to drink that evening. May Len's counsel call Olive to rebut these denials?

(c) Len also tells his counsel that a month before the alleged assault, he had quarrelled with Mick about a woman and Mick had threatened that he would 'get even' with Len some day. Len says that his cousin Percy was present at the time and can confirm this. What use, if any, can Len's counsel make of this information?

(d) Should Len's counsel put Mick's previous conviction to him? If he does so, and Mick denies it, what is likely to happen?

THE COURSE OF TESTIMONY

> **Answer plan**
>
> The question raises the following points:
> - evidence of previous identification;
> - whether the evidence about Mick's drinking is collateral to the main issue;
> - the rule concerning the finality of answers on collateral matters and the exceptions to it;
> - cross-examination of prosecution witnesses as to character.

# Answer

(a) Despite the general rule which excludes evidence of previous consistent statements (see *Roberts (1942)*), evidence of an earlier identification was admissible at common law to show that the witness was able to identify the accused at the time and to exclude the idea that any later identification in court was an afterthought or a mistake (*Christie (1914)*). The current law is contained in s 120(4) and (5). Mick can give evidence of his earlier identifications of Len, provided he indicates that to the best of his belief he made the earlier statements establishing identification, and that to the best of his belief they stated the truth.

(b) The purpose of establishing that Mick is a heavy drinker and that he had been drinking before the attack is to suggest that his identification of Len could well have been wrong as his faculties were impaired, at least to some extent, by the alcohol that he had consumed. The identification is the central issue in the case and questions designed to show that it might have been impaired by alcohol will therefore not be regarded as dealing with collateral matters. Olive can be called to rebut Mick's denial that he had had anything to drink that evening. She may also give evidence of his heavy drinking if that is a matter within her own knowledge, or of his reputation as a heavy drinker under the rule in *Rowton (1865)*. The question whether Mick is a heavy drinker is probably not a collateral matter. If true, it tends to make it more probable that he was drinking on the evening in question, and also that he drank enough to impair his ordinary powers to make an accurate identification.

(c) The quarrel with Mick is a collateral matter, but if Mick denies that it took place or that he threatened Len on that occasion, evidence may nevertheless be called in rebuttal because the effect of such evidence will be to show bias on the part of Mick against Len. Facts showing that a witness is biased against a party may be elicited in cross-examination and if they are denied, rebutting evidence can be called. Thus, in *Shaw (1888)*, evidence was held admissible to show that on a previous occasion a witness had threatened the defendant (see also *Phillips (1936)*). Both Len and Percy can therefore be called to give an account of the incident during which Mick threatened Len.

(d) Two matters have to be taken into account when deciding whether to put this conviction to Mick. The first is whether evidence of Mick's bad character is admissible under s 100 of the **Criminal Justice Act (CJA) 2003**, which relates to the bad character of non-defendants. It is possible that the prosecution will take the view that Mick's conviction should be revealed during examination-in-chief. It is for an offence of dishonesty, which could bear on his credibility as a witness, especially if he had pleaded not guilty and given evidence in his defence. If this view is not taken, the defence will have to convince the judge either that the evidence of the conviction is important explanatory evidence under s 100(1)(a), which is unlikely, or that it has substantial probative value in relation to a matter which is in issue in the proceedings and is itself of substantial importance in the context of the case as a whole: see s 100(1)(b). Whether these conditions are satisfied depends on the nature of Len's case. He appears to be saying that Mick has deliberately given false evidence incriminating him, in which case the conditions would almost certainly be satisfied. Leave of the court will still be necessary under s 100(4). The second matter is that if Len adduces the evidence under s 100(1)(b) he will have made an attack on another person's character, which will allow evidence of his own bad character, if he has one, to be given under s 101(1)(g). But since he has almost certainly brought this provision into play by his claim that Mick is a person whose testimony has been affected by a grudge, this additional attack is unlikely to have any separate significance.

If the conviction is put and Mick denies it, it may be proved against him by virtue of s 6 of the Criminal Procedure Act 1865. Proof would be made by producing a certificate of the conviction under s 73 of the **Police and Criminal Evidence Act 1984**. But it is likely that counsel for the prosecution would forestall the need for this by making a formal admission of the fact, since the information will have come from him in the first place.[1]

## Reference

1 The prosecution has a duty to disclose to the defence any previous convictions recorded against their witnesses. See *Paraskeva (1983)*.

THE COURSE OF TESTIMONY

# Question 45

Amy is prosecuted in the Crown Court for assaulting Bella, her neighbour. She pleads not guilty. The case for the prosecution is that Amy punched Bella during a quarrel in the street, causing Bella to fall and break her leg. When Amy was interviewed by the police, she told them that Bella's allegation was untrue and that on the occasion in question Bella had been about to hit her, but fell after tripping over a paving stone.

Consider the evidential issues that arise in each of the following circumstances:

(a) Amy gives evidence in her defence. During cross-examination, she states for the first time that at the time of the fall Bella was drunk. Counsel for the prosecution says: 'You've just made that up a moment ago, haven't you?' Amy replies: 'No, I haven't. The truth is, that woman needed half a bottle of gin before she could get up in the morning.' Defence counsel later wants to call Amy's cousin, Eddie, to give evidence that shortly after the incident, Amy spoke to him about it and said: 'It was that bitch Bella's own fault. She was out of her mind with drink as usual.'

(b) Amy calls her husband, Charlie. He wants to refresh his memory about the incident, which he observed, from a diary that Amy keeps.

(c) After Charlie has given evidence, Amy's brother, Dan, is called. He is asked about the incident, which he observed, but says: 'I'm sorry. I'm trying hard to remember, but it's just gone out of my head.'

## Answer plan

Part (a) involves an allegation of recent fabrication; you should refer to *Oyesiku (1971)*. It also raises the possibility that the prosecution might want to rely on s 34 of the Criminal Justice and Public Order Act 1994. Don't forget to set out the *Petkar* direction. Part (b) is a straightforward question about the use of memory-refreshing documents. Part (c) raises a number of possibilities. You should discuss the law relating to hostile and unfavourable witnesses, refreshing memory during the course of giving evidence, and the possibility of using s 23 of the Criminal Justice Act 1988.

# Answer

(a) The general rule is that evidence of a statement previously made by a witness which is consistent with his present testimony is inadmissible. Thus in *Roberts*

171

*(1942)*, a trial for murder where the defence was that a gun had gone off by accident, the accused was not allowed to call evidence to show that two days after the incident he had told his father that the death had resulted from an accident.

Exceptionally, however, evidence of such a statement can be adduced under s 120(2) of the Criminal Justice Act (CJA) 2003, in order to rebut a suggestion that the witness's oral evidence has been fabricated. At common law such evidence was admissible to rebut an allegation of *recent* fabrication, which is the allegation on these facts. By s 120(2), the earlier statement will be evidence of the truth of its contents. In *Oyesiku (1971)*, for example, counsel for the prosecution challenged the evidence of the accused's wife on the basis that she had concocted a story with her husband after his arrest. It was held that the defence should have been allowed to show that she had made a previous consistent statement about the events to her solicitor at a time when she had had no opportunity to discuss matters with her husband because he was then still in custody.

Amy was presumably interviewed by the police and failed to mention Bella's drunkenness at that stage. The prosecution could therefore ask the judge to give a direction under s 34 of the Criminal Justice and Public Order Act 1994. If he does so, he must give directions on the lines set out in *Gill (2001)* and *Petkar (2004)*, that is to say, he must identify the fact on which the defendant relies and which was not mentioned on questioning. He must direct the jury that it is for them to decide whether in the circumstances, that fact was something that the defendant could reasonably have been expected to mention. He should tell them that if they think it was, they are not obliged to draw any inferences, but that they may do so. Further, he must tell the jury that a suspected person is not bound to answer police questions, that they must not convict solely or mainly on an inference drawn from silence, and that the jury must be satisfied that there is a case to answer before they can draw any adverse inferences from silence. Finally, he should tell the jury that they can draw an adverse inference only if they are sure that the defendant was silent because he had no answers, or none that would stand up to investigation.

(b) By s 139(1) of the CJA 2003, a person giving oral evidence in criminal proceedings may, at any stage in the course of doing so, refresh his memory from a document made or verified by him at an earlier time if he states in his oral evidence that the document records his recollection at that earlier time, and that his recollection of the matter is likely to have been significantly better at that time than it is at the time of his oral evidence. Accordingly, Charlie can refresh his memory from the relevant entries made by Amy in her diary, provided he verified them at an earlier time. A witness who has used such a document must produce it for the inspection of the opposing party, who can cross-examine on it. It seems clear from *Senat v Senat (1965)* that counsel inspecting a document that has been used to refresh a witness's memory is not confined in cross-examination to those parts which were used for memory-refreshing purposes, provided it is relevant to go beyond them. But if cross-examining counsel does go beyond them, either party can apply to have the diary made an exhibit in the trial so that in due course the jury can take it into account as a whole when assessing the evidence. If the diary is made an exhibit, the entries used to refresh the witness's memory will, by s 120(3) of the CJA 2003, be evidence of any matter stated of which oral evidence by the witness would be admissible.

(c) If Dan is simply suffering from a lapse of memory, he can refresh his memory from any written statement that he made earlier: see s 139(1) of the CJA 2003. If Dan is not suffering from a lapse of memory, he may be a hostile witness, that is to say, a person who is not desirous of telling the truth to the court at the instance of the party calling him. A witness ruled hostile by the judge can be cross-examined by the party calling him with a view to showing what he said in his written statement on an earlier occasion. The power is provided by both statute and common law. By s 3 of the Criminal Procedure Act 1865, the advocate calling the witness may, by leave of the judge, 'prove that he has made at other times a statement inconsistent with his present testimony'. If the witness, as seems to be the case here, does not provide enough 'present testimony' to be inconsistent with the previous statement, he can still be treated as hostile and cross-examined on the statement by virtue of common law (*Thompson (1976)*). It is possible that Dan is 'hostile' because he is afraid to testify on Amy's behalf. If that could be proved, it would be possible to apply to have the statement put in as a piece of documentary hearsay under s 116(2)(e) and (4) of the CJA 2003. By s 119(1), such a statement will be admissible as evidence of any matter stated of which oral evidence by the witness would be admissible.

# Question 46

David is charged with raping Ellen in his flat after meeting her for the first time earlier in the evening in a public house. Ellen says that sex was never mentioned while they were in the public house. According to her, David invited her back to his flat to listen to a CD, but while this was being played, he raped her. Ellen says that she left David's flat shortly after she had been raped, and that when she arrived at her mother's house, where she lived, she told her mother that she had been raped. Her mother died before she could make a statement to the police or be interviewed by them. David's defence is that Ellen consented to sexual intercourse. He says that he met her in the public house at about 9 pm. He had never seen her before, but she came up to him and said: 'You look the sort of man I could end up in bed with. Why don't we go to your place?' David wishes to call Fergus, who was drinking in the same public house earlier that evening. Fergus says that Ellen, whom he knew only by sight, had approached him and said: 'I wouldn't mind a night with you. Let's go to your place.' Fergus says that he made an excuse and left the public house alone. David also wishes to call Gerald, who says that he had sex with Ellen at her invitation after meeting her for the first time in a different public house a week before the alleged rape by David.

Discuss the evidential matters arising. To what extent, if at all, would your advice be different if during cross-examination counsel for David put it to Ellen that she consented, and in reply she, for the first time, volunteered the information that she was a virgin before being raped by David?

### Answer plan

The following matters need consideration:
- Ellen's report of the rape to her mother;
- David's account of the meeting;
- David's claim that Ellen consented;
- Fergus's evidence;
- Gerald's evidence;
- Ellen's claim to have been a virgin.

# Answer

By s 120 of the Criminal Justice Act (CJA) 2003, previous statements of witnesses that are consistent with their testimony are admitted in certain circumstances. By sub-s (4) and (7), what were formerly known in cases where a sexual offence was alleged as 'recent complaints' are now admissible in relation to any offence if the conditions in sub-s (7) are satisfied. It is not clear whether any of the common law relating to recent complaints survives. The question is an important one on these facts because Ellen's mother is dead, and in *White v R (1998)*, the Privy Council held that it was necessary not only that the complainant should testify as to the complaint, but also that its terms should be proved by the person to whom it was made. It is therefore unclear whether Ellen could give evidence of the complaint because there is no evidence from her mother to confirm it.

David can give evidence of what Ellen said to him without infringing the rule against hearsay. The words uttered were an expression of her contemporaneous state of mind, and so fall within one of the categories of *res gestae*, a common law exception to the rule against hearsay preserved by s 118(1), para 4, CJA 2003. Alternatively, David's purpose in proving what Ellen said would be to show the effect the words had on his mind, and not the truth of what was said. In this case, the rule against hearsay would not apply (*Subramaniam v Public Prosecutor (1956)*).

The effect of s 41 of the Youth Justice and Criminal Evidence Act 1999 is that where a person is charged with a sexual offence, no evidence may be adduced by the accused about any sexual behaviour of the complainant, save in very restricted circumstances. David's evidence relates to an issue of consent, and the sexual behaviour of the complainant to which the evidence relates is alleged to have taken place at or about the same time as the event that is the subject matter of the charge against the accused. It falls within the exception contained in s 41(3)(b). A refusal of leave to adduce such evidence would clearly render the jury's verdict unsafe. Thus, both conditions referred to in s 41(2) for adducing evidence of sexual behaviour are satisfied. David's evidence is admissible.

Fergus's evidence is also evidence of Ellen's sexual behaviour and is subject to the restrictions of s 41, but it is likely to be admissible under s 41(3)(c)(ii). This allows the court to hear about other sexual behaviour of the complainant 'at or about the same time' as the alleged event which is the subject of the charge, if that behaviour is in any respect so similar to the behaviour of the complainant that took place as part of the event that is the subject matter of the charge that the similarity cannot reasonably be explained as a coincidence. In *A (2001)*, members of the House of Lords took the view that 'at or about the same time' included a period of approximately 24 hours before and after the alleged event. The incident with Fergus falls well within this period. The evidence of Ellen's encounter with Fergus is strikingly similar to David's evidence of her encounter with him. It shows Ellen's intention to have consensual sexual intercourse on that evening and should be admissible under s 41(2). (In fact, striking similarity may not be needed. In *A (2001)*, Lord Hutton observed that s 43(3)(c) contained less stringent words.) If this argument is rejected, the defence could argue that the principle of interpretation in *A* should be applied. In *A* the House of Lords held that s 41(3)(c) is to be construed by applying s 3 of the Human Rights Act 1998. The evidence should not be excluded if it is so relevant to the issue of consent that to exclude it would endanger the fairness of the trial provided for by Art 6 of the European Convention on Human Rights. Even if it were held that the encounter with Fergus did not fall strictly within the terms of s 41(3)(c), an argument based on this principle should succeed.

Gerald's evidence is likely to be inadmissible because of the requirement, under s 41(3)(c)(ii), that the evidence should be of sexual behaviour taking place 'at or about the same time' as the event which is the subject matter of the charge. If Ellen were to volunteer the information that she was a virgin before being raped by David, the defence would want to rely on s 41(5) in order to admit Gerald's evidence.

Section 41(5) allows a question, or evidence, about other sexual behaviour of a complainant to be admitted if it relates to any evidence adduced by the prosecution about any sexual behaviour of the complainant, and would go no further than is necessary to rebut or explain that evidence. The condition in sub-s (2)(b) must also be satisfied. In one sense, this evidence has not been adduced by the prosecution; it has been adduced by the defence during cross-examination. On the other hand, it has been volunteered by a prosecution witness, and it would be extraordinary if such a restricted construction were to be allowed to mislead the jury, especially in view of the decision in A. On that basis, Gerald's evidence might well be admitted.

# Chapter 11

# Opinion Evidence

## INTRODUCTION

From the standpoint of the examination candidate, opinion evidence is a tricky subject to prepare. Your examiners may show little or no interest in it, so that an opinion point comes in, if at all, only as a minor part of a question dealing largely with other matters. On the other hand, it would be possible to devote a whole problem to the subject. It would even be possible – though surely not very interesting – to invite candidates to write an essay on some aspect of opinion evidence, for example, the current state of the so called 'ultimate issue rule'. But let's assume that you have ruled out the possibility of an essay question, or at least of doing it should one turn up. How should you cope with opinion evidence as part of a problem?

In the first place, you should be careful in analysing exactly what it is that the expert is prepared to say. Break it down into a number of separate propositions if need be, because some may be more readily admissible than others.[1]

Next, you need to clarify the basis on which the opinion has been formed. For example, how much is a psychiatrist relying on what a defendant has told him? If he relies too much, he may find himself simply repeating what the defendant has said; that, obviously, would be open to the objection that it infringed the rule against hearsay.

Very often, the examiner will be vague about both these matters – exactly what the expert *is* saying and the basis for his opinion – and it will be for you to point out the difficulties.

Where you are dealing with the expert opinion of a psychiatrist or psychologist you should look at the issue to which it is directed. The reason is that evidence from either which does not amount to evidence of mental abnormality may be admitted to show, for example, the reliability of a confession. But where the issue in question is that of *mens rea*, it is most unlikely to be admitted. See *Coles (1995)*. Presumably, it is felt that to allow such evidence to be given would lead to experts deciding the issue which should properly be left to the jury. Alternatively, there may be a fear that a stage would soon be reached where experts were called on each side, the jury would be left no wiser and the expense and length of proceedings would have been increased for nothing.

Although your problem is likely to involve experts who make a living from their expertise, you may have to advise in relation to a layman who appears to be giving an opinion. Don't forget that an amateur may be an expert or that an opinion can be given by a non-expert if it is simply a short way of describing facts: see s 3(2) of the Civil Evidence Act (CEA) 1972 and *Davies (1962)*.

### Reference

1 For an example of close analysis leading to rejection of psychiatric testimony, see *Hurst (1995)*.

### Checklist

Students should be familiar with the following areas:

- opinion used as a way of conveying the sense of facts perceived;
- when expert psychiatric testimony is needed;
- who may give expert testimony;
- expert opinion on ultimate issues;
- expert evidence and the rule against hearsay – *Abadom (1983)*; s 30 of the Criminal Justice Act (CJA) 1988; s 1(1) of the CEA 1972;
- advance notice procedures in civil and criminal cases.

# Question 47

David and Jonathan are charged with murdering Salome, a prostitute. The prosecution case is that she was beaten and kicked to death by both the accused.

(a) David's defence is diminished responsibility. He says that he was one of Salome's regular clients and he acted as he did immediately after Salome said that if he did not give her £500,000 she would tell his wife of their relationship. David wishes to call Goliath, a psychiatrist. Goliath has prepared a report in which he says that he has examined David, that David described his horror at the blackmail attempt and became very emotional when speaking of his wife; in Goliath's opinion, David loved his wife dearly and would have been devastated by the break up of their marriage. Goliath adds that in two other cases in his experience, the sudden shock of a blackmail threat led to violent physical retaliation. He states that this observation has been explained in several privately circulated papers by psychiatrists who have described experiments in which they observed patterns of bodily chemical reactions which appeared to be peculiar to blackmail victims. Goliath concludes his report by saying that in his professional opinion David is not insane within the M'Naughten Rules, but was suffering at the relevant time from diminished responsibility within s 2 of the Homicide Act 1957. May Goliath testify as to all or any of these matters?

(b) Jonathan's case is that he had been with David and Salome on the occasion in question, but that he had had nothing to do with the attack. He says that when he saw what David was doing, he went into a state of shock and ran to the house of his girlfriend, Jezebel, a short distance away. Jezebel is a member of the police force. May Jonathan call her to say that when he arrived at her house, he was in a state of shock? He also wishes to call Zadok, a psychiatrist, who has examined him and who is prepared to state that in his opinion, Jonathan is a truthful man who has a peculiar horror of any sort of violence as a result of having been bullied at school. Will Zadok's evidence be admissible?

## Answer plan

(a) Since the expert's evidence is directed towards providing a defence of diminished responsibility for David, it is a good idea to outline briefly what this defence requires. The first paragraph does this, and shows that this is a case where expert evidence will be admissible in principle. But now you have to point out that there may be difficulties about the admissibility of what this expert is prepared to say. To do so effectively, you must break up what Goliath wants to say into separate heads, as follows:

- David's reaction to the blackmail attempt;
- David's reactions when speaking of his wife;
- Goliath's opinion that David loved her dearly;
- Goliath's opinion about the effect on David of the break up of his marriage;
- Goliath's description of his own experience of similar cases;
- his reference to the psychiatric experiments reported in privately circulated papers;

- his opinion as to David's sanity;
- his opinion that David was suffering from diminished responsibility.

(b) The first matter to be considered is whether Jezebel's evidence is expert testimony at all. You then need to break up Zadok's opinion thus:

- his opinion that Jonathan was truthful;
- his opinion about Jonathan's capacity for violence.

# Answer

(a) By s 2 of the Homicide Act 1957, a person who kills another shall not be convicted of murder if he was suffering from such abnormality of mind as substantially impaired his mental responsibility for his acts. It is for the defendant to prove that he comes within the section. The requirement that some abnormality of mind be established makes it clear that this is the sort of case where expert opinion evidence is receivable. As was said in *Turner (1975)*, the purpose of such evidence is to provide the court with information which is outside the experience and knowledge of a judge or jury. In *Dix (1982)*, Shaw LJ said that while s 2 of the Homicide Act did not in terms require that medical evidence be adduced in support of a defence of diminished responsibility, it made it a practical necessity if that defence was to begin to run at all. The question of admissibility in this case will therefore turn on the nature of the testimony that it is proposed that Goliath should give.

It appears that the first thing that Goliath wishes to do is to report the reactions of David when speaking of his wife, and to give his own opinion that David loved her dearly. He adds that David would have been devastated by the break up of his marriage, but whether this is an opinion formed as a result of what David told him directly, or as a result of what Goliath inferred from other things said by David, is unclear.

So far, it seems that nearly all this evidence would be inadmissible. To the extent that Goliath was repeating what David said to him, the evidence would be excluded by the rule against hearsay, although the fact that David became emotional when speaking of his wife would be admissible.[1] The questions of whether David loved his wife and what would have been his reaction to the break up of their marriage are not ones where the jury would require the special assistance of a psychiatrist. Thus, in *Turner (1975)*, the Court of Appeal held that the trial judge had rightly excluded psychiatric evidence that the defendant had had a deep emotional relationship with his girlfriend which was likely to have caused a blind explosion of rage after her confession of infidelity. As Lawton LJ said, the fact that an expert witness has impressive scientific qualifications does not by that fact alone make his opinion on matters of human nature and behaviour within the limits of normality any more helpful than that of the jurors themselves.

Then Goliath wishes to say that in two other cases in his experience the sudden shock of a blackmail threat led to violent physical retaliation, and he refers to the experiments of other psychiatrists by way of explanation. The basic question here is the same: does the jury need the assistance of this scientific evidence to determine the particular matter under consideration? At this stage, Goliath's evidence is directed to the issue whether it is more likely than not that when David killed Salome he was suffering from such abnormality of mind as substantially to impair his mental responsibility.

Is Goliath prepared to adopt the explanation of his colleagues as his own? Unless he is, there is not much point in referring to their opinions. Assuming that he does, the argument for admissibility is stronger than in relation to his earlier opinions because this is something that would not be within the ordinary knowledge of jurors. In *Abadom (1983)*, the Court of Appeal decided that an expert is entitled to draw on the work of others as part of the process of arriving at his conclusions. The fact that the work is unpublished is immaterial. Goliath may therefore rely on the privately circulated papers in forming his opinion and, as the court pointed out in *Abadom*, he ought to identify them so that the quality of his opinion may be assessed.

However, it remains necessary to be cautious about admissibility. If the judge took the view that the scientists had merely been describing ordinary human reactions in scientific terms, he would very probably conclude that their discoveries would not assist the jury. The evidence would then be excluded.

Lastly, Goliath wishes to say that David was not insane, but was suffering from diminished responsibility. The question of David's sanity is not in issue, so the first part of this opinion would be irrelevant, and therefore inadmissible. Although experts may sometimes give opinions on the ultimate issue in a case, this is not one of them. The defence provided by s 2 of the Homicide Act 1957 involves more than a simple medical issue concerning the accused's state of mind. There is also the question of substantial impairment of responsibility and this is essentially for the jury to decide (*Byrne (1960)*).

However, in *DPP v A and BC Chewing Gum Ltd (1968)*, Lord Parker acknowledged that although the question 'Do you think he was suffering from diminished responsibility?' was strictly inadmissible, it was allowed time and again without objection. Thus, on the assumption that there is some admissible evidence that Goliath can give, it is likely that he would also be allowed to say that in his opinion, David was suffering from diminished responsibility.

(b) Jezebel may certainly give evidence of Jonathan's physical and emotional condition when he arrived at her house; no special expertise is required to do this. If she wishes to give evidence that he was in a specific medical condition known as 'a state of shock', the fact that she is not medically qualified need not prevent her from doing so. It would be enough that she had acquired the necessary medical knowledge as part of her police training and experience. *Silverlock (1894)* is authority for the proposition that an appropriate professional qualification is not essential for an expert witness. In that case a solicitor who had studied handwriting as a hobby was allowed to give evidence as a handwriting expert.

Zadok will not be able to give his opinion that Jonathan is a truthful man. *Toohey v Commissioner for Metropolitan Police (1965)* establishes that medical evidence will be admissible to show that a witness suffers from some disease, or defect or abnormality of mind that affects the reliability of his evidence. But subject to this, it appears that only in the most exceptional cases will psychiatric testimony be admissible concerning the truthfulness of the accused.[2]

Two problems arise in connection with Zadok's opinion about Jonathan's capacity for violence. The first is whether it is in principle admissible at all. There is little to suggest that English courts are likely to follow the example set by the Supreme Court of Canada in *Lupien (1970)*, which held admissible evidence showing that the defendant had a temperament which would have made his participation in a particular form of conduct very unlikely. In *Reynolds (1989)*, the Court of Appeal took the view that psychiatric evidence about personal traits, such as the habit of fantasising, was inadmissible because the jury could use its common sense about such matters. It is likely that a court would regard an aversion to violence in the same light.

Even if this basic problem can be overcome, a second one remains: on what basis was Zadok's conclusion reached? If it was merely on what Jonathan said to him during a consultation it would be likely to fall foul of the rule against hearsay. At least in *Lupien (1970)* the defendant had been subjected to psychiatric tests for the purpose of determining the issue in question.

## References

1 What is relevant is David's state of mind at the time of the offence. Light can be thrown on this by David's emotional reaction when talking to Goliath about his wife, but not, according to English law at any rate, by his account to Goliath of what his state of mind was at the time when he killed Salome. If David wants this to go before the jury, he will have to testify.

2 One such case was *Lowery v R (1974)*, where two co-accused blamed each other for a murder and the Privy Council held that the trial judge had properly admitted the evidence of a psychologist, who had carried out tests on both defendants, to show that the testimony of one was more likely to be true than that of the other. Nothing of the kind arises here; David accepts that he killed Salome and has not tried to implicate Jonathan.

# Chapter 12

# Privilege and Public Policy

## INTRODUCTION

The first thing to get straight is the difference between these two concepts. A *privilege* is a right that the law gives to a person allowing him to refuse to testify about a certain matter, or to refuse to produce a document or piece of real evidence. *Public policy* (often now referred to as 'public interest immunity') comes into the picture where it is thought that the disclosure of evidence would be damaging in some way to the general good. The most obvious example is where national security would be compromised if the evidence in question had to be given, or the disclosure made.

There are four privileges which you ought to study. The first is the privilege against self-incrimination. One theoretical topic that could come up as an essay question is whether such a privilege should exist at all. You should note that this is not the same question as whether the accused should have a right to silence. Some writers do refer to 'the privilege against self-incrimination' in the broad sense of a 'right to silence', but this is confusing and it will be better if you keep the two ideas distinct.

The classic context for the operation of the privilege against self-incrimination is a *civil* action where one of the witnesses is being cross-examined about conduct that would amount to a criminal offence. For example, suppose I sue a storage company for the loss of my valuable furniture which was in store with them, and it is my case that the furniture was destroyed when the company deliberately set fire to the premises to collect on an insurance policy. In those circumstances, the privilege might well be invoked at some stage of the hearing by a witness for the company who was being cross-examined.

You should note the increasing number of statutory exceptions to this privilege.

Legal professional privilege is also of considerable importance. Note the various circumstances in which this applies, especially those cases where the communications are not directly between lawyer and client, but between lawyer and third parties on behalf of the client.

This privilege can be 'waived' by accident. What happens is that, in any large action, the task of preparing documents for disclosure is so great that quite often one side shows the other privileged documents by mistake. By r 31.20 of the *Civil Procedure Rules 1998*, inadvertently disclosed privileged documents may only be used with the consent of the court. Some knowledge of the former law that governed the granting of injunctions to restrain the use of such documents is likely to be helpful in judging whether consent will be given.

Two more privileges ought to be studied. One is the limited privilege that has been given in respect of a journalist's sources. (See s 10 of the *Contempt of Court Act 1981*.) The other is the privilege that attaches to 'without prejudice' statements. With the latter, remember that if the negotiations result in agreement there is no longer any need for 'without prejudice' protection. It follows that, if there is any subsequent litigation concerning that agreement, you are free to use the documents marked 'without prejudice' as evidence of the agreement and its terms (*Tomlin v Standard Telephones and Cables Ltd (1969)*). But note also *Rush and Tomkins Ltd v GLC (1989)*, which makes evidence of negotiations inadmissible in any subsequent litigation connected with the same subject matter. This is particularly likely to affect a situation where a main contractor reaches a settlement with one of several sub-contractors.

Public policy questions are not ones that many candidates answer well, and unless you have also studied public law it is, perhaps, better to avoid the topic in the examination. I have nevertheless suggested in the checklist some areas with which you might make yourself familiar. The subject of police informers is interesting, topical and not too difficult to master. It is also a subject that might feature as part of a wider question.

## Checklist

Students should be familiar with the following areas:
- the privilege against self-incrimination;
- legal professional privilege;
- s 10 of the Contempt of Court Act 1981;
- 'without prejudice' statements;
- public policy considerations involving national security, affairs of state, and the proper functioning of government and its services;
- public policy considerations in respect of information in the possession of the police relating to the investigation of crime;
- public policy considerations in respect of confidential or personal statements made in official reports or inquiries.

# Question 48

'The fact that evidence which is relevant and otherwise admissible may be excluded by public policy or privilege gives to the two subjects an appearance of similarity which is misleading. The rules and their operation are quite distinct, and any superficial identity of result is more than outweighed by substantial and far reaching differences.'

Discuss.

## Answer plan

Sometimes, the examiner sets quite a lengthy quotation as the subject for an essay. To write an effective essay, it is of course vital that you should read the quotation carefully, probably at least twice, in order to determine exactly what it means. All too often I have read scripts where it seemed as if the candidate had glanced at the quotation, had seen that it had something to do with public policy, and had assumed he would pass if he regurgitated his lecture notes on *Conway v Rimmer (1968)*, etc. I emphasise again that the examiner is looking for an argument, not an exposition of basic law. If you fail to provide an appropriate response, you will fail the question.

What is this particular quotation about? First, the writer refers to the fact that the rules of both privilege and public policy have the effect of excluding evidence that would otherwise be relevant and admissible. To that extent, the two sets of rules appear to be alike, but, he goes on, the fact that the rules have the same *result* does not mean that there are any other similarities. Similarity of result need not involve similarity in the way the result is reached. This is certainly true in some matters; is it true in this case? In other words, what are the differences and similarities between the rules relating to privilege and those relating to public policy?

It probably strikes you that the idea contained in the quotation is basically correct. But it is not very interesting to say so at once, and the key to producing a really competent answer is to argue a little *against* the idea contained in the quotation. This is done here by arguing that there is not only a similarity in outcome, but a similarity in the way the rules are operated.

You can then move on to make obvious points about waiver, use of secondary evidence and persons entitled to make the claim. You conclude by agreeing with the proposition contained in the quotation. But you do so with reservations, and have shown some independent thought on the subject.

In summary, therefore, the essay is constructed as follows:
- difference between outcomes and the means of achieving them;
- argument for similarity of means based on the balancing of potential harms;
- place of balancing interests in privilege and public policy;
- potential differences between privilege and public policy: waiver and use of secondary evidence;
- persons who can claim privilege and raise issues of public policy;
- concluding remarks on the quotation.

# Answer

Similarity of outcomes does not necessarily involve similarity in the way the outcomes under consideration were achieved. Dr Crippen died by hanging and Louis XVI lost his life by means of the guillotine. The outcome in each case was the same: death. However, the procedures preceding those outcomes and the methods by which death was achieved were vastly different. It does not, therefore, appear to be a very impressive argument for similarity between the rules relating to privilege and those relating to public policy that they achieve the same outcome.

However, it can be argued that there is more than identity of outcome, and that in fact there is similarity in the way the rules are operated. If a claim to privilege succeeds, it does so because when you balance the harm that will follow if the privilege is upheld against the harm that will follow if it is not, the latter is found to be greater. Yet this is the very same principle that operates in the sphere of public interest immunity.

When privilege is being considered, this balancing exercise operates in a way about which it is difficult to generalise, but which may best be described as 'oiling the wheels of the administration of justice'. For example, for each party to have his case presented as well as possible within our adversarial context, it is necessary that the lawyers on each side be fully acquainted with all the relevant facts. To achieve this, it is vital that the client should be able to trust the lawyer. This could not be the case if what he said to his own lawyer could be used against him, and this gives rise to rules about legal professional privilege.

The fact that justice can be done by disputants themselves, and not only by courts, is recognised by rules which encourage parties to settle their quarrels without recourse to litigation. So, for example, we find that there are rules which say that admissions made by parties while trying to reach a settlement cannot afterwards be proved against them if negotiations break down and the matter has to go to court.

On another level, there may be public interests which conflict with the doing of justice in a particular case. Thus, the public interest in the detection of crime or in the maintenance of national security may require non-disclosure of certain matters, even though this may harm an individual litigant by depriving him of vital evidence.

In both types of case, there is a balancing of interests. Is the interest in rectitude of decision outweighed by the interest in keeping the administration of justice working as well as possible, both inside and outside the courts? Is the interest in doing justice to the parties in a particular case outweighed by some wider public interest? So far, it seems that although the situations giving rise to such problems of balancing may be very different, the principle that is operating in each case is essentially the same. Have we found a common feature other than outcome that would disprove the contention expressed in the passage quoted?

Closer examination suggests that although the balancing of interests is indeed a feature common to both the law of privilege and the law relating to exclusion on grounds of public policy, this does not disprove the contention. The reason for this is that it is too common a feature of evidence law, for it can be used to account for all the ordinary rules of exclusion, such as those governing hearsay evidence or evidence of the accused's criminal propensity. The public may be said to have an interest in the full disclosure of relevant information in a criminal trial, but it also has an interest in rectitude of decision. This latter interest may be served better by concealing some information, because, if it were disclosed, its capacity to mislead the jury would increase the chances of misdecision. Thus, it may be said that a balancing exercise takes place in which greater weight is given to one interest rather than the other, depending on the amount of harm likely to result.

On the other hand, there appear to be quite strong arguments to justify the contention expressed in the passage quoted.

Matters covered by public policy are those where the safety or well being of citizens generally is concerned. Privilege, by contrast, covers matters that directly affect only the particular litigant or witness. This gives rise to differences in the way in which the law deals with two subjects: waiver and the use of secondary evidence.

A party or witness who has a privilege may always waive it voluntarily and, in such a case, the once privileged document or testimony will be treated in the same way as any other evidence in the case. But, because public policy objections exist, in theory, for the benefit of citizens generally there is some difficulty with the idea that objections of this type can be waived. Thus, in *Rogers v Home Secretary (1973)*, Lord Simon said that once the public interest which demands that evidence be withheld has been found weightier than the public interest requiring courts to have access to all relevant material, the evidence cannot in any circumstances be admitted. It is not a privilege that may be waived, either by the Crown or by anyone else.

However, in *Alfred Crompton Amusement Machines Ltd v Customs & Excise Commissioners (No 2) (1974)*, Lord Cross thought that waiver could be allowed if a person or party, such as an informer, for whose benefit the objection was made volunteered to testify or disclose the evidence. One way of analysing such an odd situation would be to say that it was not a case of waiver at all, but one where the public interest had just disappeared, because the interest in question is that of protecting a person from having to disclose certain information *against his will*.[1] This approach was adopted by the Court of Appeal in *Savage v Chief Constable of the Hampshire Constabulary (1997)*, where it was held that a police informer could waive his anonymity in order to sue the defendant on an alleged contract to make payments to the claimant in return for information.

The courts have recently brought the operation of public interest immunity more closely into line with that of privilege in respect of waiver. An important distinction used to be that, while a privilege could be waived, a claim to public interest immunity could not. As Lord Scarman said in *Air Canada v Secretary of State for Trade (1983)*, when the Crown puts forward a public interest immunity objection, it is not claiming a privilege but discharging a duty. Similarly, in *Makanjuola v Commissioner of Metropolitan Police (1992)*, Bingham LJ said that public interest immunity 'is not a trump card vouchsafed to certain privileged players to play as and when they wish'. He added that it could not, in any ordinary sense, be waived, because although rights can be waived, duties cannot. On that approach, it followed that where a litigant held documents in a class that was *prima facie* immune, he should (save in a very exceptional case) assert that they are immune and decline to disclose them. The ultimate decision about where the public interest lay was not for him, but for the court.

However, this approach, coupled with a claim to immunity based on the class into which a document fell, rather than on its specific contents, led to undesirably wide public interest immunity claims by ministers. The practice was criticised in the Scott Report,[2] and the central government has now effectively abandoned class claims.

Further, in *R v Chief Constable of West Midlands Police ex p Wiley (1995)*, the House of Lords held that a class claim cannot be made in respect of documents compiled as part of the investigation of a complaint against the police, and it seems likely that class claims generally will be reduced in future. After *ex p Wiley*, it is clear that if a minister believes that the overriding public interest requires government documents to be disclosed, he is not obliged to request immunity for them. It appears that ministers must now consider, before making a claim for public interest immunity, whether the public interest is better served by disclosure than by concealment. It looks very much as if they are expected to exercise a discretion in deciding whether or not to waive public interest immunity.

The second main difference between information affected by privilege and information affected by public policy is in relation to the use of secondary evidence.

# Privilege and Public Policy

When public policy requires that information be concealed, the documents which are the immediate subject of the exclusion are obviously affected but, in addition, it is not possible to prove their contents by secondary means. Privilege, however, attaches only to an original document or communication. Subject to the possibility of protection under the law relating to confidentiality, secondary evidence is in principle admissible. Thus, an opponent may be able to prove facts contained in a privileged document by producing a copy, or by calling a witness to give oral evidence of its contents.

A final point of distinction between claims based on privilege and claims based on public policy is that in the case of privilege the claim must be made by the person who is entitled to the privilege, but an objection made on grounds of public policy may be made by someone who is not even a party to the proceedings. The court may even do so of its own motion.

Thus, it can be seen that, despite superficial similarities in both effect and operation, there are significant differences between the rules relating to privilege and public policy and between the ways in which those rules operate.

## References

1. Lord Denning has on several occasions said that there could be waiver of objections based on public policy. In *Campbell v Thameside Metropolitan Borough Council (1982)*, he proposed a distinction between claims affecting documents which must be kept secret on such grounds as those of national security or the preservation of diplomatic relations, and documents in a lower category which are kept confidential in order that persons should be candid in their reports or for other good reasons. In these latter cases, he suggested, immunity should be capable of being waived either by the maker or by the recipient of the document.

2. *Report of the Inquiry into the Export of Defence Equipment and Dual-Use Goods to Iraq and Related Prosecutions*, 1996, HC 115, 15 February.

# Question 49

Answer BOTH parts of this question:

(a) Francis is being prosecuted for possession of cannabis which has been found at his house. When the police raided the premises, they discovered a small quantity of the drug wrapped in silver paper at the bottom of a pile of underclothes which lay on the floor. Francis denies the charge. He says that he is an asthmatic and unable to smoke, but that writers, artists and students are frequent callers at his house and that any one of them could have dropped the package. He suspects that the police were tipped off by George. George has been employed by Francis as a general handyman for the last eight years. In the past, he has been sentenced to terms of imprisonment; he is now an alcoholic and has often made false allegations against Francis when drunk.

May the defence require the police to disclose the name of their informer?

(b) Harry is being prosecuted for supplying drugs. The only evidence against him is that of four police officers. Two officers, Ian and John, give evidence that while keeping watch in private premises, they observed Harry selling drugs. Two others, Kate and Larry, give evidence that while keeping watch in an unmarked police vehicle, they also observed Harry selling drugs.

May the defence cross-examine Ian and John to discover the exact location of their observation point in order to test the quality of their observations?

May they cross-examine Kate and Larry to discover the colour, make and model of their vehicle and the times of their alleged surveillance?

## Answer plan

This is a straightforward question involving cases on the public interest in non-disclosure of information concerning police investigations.

Part (a) deals with the traditional problem of the informer. The basic rule stated in *Marks v Beyfus (1890)* must be your starting point; it will be useful to refer to what Lawton LJ said in *Hennessey (1978)* about the reason for that rule. Don't rush things; deal with the basic rule first and turn to the exception only after that. Then comes the factual problem: is disclosure necessary to show the accused's innocence? The point is best made here by a comparison of *Agar (1990)* and *Slowcombe (1991)*. Don't forget though to provide your own conclusion on the facts of this question; the cases you have cited are useful illustrations of a principle, but no more.

Part (b) is even more straightforward and is designed to test the candidate's knowledge of *Rankine (1986)*, *Brown (1987)* and *Johnson (1988)*.

# Answer

(a) The basic rule is that in public prosecutions witnesses may not be asked, and will not be allowed to disclose, the names of informers or the nature of the information given. Thus, in *Marks v Beyfus (1890)*, an action for malicious prosecution, the Director of Public Prosecutions, who had been called as a witness, refused on grounds of public policy to give the names of his informants or to produce the statement on which he had acted in directing the earlier unsuccessful prosecution of the plaintiff. His objection was upheld by the trial judge, and the plaintiff was unsuccessful in his appeal. Lawton LJ stated in *Hennessey (1978)* that the rationale of the rule is that informers need to be protected, both for their own safety and to ensure that the supply of information about criminal activities does not dry up.

However, in *Marks v Beyfus (1890)*, Lord Esher qualified this basic rule by stating that it could be departed from if the disclosure of the name of the informant was necessary or right in order to show the prisoner's innocence. In such a case, one public policy would be in conflict with another, and the policy which said that an innocent man should not be condemned when his innocence could be proved had to prevail. However, it is for the accused to show that there is a good reason for disclosure (*Hennessey (1978)*).

An example of a case where disclosure was considered appropriate is *Agar (1990)*. In that case, a prosecution for possession of drugs, the Court of Appeal said that the trial judge should have ordered the informer's disclosure because it was necessary for the support of the accused's defence that the informer and the police had acted together to frame him.

But it may well be the case that knowledge of the informer will not affect the defence, and then disclosure will not be ordered. An example is *Slowcombe (1991)*. Following a tip off, the defendant had been arrested in possession of a shotgun outside a sub-post office. He claimed to have been recruited by V, and to have been told by him that there was an accomplice working in the post office who would hand over the money, but that the gun was necessary for the sake of appearances. The defendant argued accordingly that he was not guilty of conspiracy to rob, but only of conspiracy to steal. The judge refused a defence application to ask a police officer whether their informer had been V. The Court of Appeal upheld this decision. If V had not been the informer, the defendant's story could still have been true. If it had been V, that would not establish that the defendant had been told that only a theft was planned. V could have conspired with the defendant to commit robbery, but then have turned informer. Disclosing the name of the informer could contribute little or nothing to the issue the jury had to consider: might the defendant's explanation have been true?

The issue in the case of Francis is whether his explanation for the presence of the cannabis might be true. Knowing that George was the informer can contribute nothing to the resolution of this question. If Francis were to suggest that George planted the cannabis and then tipped off the police, the position would be different, but that does not appear to be his case.

It is unlikely, therefore, that the defence application would succeed.[1]

(b) It was held in *Rankine (1986)* that the rule in *Marks v Beyfus (1890)* also protects the identity of persons who have allowed their premises to be used for police observation, and the identity of the premises. Even if the accused argues that identification of the premises is necessary to establish his innocence (as it surely would be in this case), the judge may still refuse to allow the question to be put. For example, in *Johnson (1988)*, where the accused was charged with supplying drugs, the only evidence against him was supplied by police officers who had kept observation from private premises. The defence applied to cross-examine about the exact location in order to test whether the officers could have seen what they said they did. The trial judge nevertheless ruled that the exact location should not be revealed and the Court of Appeal upheld this decision.

But the prosecution must have first provided a proper evidential basis to support their claim for protection of identity. In *Johnson (1988)*, Watkins LJ stated the following as minimum requirements:

- the police officer in charge of the observations must testify that he had visited all the observation places to be used and ascertained the attitude of their occupiers, both as to the use to be made of them and to possible subsequent disclosure;
- a police officer of at least the rank of chief inspector must testify that immediately prior to the trial he visited the places used for observation and ascertained whether the occupiers were the same as when the observation took place and, whether they are or not, the attitude of those occupiers to possible disclosure of their use as observation points.

In *Johnson (1988)*, the prosecution called evidence as to the difficulty of obtaining assistance from the public and the desire of the occupiers, who had been occupiers throughout, that their names and addresses should not be disclosed because of fear for their safety. Assuming that similar evidence is available in this case, the defence will not be permitted to cross-examine Ian and John about the exact location of the premises which they used.

But the object of keeping the identity of the premises secret is to protect the owner or occupier. Where this consideration does not apply, cross-examination may be permitted on detailed aspects of surveillance. Thus, in *Brown (1987)*, where officers gave evidence that they had kept observation from an unmarked police vehicle, it was held that the defence was entitled to information relating to the surveillance and to the colour, make and model of the vehicle.

The defence will therefore be entitled to ask Kate and Larry about these matters.

### Reference

1 But for what happened in the case on which this question is based, see Farson, D, *The Gilded Gutter Life of Francis Bacon*, 1993, Chapter 12.

# Question 50

Cedric was employed by AB Ltd, a company engaged in the manufacture of meat pies. One day, his hand was caught in a mincing machine and he suffered grave injuries, because of which he decided to sue AB Ltd for compensation. When AB Ltd learned of the accident, they obtained a report from an independent safety expert in accordance with their usual practice when accidents occurred on their premises. Copies of this report were sent to the board of directors and to the legal department of the company.

Cedric wrote a letter to Derek, his solicitor, setting out his account of the accident in which he admitted that he had not complied with safety regulations when operating the mincing machine because he had been 'chatting someone up' at the time. Enid, Derek's secretary, took a photocopy of this letter and gave it to her lover Fabian, who is a director of AB Ltd.

Cedric wishes to obtain a copy of the safety expert's report. He suspects that his employers may have obtained a copy of his letter to Derek and is afraid that they may use it against him. Advise Cedric.

## Answer plan

A relatively straightforward question about privilege. You need to discuss the following points:

- the safety expert's report – legal professional privilege in relation to third party communications;
- is Cedric's admission privileged?;
- will AB Ltd be allowed to use the photocopy of the letter sent by Cedric?

# Answer

Communications which are made between a party or his legal advisers and a third party will be privileged provided the dominant purpose in making the communications was to obtain or provide advice in connection with pending or contemplated litigation. The requirement that advice in such a connection be the dominant purpose of the communication was established by *Waugh v British Railways Board (1980)*. In that case, the claimant sued the defendants under the **Fatal Accidents Act 1976** in respect of the death of her husband which had occurred in a railway collision. Her advisers wished to obtain discovery of an internal report prepared by the defendants for submission to the railway inspectorate and the ministry. Another object of the report was to provide information for the Board's solicitor to enable him to advise the Board. The House of Lords held that the Board was not entitled to claim privilege in respect of this report. To attract such privilege, preparation for the purposes of intended or contemplated litigation had to be 'at least the dominant purpose' for bringing a document into existence. But the report in *Waugh's* case had been prepared not only for the purpose of litigation but for other major purposes in relation to the safe running of railways. Submission to the solicitor had not been shown to be the dominant purpose of making the report; therefore it was not privileged.

Whether such a document is privileged will turn on the facts of each individual case. But, on the facts given, it looks as if assistance in litigation was only one of the objects of AB Ltd in obtaining the safety expert's report, and that the maintenance of safe working practices was equally important. The report is thus unlikely to be privileged.

All communications between solicitor and client made for the purpose of giving or receiving legal advice are privileged (*Waugh v British Railways Board (1980)*). It is clear that the letter which Cedric wrote to Derek was privileged for this reason.

However, privilege attaches only to the original letter sent by Cedric. In principle, secondary evidence of a privileged document is admissible. Thus, in *Calcraft v Guest (1898)*, it was held that the defendant was entitled to put in evidence copies which he had made of certain proofs of evidence. By r 31.20 of the **Civil Procedure Rules 1998**, inadvertently disclosed privileged documents may only be used with the consent of the court. But, this document has not been *inadvertently* disclosed. Use of a document that is an admissible piece of evidence may be restrained on the ground that it contains confidential information. In *Lord Ashburton v Pape (1913)*, the plaintiff opposed the defendant's discharge from bankruptcy. The defendant obtained by trickery a number of relevant documents from a clerk in the employment of the claimant's solicitors. Having obtained them, he took copies. The Court of Appeal held that the plaintiff was entitled to an injunction requiring the defendant to deliver up all originals and restraining him from making any use of the copies or of the information which he had obtained. Provided the privileged documents or copies of them have not already been used as secondary evidence in the litigation, the party entitled to the privilege will be able to obtain a similar injunction (*Goddard v Nationwide Building Society (1987)*).

Cedric's solicitors will therefore be able to obtain an injunction restraining the use by AB Ltd of the photocopy that was given to Fabian and of the information contained in it.

# CHAPTER 13

# REVISION

## INTRODUCTION

So far, each chapter has dealt very largely with one topic in the law of evidence. Essay questions in an examination are usually on a specific topic, but that is not generally the way in which examiners set problem questions. In these you are very likely to be given a scenario that will test your knowledge of the law more widely. It is important to get some experience in answering questions of this kind, and the object of this chapter is to provide this opportunity.

First, you have to choose the questions that you want to do. This means that you have to read all of them, carefully, at the beginning of the examination. You might think that, having made your decision, you should plunge at once into writing an answer to the first question of your choice. But this is not the best way to proceed. Almost certainly, you know more evidence law than you think you do. But you probably cannot recall it all at once. So you need to give your brains the best opportunity to recall what you know. You can do this by planning your answers to *all* the questions that you intend to answer before writing a full answer to any of them.

How does this help? I expect that you have sometimes had the experience of trying to remember something in ordinary conversation. Perhaps you are telling a friend about an old film that you once saw and liked. You can remember some of its details, and perhaps its title, but you cannot remember who starred in it. Ten minutes later you are talking about something completely different – and suddenly you remember the name that you were trying to recall earlier. What seems to happen is that subconsciously your brain carries on its task of recall even though you have, apparently, dismissed the subject from your mind. This is what can happen in examinations. If you alert your brain by making as thorough a preparation as you can of questions 4–7 at the start, when you are writing your full answer to question 4, you may very well find that something comes into your head about some law you could not at first remember in connection with question 6. It will be the work of a moment to add this to your answer plan for question 6, and then continue writing your full answer to question 4. You will not, of course, find that you have been distracted from question 4 because you will already have on rough paper an answer plan to follow for that question.

Moral: at the very start of the examination make as good an answer plan as you can for *all* the questions that you intend to answer.

Next, how should you tackle a problem question? After you have read it through once, go through it again and break it up mentally into defendants and pieces of information. (I am assuming that the problem is about evidence in a criminal trial.) It's a good idea to deal with each defendant separately, and to consider the significance for evidence law of each piece of information that you are given. That means that you should be thinking initially about its relevance for the case as it affects a particular defendant and any co-defendants. In criminal problems, it helps to put yourself in the shoes of counsel for the prosecution and then in those of counsel for the defence. For example, you might ask yourself of a piece of information, 'If I were prosecuting, why would I want this information to go before the jury?' And then, 'If I were counsel for the defence, what arguments would be available to me to get this piece of information excluded?'

But, as I have said before in this book and elsewhere, evidence law is not concerned only with questions about the admissibility of evidence. It is also concerned with directions that a judge should give during his summing-up to the jury about how to treat specific items of evidence that have been admitted, but which for various reasons require careful handling. If, for example, identification evidence has been admitted, a *Turnbull* direction will be required. And don't think you can satisfy the examiner by saying that, and no more. The examiner wants to see if you know what a *Turnbull* direction should contain. What directions should be given if s 34 of the Criminal Justice and Public Order Act 1994 applies? Don't just mention *Petkar*; find some means of remembering what points were made in that case, and summarise them for the examiner. Where this sort of memory work is needed, try to make a list of key words, one for each point that the judge should make, and turn the initial letters of those words into a single word that you can remember. The army used to be good at this sort of thing. When I was at school, we were taught in the Combined Cadet Force how to give an order to fire at a specific target. You had to specify the group of soldiers whom you wanted to carry out the order; you had to specify the range of fire, you had to indicate where they should be firing; and you had to indicate the target. Group – Range – Indication – Target: GRIT. We all remembered it then, and I can remember it now, even though after leaving school I never had to give an order to anyone to fire a gun at anything. Work out something on those lines to help you remember the contents of judicial directions. It's quite fun to try, and the very process of trying should help to fix the details in your mind. A variant of this system is to use the initial letters of your key words to make up a memorable sentence. For example, 'Every good boy deserves flogging.' It's memorable because it's nonsense. But it helps you to remember the sequence E, G, B, D, F, and if you have studied music you will know the significance of that.

One way to use the questions in this chapter would be to read the question and then without looking at the answer plan, try to work out your own plan. Then compare it with the plan in the book, look up what you have forgotten, and finally write your answer without reference to books or notes in roughly the time that you would have to answer a question in the examination. (Don't forget to deduct your initial preparation time when working out the time available for each question.)

Here, then, are three more questions, but of a kind more like the ones that you will encounter in your examination.

# Question 51

Alex and Ben are charged with being jointly concerned in the importation of heroin during April this year. They are separately represented. Each intends to plead not guilty and to give evidence in his own defence. Alex had an interview with the police in which he denied everything, and in the course of which he said, 'I have never been involved with drugs, but Ben is well known for dealing in them.' When the police lawfully searched Alex's flat they found a small quantity of cannabis in a bathroom cabinet. When they lawfully searched Ben's house they discovered £2,400 in used bank notes in a chest of drawers. They also discovered a notebook in which Ben had written, 'Alex arriving with the stuff on 4 April. Meet him at Dover 10.35 a.m.' Alex has no previous convictions. Ben has a spent conviction for assault.

Discuss the evidential matters arising.

## Answer plan

The question requires consideration of six matters.

- Alex's interview with the police. Is it admissible? If so, what is its evidential status in relation to (i) Alex; (ii) Ben?
- The discovery of the cannabis at Alex's house. Is it relevant? Is it admissible? If it is both relevant and admissible, does a special direction have to be given to the jury? (This last question can be answered only if you appreciate why this evidence is relevant.)
- The discovery of cash in Ben's house. Relevance and admissibility?
- The notebook entry. Relevance? If relevant, against whom is it admissible?
- Alex's good character – *Vye* direction.
- Ben's spent conviction. What application might the prosecution make about it? Would the application be likely to succeed? Is a *Vye* direction possible?

# Answer

Alex's interview with the police contains wholly exculpatory statements. It was held by the Court of Appeal in *Pearce (1979)* that it is the duty of the prosecution to present the case fairly to the jury, and that it would be unfair to give evidence of a defendant's admissions but exclude answers favourable to a defendant. The Court held, however, that a wholly exculpatory statement is not evidence of the truth of its contents, but only of the defendant's reaction when questioned by police. Insofar as the statement implicates Ben, it is merely hearsay and not evidence against him (*Gunewardene, 1951*).

The discovery of the cannabis is unlikely in itself to be held relevant to the current charge, which concerns a far more serious offence with a much more dangerous drug. But the court may well consider it relevant because it shows Alex to have been lying when he supported his denial of involvement by saying that he had never been involved with drugs. A similar situation arose in *Peters (1995)*, where the defendant was charged with importing amphetamines. In police interviews he denied any knowledge of the presence of the amphetamines found in his car and said that he had no connection with drugs in any form. A search of his home revealed small quantities of cannabis and some drug-related equipment. The Court of Appeal held that these discoveries were admissible because they tended to show that his denial of any connection with drugs was untrue.

If the evidence is admitted for this purpose, the judge should give a *Lucas (1981)* direction to the jury. As developed in *Burge and Pegg (1996)*, such a direction should contain two elements. First, it must be admitted by the defendant, or the jury must find it proved beyond reasonable doubt, that the defendant lied when he said that he had never been involved with drugs. If the jury are satisfied that he did lie, they should be warned that the mere fact that the defendant has lied is not in itself evidence of guilt, because defendants may lie for innocent reasons. For example, in this case Alex might have lied in an attempt to strengthen an otherwise true defence.

Can the prosecution make use of the discovery of cash in Ben's house? It could be circumstantial evidence of his involvement in the offence. On the facts it is difficult to tell. There appears to be no direct evidence of dealing by Ben, or of his possession of the heroin with intent to supply. In *Wright (1994)* the discovery of £16,000 in cash and a gold necklace worth about £9,000 was held to be relevant and admissible where the defendant was charged with possession of crack cocaine with intent to supply. In *Grant (1996)* the defendant, charged with possession of crack cocaine with intent to supply, was found with just over £900 in cash in his possession. The Court of Appeal held that the finding of the money in conjunction with a substantial quantity of drugs was capable of being relevant to intent to supply and could properly be admitted. The facts of this case, however, are different. Both defendants are charged merely with being concerned in the importation of heroin, and the only drugs that appear to have been found in the possession of either of them related to Alex alone, and the drug in question was not heroin. The admissibility of the discovery of the cash is likely to turn on what other evidence is available to show Ben's involvement in the offence.

One other item of evidence is the notebook entry in Ben's handwriting. This is relevant because it might be inferred from the entry, assuming it can be shown to refer to the month mentioned in the indictment, that Ben was engaged in some transaction that involved meeting Alex 'with the stuff' at Dover. It is certainly evidence admissible against Ben. Is it also admissible against Alex? A court would very probably find that it was, on the basis that the statement was made by Ben in furtherance of their common enterprise. *Devonport and Pirano (1996)* is a case supporting this rule. In that case five defendants were convicted of conspiracy to rob a bank. One of the pieces of evidence was a document found in the possession of the girlfriend of one of the defendants. The prosecution case was that it had been dictated to the girlfriend by one of the defendants, and that it showed the proposed division of proceeds from the robbery that was being planned. It referred to all five defendants, but the only person with any knowledge of the document had been the person who had dictated it and the girl who had written it. The Court of Appeal held that it was evidence against all the conspirators if it had been brought into existence in furtherance of the conspiracy, provided there was some further evidence beyond the document itself that the other defendants had been involved in the conspiracy. Defendants do not have to be charged with conspiracy for the rule to apply; a joint charge in relation to a common enterprise will be enough. The entry in Ben's notebook appears to be a reminder to himself to meet Alex. If so, it is evidence of having been made in furtherance of the common enterprise. It will be admissible against Alex also, provided there is some additional evidence of involvement on Alex's part. This common law exception to the hearsay rule was preserved by s 118(1), para 7, **Criminal Justice Act (CJA) 2003**.

Alex is of good character, and the judge must give a *Vye (1993)* direction to the jury about the significance of this. He must tell them that good character is relevant to Alex's credibility as a witness, and is also relevant to the question whether he is likely to have behaved as alleged by the prosecution.

Ben's position is slightly more complicated. Although the offences are very different, if Ben pleaded not guilty and gave evidence at the earlier trial he must have been disbelieved. It might be argued, if he gives evidence in the current case, that his conviction is relevant to the question whether he has a propensity to be untruthful, and so admissible under s 101(1)(d) CJA 2003. The defence could argue strongly, however, that the conviction should not be admitted for this purpose, under both s 101(3) and s 103(3). Further, in *Hanson (2005)* the Court of Appeal said that a disposition would often not be established by only one previous conviction.

If the prosecution makes no application, or fails in its application, the defence may apply to have Ben treated as being of good character for the purposes of the current trial. In *Gray (2004)* the Court of Appeal said that if a defendant has a previous conviction which, because of its age or nature, may entitle him to be treated as being effectively of good character, the trial judge has a discretion to treat him in this way. If he does so, a full *Vye* direction must be given. It was also said that where the previous conviction is irrelevant in relation to the offence charged, the judge's discretion ought to be exercised in favour of the defendant.

# Question 52

Charlie is charged with the murder of David, the husband of Charlie's mistress, Ella. The case for the prosecution is that Charlie and David met by agreement to discuss Charlie's relationship with Ella, and that during the meeting Charlie killed David by striking him on the head with a cricket bat. When interviewed by the police, Charlie refused, on legal advice, to answer any questions. He now intends to plead not guilty and to give evidence that he struck David in self-defence when David tried to attack him with a knife. He wishes to call Fergus, a psychiatrist, to say that Charlie must have been acting in self-defence because he has an abnormally placid temperament and a pathological fear of violence. The police took statements from Ella and from Charlie's wife, Geraldine. The prosecution wishes to call both women as witnesses, but neither is now willing to testify.

Discuss the evidential matters arising.

## Answer plan

There are five points that need to be considered.

- the significance of Charlie's refusal, on legal advice, to answer police questions;
- the evidential burden where self-defence is raised;
- the admissibility of Fergus's evidence (a) that Charlie must have been acting in self-defence; and (b) that he had (i) an abnormally placid temperament; (ii) a pathological fear of violence. (Note the importance of breaking up into distinct propositions what Fergus intends to say.);
- Ella's competence and compellability;
- Geraldine's competence and compellability.

# Answer

Charlie, albeit on legal advice, has failed to answer police questions. In particular, he has failed to tell the police on being questioned that he was acting in self-defence when he struck David. This potentially brings him within the scope of s 34 of the Criminal Justice and Public Order Act 1994, and the question arises of how the judge should direct the jury about this.

He should follow what was laid down by the Court of Appeal in *Petkar (2004)*. So he must identify the facts on which Charlie relies and which were not mentioned on questioning. The obvious fact is that he was acting in self-defence, but there may be others as well. He must identify the inferences which it is suggested might be drawn from failure to mention such facts, to the extent that they may go beyond the standard inference of late fabrication. The jury should be told that, if an inference is drawn, they should not convict wholly or mainly on the strength of it. They should be told that an inference should be drawn only if they think it is fair and proper, and it should be drawn only if the only sensible explanation for failure to mention facts relied on is that the defendant had no answers, or none that would stand up to scrutiny. Moreover, an inference should be drawn only if, apart from a defendant's failure to mention facts relied on, the prosecution case is so strong that it clearly calls for an answer by him. The jury should be reminded of the evidence on the basis of which they are invited not to draw any inferences from silence.

A special direction must be given, because Charlie's silence was on legal advice. In *Betts and Hall (2001)* the Court of Appeal held that adverse inferences could not be drawn from silence where the defendant had honestly relied on legal advice in his refusal to answer questions, and was not simply using the advice as a cloak behind which to hide. But in *Howell (2003)* the Court of Appeal held that genuine reliance on legal advice was not of itself enough to avoid the application of s 34. The Court said that what was reasonable depended on all the circumstances. Even where silence was advised, there must always be soundly based objective reasons for that advice. In *Knight (2003)* the Court of Appeal observed, *obiter*, that if there was any conflict between *Betts and Hall* and *Howell*, *Howell* was to be preferred. Although in *Robinson (2003)* another division of the Court of Appeal seemed to prefer the approach taken in *Betts and Hall*, it was later confirmed in *Hoare (2004)* and *Beckles (2004)* that *reasonable* reliance on legal advice is necessary to prevent the drawing of adverse inferences, and this is reflected in the amended Judicial Studies Board specimen direction on s 34.

The jury may well find themselves having to ask whether it was reasonable to rely on the legal advice to remain silent when his explanation for what took place was so obviously important.

A defendant who raises the defence of self-defence has an evidential burden in respect of that defence *(Lobell, 1957)*. That is to say, in order for self-defence to be a live issue for the jury's consideration, there must be some evidence to support it. That evidence can, of course, be provided by Charlie himself in the course of testimony.

The evidence to be given by Fergus raises some difficulties. In principle, an expert can give evidence of his opinion on matters that would not fall within the competence of the members of the jury *(DPP v A and BC Chewing Gum Ltd, 1968)*. However, the question whether Charlie might have been acting in self-defence can be regarded as the ultimate issue in this case, and is clearly a matter entirely for the jury. Fergus will not be allowed to say that Charlie must have been acting in self-defence. He also wants to say that Charlie has an abnormally placid temperament. In *Coles (1995)* the Court of Appeal held that expert evidence is inadmissible to enable a jury to reach a decision about the existence of *mens rea*, unless the evidence is related to the mental health or psychiatric state of the defendant. Unless the statement that Charlie has an abnormally placid temperament can be said to amount to evidence of mental abnormality, Fergus will not be able to give evidence of this either. If by 'a pathological fear of violence' Fergus is referring to a recognised mental abnormality, he will be able to give evidence of this, but not otherwise.

By s 53(1) of the **Youth Justice and Criminal Evidence Act 1999**, at every stage in criminal proceedings all persons are (whatever their age) competent to give evidence. There is nothing to suggest that for any reason Ella is unable to fulfil the very simple conditions set out in s 53(3). The general rule at common law is that all competent witnesses are also compellable (*Hoskyn v Commissioner of Police for the Metropolis, 1979*). No relevant exception applies to her. She can therefore be compelled to give evidence. It will be necessary to discover why she is unwilling to give evidence. If she does so through fear, her written statement may be admissible under s 116(2)(e) **Criminal Justice Act (CJA) 2003**. Under that provision it would still be necessary for the court to give leave for her evidence to be given in this way, and in deciding whether or not to do so, the court must have regard to the matters set out in sub-s (4). The nature of the fear will have to be ascertained, but by sub-s (3) the term is to be widely construed.

The same rules about competence will apply to Geraldine, but she is in a special position so far as compellability is concerned. By s 80(2A) of PACE the spouse of a defendant is compellable to give evidence for the prosecution in respect of a 'specified offence'. The specified offences are set out in sub-s (3). They do not include the murder of an adult person. Accordingly, Geraldine cannot be compelled to give evidence for the prosecution against Charlie. If, however, she is unwilling to do so through fear, the same principles would apply to the use of her written statement as have been outlined in relation to Ella.

# Question 53

Harry and Irma, both aged 18, had known each other for some years. The case for the prosecution is that they both went to the same party, and towards the end of the evening Harry offered Irma a lift home in his car, and she accepted. It is alleged that at some stage Harry stopped the car, dragged Irma into a field, and raped her. Irma says that she was so stunned by what had happened that afterwards she got back into the car with Harry and let him drive her home. Jack, her elder brother, says that when Irma arrived there was mud in her hair and on her clothes. He said to her, 'Irma, what have you been up to? Mind you tell me the truth, or I shall have to report this to Mother.' Irma replied, 'Oh Jack, that bastard Harry raped me in a field!' Jack gave a written statement to the police, but has since gone back-packing abroad and cannot at present be traced. When Harry was interviewed by the police he said, 'I'll tell you everything. She was going on and on about how she was excited at the thought of sex in the open air. When we reached a field she tried to stop the car. We nearly had an accident. I did have sex with her, but I'd never have done so if she hadn't been begging for it.' Jack wishes to call Ken and Larry to say that a short while ago they had sex with Irma on separate occasions, and that she had insisted on having sex in the open air. She had sex in a park with Ken, and with Larry she had sex on a building site. Jack's solicitor has recently heard that last year Irma made an allegation of rape against Mike, who used to be her geography teacher, but that she subsequently withdrew the complaint.

Discuss the evidential issues that arise.

## Answer plan

Four matters need to be discussed:

- Jack's evidence. If he is available in time for Harry's trial, will he be able to give evidence of what he heard and saw? What directions would the judge have to give to the jury about this evidence? If he is not available, can the prosecution use the written statement that he gave to the police?
- Harry's interview with the police. Is it admissible? What is its evidential status?
- Can Ken and Larry be called to give evidence for the defence?
- What use, if any, can be made of the information that Harry's solicitor has recently obtained?

# Answer

If Jack is available at Harry's trial he would in principle be able to give evidence of how Irma's physical condition when she came home. But it does not look as if this would assist the prosecution to any degree. Harry has admitted having consensual sex with her in a field, and her muddy condition is as consistent with that as with rape. On the other hand, the prosecution may be able to adduce evidence of what she told Jack. It could be argued that her allegation against Harry falls within s 120(4) and (7) CJA 2003. The only problem might be with sub-s (7)(e); the defence could argue that Jack's words, 'Mind you tell the truth, or I shall have to report this to Mother' constituted a threat that would make her allegation inadmissible under that sub-section.

If the words are held not to constitute a threat, the question arises whether the prosecution can use the written statement made by Jack if is still unavailable at the time of Harry's trial. The provisions that would make a written statement by him admissible in principle can be found in s 116(2)(c) or (d). However, s 121 would also apply, because the significant part of Jack's evidence involves the report of an oral statement made to him by Irma. To allow the statement containing this to be given in evidence would be to allow multiple hearsay. The only condition of admissibility that might apply in this case would be s 121(1)(c), and it may be doubted whether a statement confirming the oral evidence of Irma would be regarded as having such a high value that the interests of justice would require it to be admitted. If evidence of Irma's complaint were to be given, whether orally or by way of Jack's written statement, it would be the judge's duty to warn the jury that an earlier complaint by a rape complainant cannot provide independent confirmation of the complainant's own evidence *(Islam, 1999)*.

Harry's interview with the police will be admissible. Insofar as it contains an admission that he had sex with Irma, it will be admissible as a confession under s 76(1) **Police and Criminal Evidence Act (PACE) 1984**. Insofar as it contains exculpatory matters – she was a willing, indeed an eager, partner – it will be admissible by virtue of the principle settled in *Pearce (1979)* that the prosecution must in fairness adduce evidence of exculpatory as well as inculpatory statements by the accused. What Harry produced was a 'mixed' statement, which, following *Sharp (1988)* and *Aziz (1995)*, will be treated as evidence of the truth of all its contents, though the judge may point out that the exculpatory part should not be given the same weight as the inculpatory part.

Whether Ken and Larry can be called for the defence will depend on the application of s 41 of the **Youth Justice and Criminal Evidence Act 1999**. The basic rule laid down in s 41(1) is that there can be no evidence or cross-examination about any sexual behaviour of the complainant without the leave of the court, which can be given only under sub-s (3) or (5). Sub-s (5) is inapplicable here. The defence is consent; there is no suggestion that it is anything else, such as an honest belief where consent did not in fact exist. The evidence of Ken and Larry can be given, therefore, only if it falls within the exceptions contained in sub-s (3)(b) or (c). It does not sound as if the events involving Ken and Larry can be admitted under sub-s (3)(b). In *A* (2001) members of the House of Lords observed that 'at or about the same time' would not normally be construed so as to refer to a time much more than 24 hours before or after the alleged offence. Reliance would have to be placed on sub-s (c), which imposes a test of similarity. Although, as was observed in *A*, the test is not the old test of *striking* similarity that was once applied in similar fact cases, it was at least doubtful whether a preference for sex in the open air would be held sufficiently unusual to meet the requirement of the sub-section. *A* decided that s 41(1)(c) was to be construed in accordance with the **Human Rights Act 1998** so as to allow evidence to be given where its exclusion would deny a defendant his right to a fair trial. But the evidence in *A* was of the *defendant's* previous sexual relationship with the complainant. A complainant's relationship with other men is very unlikely to be admitted under the principle acknowledged in that case. It is unlikely, therefore, that Ken and Larry will be allowed to give evidence.

It has been emphasised by the Court of Appeal on several occasions, for example in *W (2005)* and in *E (2005)*, that while evidence of a previous false complaint by a complainant is not evidence of sexual behaviour within s 41, there must be a proper evidential basis for asserting not only that the complaint was made, but also that it was untrue. In the absence of evidence that the earlier complaint was untrue, it will amount to evidence of sexual behaviour and will fall within s 41. It follows that in the absence of evidence that the complaint made against Mike was untrue, evidence that it was made will be inadmissible.

# INDEX

act of gross indecency in a public place 151–153
admissibility 2–4, 196–205; admissible evidence 181–182; argument for 134; cautious about 181
advance notice procedures in civil and criminal cases 178
arbitrator, powers of 9

'background evidence' 134
balancing of interests 187
burden of proof 15–29; basic rule about 21–23; circumstances and 24; legal versus evidential 15; of proof, in civil cases 16–17; proper direction on 21–23; reversal of 17–19, 27; rule affecting 34
Burglary 121
business and other documents exception (s 117) 60

character evidence 127–165; in criminal trials 127; from previous conviction 132–134; *see also* evidence of bad character; evidence of good character
civil cases: advance notice procedures in 178; factual issues in 2–4
civil trial, evidence law in 36–38
co-defendant(s): adduce evidence of 160; issue between 158–159
common law: common law hearsay rules 46; statutory powers of exclusion and 60
communications: between solicitor and client 194; third party communications legal professional privilege in 193–197
compellability 31–40; of accused's spouse 32–33
competence 31–40; of accused's spouse 32–33; of children in civil and criminal cases 32

confessions: admitted confession 111, 115, 118; confession, excluding 99; confession, recognizing 98; definition 100, 112; ill-gotten evidence and 97–126; impact on the case as a whole 98–99; inadmissible confession, evidence via 112; made in the absence of a solicitor 114; possibility of 112; in s 82(1) of PACE 1984, 115, 120
conviction: evidential value of 154–157; spent convictions 147
corroboration law, abolition of 78
course of testimony 167–176
criminal cases: advance notice procedures in 178; factual issues in 2–4
Criminal Justice Act (CJA) 2003; effect of reforms in 46–48; in reforming the law relating to hearsay 70; rule against hearsay and 46–49; 'safety-valve' 70
Criminal Justice and Public Order Act (CJPOA) 1994 100–104; counter arguments 101; on right of silence in police station 100–104, *see also under* right of silence; s 34, arguments in favour of 101; s 35 and the burden of proof 101; s 35 effect 101; s 35 justification of 101
criminal trial, evidence law in 36–38
cross-examination 101, 148–149, 154–155; of a defendant 154; of the parties as to credit 168; of prosecution witnesses as to character 169–170

defence: of provocation 6; self-defence as 21
defendant: cross-examination of 154; evidential burden on 22; personal characteristics of 125; prosecution and, issue between 137, 150, 157; silence of 125
description evidence 93
documentary hearsay evidence 71

207

earlier convictions, relevance and admissibility of 133
elements of the offence and defences, distinction 17–18
European Convention on Human Rights 17–20; elements of the offence and defences, distinction 17–19; *mala in se* and *mala prohibita*, distinction 17–19; Parliament's decision, deference to 17–18
evidence: in absence of identification 51; of bad character 127–139, 158, 170; basic concepts 1–13; defendant's 22, 128; evidence law, in criminal and civil trials 36; evidential burden 15, 21, 200–202; of good character 132, 151–153; via inadmissible confession 112; of inequality of bargaining power 7; meaning of 16–17; of the previous conviction 154–157; of propensity 132, 141; of a statement 44
expert testimony 178–182; *see also* description evidence; identification evidence; uncorroborated evidence; voice identification

fairness concept 104–105; of the proceedings 124; *see also* unfairness
finality of answers to collateral questions 168
fraudulent misrepresentation 25
freedom of contract 7

generalization 3
'golden thread' principle 17

hazardous evidence 75–95; mandatory warnings to the jury 76
hearsay 41–73; admissible by agreement 59; admissible by statute 59; admissible under any preserved common law rule 59; admissible in the interests of justice (the 'safety-valve') 59; in civil and criminal proceedings 41; common law rule against 42; and CJA 2003, 46–49, *see also* rule against hearsay; CJA 2003 in reforming the law relating to 70; defendants' statements 66–67; definition 41; definition in s 114(1) of the CJA 2003, 43; extension of 47; 'hearsay fiddles' 71; oral and documentary hearsay 70; *res gestae statements* 59, *see also separate entry*; 'safety-valve' exception 43; *statements in furtherance of a common enterprise* 60; unavailability exception 43

identification evidence/parade 52, 77, 86; convicting on 137; description evidence and, distinction 93; difficulty with 86; pre-trial identification of suspects, procedures for 87–88; *see also* mistaken identification
ill-gotten evidence, confessions and 97–126
immunity 188–190
'implied assertions': abolition of 70; concept of 48, 71
imprisonment, risk of 19
improperly obtained evidence 104–108
informer, traditional problem of 190–192
innocence, presumption of 17, 19
interpretation: guidelines for 28; substantial questions of 27
intoxication 6
irrelevance 7

judicial notice 4; doctrine of judicial notice 9; English law and 8–10; evidence and 8–10; inquiry and 10; law on 8–10; law on, problem with 8–9; limited view of 10; in litigation 9; local or special knowledge and, distinction 8; rationale of, theories about 9; rationales for 8–10

law of evidence, Thayer definition 5
legal burden 15; on the accused person 16–20
'legalistic backwater' 70
legal professional privilege: in third party communications 193–197
legal relevance: concept 4–8; court's reluctance in 6; difficulties presented by 5–8; judicial decisions about 5–8; in the law of evidence 7; recognition, lack of 7; Thayer's rejection of 5–8; to unfairness to defendants 7; usefulness 5–8
life imprisonment 19

*mala in se* and *mala prohibita*, distinction 17
mandatory warnings to the jury 76
'matter stated', definition of 41, 43, 46
mental abnormality, evidence of 202
mistaken identification 92–100; protecting against, ways of 92; risk in 92–100

'natural selection' 75
'negative hearsay' 43

offences 17–19; categories of 164; classification, difficulty in 18; constituent element of 19;

# Index

as criterion for reverse burdens of proof 18; defendant's propensity to commit 164; essential element of 29; maximum penalty for 19

opinion evidence 177–182

oppression 109; definition 109–110; evidence of 110; quick dismissal of the possibility of 116; seriousness of the conduct needed to constitute 121

oral evidence in criminal proceedings 172

outcomes: outcomes and the means of achieving them, difference between 186; similarity of 186–189

Parliament's decision, deference to 17–18

Police and Criminal Evidence Act 1984: limited protection of s 78(1) 105; protecting defendants against improperly obtained evidence 104–108

police investigations 190–192

'the preponderance of probability' 25

preserved common law exceptions (s 118) 60

presumptions: allocation of 33–34; classifications 32–33; competence and compellability and 31–40; conflicting presumptions 32; conflict of 35; of death 32–33, 39; of innocence 35; 'irrebuttable presumption of law' 31; in Law of property act 39; of legitimacy 32–33, 35, 39–40; of marriage 32; 'presumption of fact' 31; 'the presumption of innocence' 32; of regularity 32–33; *res ipsa loquitur* 32; theoretical basis for recognizing 32; universal competence and compellability, general rule of 32–33

previous consistent statements 168

previous convictions 164–168; evidence of 154, 163

previous identification, evidence of 169–170

previous inconsistent statements 168

*prima facie* hearsay 71

privilege and public policy 183–194; that attaches to 'without prejudice' 184; legal professional privilege 184; limited privilege 184; place of balancing interests in 186; potential differences between 186; against self-incrimination 183

proof: burden and standard of 15–29; *see also under* burden of proof; standard of proof

proposition, superficial attractiveness of 33

psychiatric testimony 178–182

public interest immunity 188

'rebuttable presumption of law' 31

refreshing memory 168–173

relevance of evidence 3, 42, 129, 147, 197–205; apparent 'rules' about 5–8; of a false alibi 49–52; judges' decisions about 7; in the rule against hearsay, importance of 43; statutory framework for determining 6; weight and 5–8; *see also* legal relevance

reliability: of evidence 106–107; reliability point 112

*res gestae statements*: categories 59–60; declarations 60; retention of 70; spontaneous exclamations 60; statements of the person 60

reverse burdens of proof 17–19, 27

revision 195–205

right of silence 149; in police station, CJPOA 1994 on 100–104

rights of inheritance 38

rule against hearsay: questionable validity of 46–48; scope of 59; traditional reasons for 46–48

safety expert's report 193–197

'safety-valve' 70–71; exception, in CJA 2003 43; 'safety-valve' exception (s 114) 60

self-defence, as defence 21

self-incrimination, privilege against 183–194

silence, inference from 149

'special motive' point 112

spent convictions 147

standard of proof 15–29; in criminal cases 16–17; proper direction on 21–23

'statement', definition of 41, 43

*statements in furtherance of a common enterprise* 60

supplementary provisions (ss 121–125) 60

third party communications: legal professional privilege in 193–197

unavailability exception 60; in CJA 2003 43

uncorroborated evidence 82

unfairness: unreliable evidence as a source of 105

unfavourable and hostile witnesses 168

unreliable evidence: as a source of unfairness 105

voice identification 93

warnings 76, 78–81; informal warning 77, 82

'without prejudice' statements 184–194

209